A Life That Is Good

A Life That Is Good

The Message of Proverbs in a World Wanting Wisdom

Glenn Pemberton

William B. Eerdmans Publishing Company
Grand Rapids, Michigan

Wm. B. Eerdmans Publishing Co.
4035 Park East Court SE, Grand Rapids, Michigan 49546
www.eerdmans.com

Published 2018
Printed in the United States of America

27 26 25 24 23 22 21 20 19 18 1 2 3 4 5 6 7 8 9 10

ISBN 978-0-8028-7567-9

Library of Congress Cataloging-in-Publication Data

Names: Pemberton, Glenn, author.
Title: A life that is good : the message of Proverbs in a world wanting wisdom / Glenn Pemberton.
Description: Grand Rapids : Eerdmans Publishing Co., 2018. | Includes bibliographical references and index.
Identifiers: LCCN 2018022307 | ISBN 9780802875679 (pbk. : alk. paper)
Subjects: LCSH: Bible. Proverbs–Criticism, interpretation, etc.
Classification: LCC BS1465.52 .P43 2018 | DDC 223/.706–dc23
LC record available at https://lccn.loc.gov/2018022307

Unless otherwise indicated, all biblical citations are from the New Revised Standard Version (NRSV).

Other Bible Translations: ASV, CEB, CEV, ERV, ESV, HCSB, KJV, MEV, NASB, NCV, NIV, NJPS, NLT, RSV

To our children
by blood and by love:

Taylor, Simeon, Wade,
Lannea, David, T'auna, and Steven

Contents

Foreword

Many students of the Bible treat the book of Proverbs as an afterthought in the Bible, an alien presence when compared to other books. After all, references to the great events of redemption (the patriarchs and matriarchs, exodus, conquest, and more) seem missing. Explicit references to covenant and law, prophets and priests are hard to find. While the prophets speak with a resounding "word of the Lord," the sages who produced the book of Proverbs talk about their experiences, observations, and the traditions of those who came before them. Furthermore, when read in the light of similar writings from Egypt and elsewhere in the ancient Near East, the proverbs of the book show a remarkable similarity to those produced by their pagan counterparts.

In a word, many scholars feel that the sages of Proverbs are a more kindred spirit to ideas outside the Bible than to the other voices within the Bible. As one author put it recently,

> Ancient Israel's sages had no qualms incorporating the wisdom of other cultures. Biblical wisdom seeks the common good along with the common God. Wisdom's international, indeed universal appeal constitutes its canonical uniqueness. The Bible's wisdom corpus is the open door to an otherwise closed canon.[1]

As a result of such thinking, the book of Proverbs, along with other wisdom books like Ecclesiastes and Job, are often treated as out of the mainstream theology of the Old Testament.

That does not mean that Christian readers fail to appreciate Proverbs, however. Indeed, it is not uncommon to find people carrying a Bible that contains the New Testament with only the books of Psalms and Proverbs from

1. W. P. Brown, *Wisdom's Wonder: Character, Creation, and Crisis in the Bible's Wisdom Literature* (Grand Rapids: Eerdmans, 2014), 3.

the Old Testament. After all, it is thought, Proverbs has the benefit of giving us some pretty concrete guidance for how to live life in a way that will lead to success and maybe even prosperity.

Both of these perspectives, that Proverbs is an outlier within Old Testament theology and that Proverbs carries special weight on account of its concrete wisdom, demonstrate the need for people to better understand the book of Proverbs. While they capture an aspect of truth about the book, they are in the final analysis the result of a very superficial interpretation. For this reason, I am happy that Glenn Pemberton has brought his considerable insight to bear on the book of Proverbs. He combines his incisive theological sense along with a lively writing style to produce this wonderful book that will open up new depths of the book of Proverbs to his readers.

I have been impressed with Dr. Pemberton's thinking and writing for a long time. In particular, his previous studies of the Psalms, especially the laments and psalms of confidence, have opened up for me new dimensions of understanding. Dr. Pemberton is helpful because he allows his real life experience to inform his study, so he can explain to us not only about the meaning of the biblical text in its ancient context, but also how that ancient meaning impacts us today.

I am excited and encouraged that you have chosen to read this book along with the book of Proverbs. As a result, your mind and heart will mature as you walk the path of life toward a deeper relationship with God.

TREMPER LONGMAN III
Distinguished Scholar
and Professor Emeritus
Westmont College

Preface and Acknowledgments

As I reflect on the development of this book, it is difficult to remember when the ideas first crossed my path—in courses taught by John Willis, doctoral exams, or my dissertation supervised by David Peterson,[1] or in the writings of Michael Fox, William Brown, Leo Perdue, and Dave Bland. I owe a great debt to these and other sages who have profoundly influenced my understanding of Proverbs and Israelite wisdom. My work has also been enriched by time spent with churches throughout Oklahoma, Texas, Kansas, and Colorado, as well as my university students who challenged me with their questions and their insights. A seminal moment in this long process came at a 2009 seminar hosted by Dave Bland and David Fleer at Lipscomb University, Tennessee, "Preaching Character: Reclaiming Wisdom's Paradigmatic Imagination for Transformation." Over three days, presentations from Scot McKnight, Tremper Longman III, Richard Ward, Tom Long, myself, and others received enthusiastic engagement from participating pastors and preachers.[2] Together, all of these voices so fill my mind that I am wise enough to know that the majority of my thoughts are not original, but may be traced back to ideas from these mentors, writers, churches, students, colleagues, and pastors, ideas that have been simmering and maturing in my mind for many years.

During this same period, I also presented research on Proverbs at regional and national conferences, and subsequently published several of these papers in journals and monographs. Three of these studies, in part or whole, lie beneath chapters in this book:

1. Glenn Pemberton, "The Rhetoric of the Father: A Rhetorical Analysis of the Father/Son Lectures in Proverbs 1–9," (PhD dissertation, Iliff School of Theology and University of Denver, 1999).

2. See Dave Bland and David Fleer, eds., *Preaching Character: Reclaiming Wisdom's Paradigmatic Imagination for Transformation* (Abilene, TX: Abilene Christian University Press, 2010).

- Chapter two, "Daughter Divine: Proverbs's Woman Wisdom," for *The Priscilla Papers*, edited by J. Miller. Minneapolis: Christians for Biblical Equity, forthcoming 2018.
- Portions of chapter three, "Proverbs, Persuasion, and Preaching." In *Preaching Character: Reclaiming Wisdom's Paradigmatic Imagination for Transformation*, edited by Dave Bland and David Fleer, 65–82. Abilene, TX: Abilene Christian University Press, 2010.
- Chapter four, "It's a Fool's Life: The Deformation of Character in Proverbs," *Restoration Quarterly* 50 (2008): 214–24.

I express my gratitude to each of these publications and their editors for permission to edit and rework these papers to suit the purposes of this volume.

While working on this project, my life took a major turn when I made the difficult yet inevitable decision to retire from teaching due to my health. For many years my colleagues in the undergraduate department of Bible, Missions, and Ministry, Abilene Christian University (ACU), especially Rodney Ashlock, chair of the department, and Jack Reese followed by Ken Cukrowski, deans of the College of Biblical Studies, have walked with me as I descended into the labyrinth of severe chronic pain (CRPS/RSD). Their provision of physical accommodations and a restructured workload along with their compassion and constant encouragement enabled me to do the work I love for as long as possible—and even beyond. Working toward the same goal, my medical team has and continues to provide me with the best care possible: Corey Brown (DPM), Robbie Cooksey (DO), Larry Norsworthy (PhD, LCP, BCPM), Gary Heath (MD), Shona Preston (FNP, BC), Edgar Reyther (RMA), and Daniel Vaughan (MD). For all these friends—their wisdom, compassion, and determined refusal to give up on me or allow me to give up on myself—I will be forever grateful.

Over the past year, I have tried to reframe my identity from a "disabled person" to a "writer." I do enjoy writing and reading, even with the limitations of CRPS. The recent surge in the next big thing—*blogs*—now requires every writer (and their basset hound) to keep an active blog site. So instead of burying my head in the sand, as I would prefer, I have taken the plunge into the wild world of blogging with technical support from the Siburt Institute at Abilene Christian University. I invite you to visit me at "Seasons: A Time for All Things" (http://char.is/glennpemberton/), where you will find curriculum for adult Bible classes, book recommendations for preaching and teaching from the Old Testament, a collection of my prayers, audio and video links to seminars and sermons, short textual and topical studies, and coordinated with the release of this book—new posts with additional studies in Proverbs, and responses to your questions or comments regarding this book.

I've learned through my reading that most writers have a first reader we trust to tell us the truth, even when we don't want to hear it. For me, my wife, Dana, takes this role with graciousness and unflinching truthfulness. While equally stunned with me by the speed and extent to which my CRPS has grown, she has helped me reimagine life as a writer: carving out physical space for me to write, acquiring adaptive furniture and technology, and most of all—believing in me. Writing is lonely business, CRPS even lonelier. Having someone who believes in you won't take the pain or loneliness away, but it certainly makes it endurable. Thank you, Dana—you remain the great surprise and love of my life.

Finally, I express my thanks to Mitchell Gordon, a student in the Graduate School of Theology (ACU) for his assistance in the preparation of the final manuscript and indexes. I am also grateful for the team at Eerdmans, especially my editor Andrew Knapp for his encouragement throughout this project, appropriately challenging weak conclusions, and saving me from many embarrassing mistakes. We may not agree at every point and errors that have slipped through are entirely my own, but I have found the truth and benefit in what the sages said: "Iron sharpens iron" (Prov. 27:17).

Glenn Pemberton
Abilene, TX
February 2018

To Readers, Group Leaders, and Teachers

This book is written primarily for faith-based discussion groups and Bible classes, with secondary consideration for undergraduate university courses on Israel's wisdom literature or Proverbs and for individual readers. Consequently, at the end of each chapter I provide at least five discussion questions. For those who want to read the biblical texts (*may your number grow like the weeds in my flower garden*), I have provided two lists at the beginning of each chapter under the title "To Prepare for Reading This Chapter." The first list includes *every text* in Proverbs on the topic of the chapter (occasionally with references to other biblical texts). The second is a thinner version of the first.

Finally, I conclude each chapter with a "Project Challenge" for ambitious groups to pursue together or individually. Naturally, in university courses the instructor may use this chapter-end material in diverse ways, for example assign proverbs to read before or after reading the chapter, require notes or short essays on the discussion questions, use these questions for potential quizzes, or adapt challenge questions for individual or group research projects.

Many books and commentaries on Proverbs include brief subject studies, from a single paragraph to one or two pages on each topic. Their primary purposes, however, whether introducing the wisdom movement in Israel or commenting on every verse, prevent what I attempt to do here. I do recognize the importance of context, or perhaps the purposeful lack of organization in Proverbs (see chapter 3). But I also recognize our practical need to identify and organize all that the sages have to say about key issues affecting our lives. Consequently, the method behind my approach in this book might best be described as preparing and serving a meal. In each chapter, I attempt to set out all that the sages have to say on a particular topic with enough organization that the raw ingredients (individual proverbs) come together to provide distinct dishes (organized sets of information). Each chapter serves one decent meal. However, some of the most important digestion of the content is left for the discussion questions. Of course I raise these issues with at least partial proposals or solutions in the chapters. But my hope is that a conversation that includes each person's reading and experience will stimulate the full-bodied discussion of the topic needed by our communities of faith today.

Abbreviations

ASV	American Standard Version
BCE	before Common Era
CEB	Common English Bible
CEV	Common English Version
cf.	*confer*, compare
ch.	chapter
chs.	chapters
e.g.	*exempli gratia*, for example
ERV	Easy-to-Read Version
ESV	English Standard Version
etc.	*et cetera*, and so forth, and the rest
HCSB	Holman Christian Standard Bible
KJV	King James Version
lit.	literally
MEV	Modern English Version
NASB	New American Standard Bible
NCV	New Century Version
NIV	New International Version
NJPS	New Jewish Publication Society Translation
NLT	New Living Translation
NRSV	New Revised Standard Version
RSV	Revised Standard Version
v.	verse
vv.	verses

THE BOOKS OF THE OLD TESTAMENT

Genesis	Gen.	Song of Songs	Song
Exodus	Exod.	Isaiah	Isa.
Leviticus	Lev.	Jeremiah	Jer.
Numbers	Num.	Lamentations	Lam.
Deuteronomy	Deut.	Ezekiel	Ezek.
Joshua	Josh.	Daniel	Dan.
Judges	Judg.	Hosea	Hosea
Ruth	Ruth	Joel	Joel
1–2 Samuel	1–2 Sam.	Amos	Amos
1–2 Kings	1–2 Kgs.	Obadiah	Obad.
1–2 Chronicles	1–2 Chr.	Jonah	Jonah
Ezra	Ezra	Micah	Mic.
Nehemiah	Neh.	Nahum	Nah.
Esther	Esther	Habakkuk	Hab.
Job	Job	Zephaniah	Zeph.
Psalms	Ps. (plural Pss.)	Haggai	Hag.
Proverbs	Prov.	Zechariah	Zech.
Ecclesiastes	Eccl.	Malachi	Mal.

THE BOOKS OF THE NEW TESTAMENT

Matthew	Matt.	1–2 Thessalonians	1–2 Thess.
Mark	Mark	1–2 Timothy	1–2 Tim.
Luke	Luke	Titus	Titus
John	John	Philemon	Phlm.
Acts	Acts	Hebrews	Heb.
Romans	Rom.	James	Jas.
1–2 Corinthians	1–2 Cor.	1–2 Peter	1–2 Pet.
Galatians	Gal.	1, 2, 3 John	1, 2, 3 John
Ephesians	Eph.	Jude	Jude
Philippians	Phil.	Revelation	Rev.
Colossians	Col.		

PART ONE

The Sages, Their Book, and Wisdom

CHAPTER 1

The Sages and Their Book

If it be knowledge or wisdom one is seeking,
then one had better go direct to the source. And the source is not
the scholar or philosopher, not the master, saint, or teacher,
but life itself—direct experience of life.

—Henry Miller[1]

The sages of Israel teach that those who would be wise
must aim, not at power, but at goodness.

—Ellen Davis[2]

TO PREPARE FOR READING THIS CHAPTER

1. Read Proverbs 1:1–7 in several translations.
2. On the different ways or people through whom the Lord spoke to Israel, see Jer. 18:18; Ezek. 7:26; Matt. 23:34–35.
3. On the idea of *wisdom* in Proverbs, read the following: 2:10; 3:13; 4:5, 7; 5:1; 10:8, 13, 14, 23; 12:15; 13:10; 14:6, 8, 33; 15:2, 7; 16:16, 21, 22; 18:15; 19:8, 20; 20:18; 21:11; 23:23; 24:3, 5–6; 25:12; 28:7.

Our path to the house of wisdom begins during the crisis of the Babylonian invasion into the nation of Israel and the desperation brought on by the siege of Jerusalem. An unusual place to begin, I admit, but a site that provides a firm surface for the foundation we must establish for the sages. The stakes for the prophet Jeremiah were high, in large part because of the unpopular message he had been

1. Henry Miller, *The Books in My Life* (New York: New Directions, 1952), 11.
2. Ellen Davis, *Proverbs, Ecclesiastes, and the Song of Songs*, Westminster Bible Companion (Louisville: Westminster John Knox, 2000), 27.

spreading around town: *if you want to survive this siege, you must surrender to the enemy* (Jer. 21:9, 38:17–18). His opponents were livid and discussed what to do about Jeremiah—specifically his treason for advocating surrender and his influence over those terrified by the events. And what to do was obvious: find a way to silence him in a grave; *put him to death using legal means*. After all, he was only one small link out of many that connected the people to their God. They said,

> *Come, let us make plots against Jeremiah—for instruction shall not perish from the priest, nor counsel from the wise* (hokmah), *nor the word from the prophet. Come, let us bring charges against him, and let us not heed any of his words.* (Jer. 18:18)

The leaders could not imagine that taking one out of the dozens of prophets, priests, and sages (the wise) could possibly silence the word of God. Others would fill the void left by Jeremiah.

Another prophet, Ezekiel, a contemporary of Jeremiah who was already living in exile in Babylonia, could also see the disaster not as a future event but already in the process of happening. What Jeremiah's Israelite enemies could not imagine had, in fact, already begun:

> *Disaster comes upon disaster,*
> *rumor follows rumor;*
> *they shall keep seeking a vision from the prophet;*
> *instruction shall perish from the priest,*
> *and counsel from the elders.* (Ezek. 7:26)

Ezekiel, coincidentally, identifies the same three sources of God's word: the prophets, the priests, and the sages—the "counsel from the elders," a typical expression of wisdom. Six hundred or more years later as he neared his own death, Jesus stood with Jeremiah and Ezekiel in giving the same list of people whom God will send and God's people will destroy:

> *Therefore I send you prophets, sages, and scribes, some of whom you will kill and crucify, and some you will flog in your synagogues and pursue from town to town, so that upon you may come all the righteous blood shed on earth . . .* (Matt. 23:34–35)

Jeremiah, Ezekiel, and Jesus recognize more than one sanctioned voice in ancient Israel and more than just one way the Lord speaks to people: priests, prophets, and *sages*. In fact, they suggest that describing the fullness of the Lord's word requires more than one perspective or one group. This observation may appear insignificant, but allow me to suggest that as we begin to comprehend what this means for us, the ground will begin to shake with tremors until finally an earthquake changes the entire landscape of how we think about God and living by faith today. Even those of us who have been working with this material for years—we are still trying to grasp what wisdom brings to the table.

Opposed to a monolithic, single perspective that values only one way of understanding God and living by faith, the texts above identify three distinct orthodoxies, or true or correct ways of thinking about God and life with God. The priests and prophets are the most well-known. The sages are not only the least familiar, but are often dismissed or not recognized as valid sources of theology, or words about God and faith. Consequently, our work here will begin by using the priests and prophets to build an understanding of the sages and wisdom. Figure 1.1 provides a helpful guide for taking notes and creating a comparative guide of similarities and differences among the three groups. Along the way, we will also establish a working definition of wisdom, examine the prologue of Proverbs (Prov. 1:1–7) , and conclude with a brief tour of the prologue and the landscape ahead (Prov. 1–9).

The Priests

The first group mentioned in Jeremiah 18:18 are the priests, the only unit restricted by age (30–50 years old, Num. 4:34–35), heritage (the descendants of Aaron), and gender (males only), though women did serve at the entrance of the tabernacle (1 Sam. 2:22). The priests had many different jobs and responsibilities that ranged from making sacrifices at the temple (Num. 18:5–7), serving as health and building inspectors of sorts in Israel (Lev. 13:1–59; 14:34–40), and acting as judges of a supreme court at the temple (Deut. 17:8–9). Priests were also responsible to teach the people how to distinguish what is holy from what is common and what is clean from what is unclean. They were to teach the *Torah*, the law or instruction (Lev. 10:11), for the purpose of keeping God's place/space ritually clean so that God could live with his people (Lev. 15:31). The priests told the stories of Israel's ancestors and spoke of the covenants God made with them. They viewed life with God through the lens of ritual purity and holiness (Lev. 17:10–11; 20:7–8; 22:31–32), worship, and obedience to the *Torah* (Deut. 5:33; 8:1; 11:8–9).

If we were to ask a priest how he knew about God and the life of faith, his reply would be simple: *Torah* or the Law of Moses (Gen. to Deut.). A priest would *never* say, "The Lord has told me or shown me" (unless the priest was also prophet; see below). Instead, a priest would point to the *Torah* and say, "This is what the Torah says or teaches." So it is no surprise that the biblical texts most associated with the priests are the five books of *Torah*, the first five books of the Old Testament. Finally, what persons or groups today are most similar to Israel's priests in their perspective (lens of faith), concerns, and practices? For example, pastors or preachers are similar to the priests in how they look to Scripture for God's word and in their concern for worship.

The Three Orthodoxies in Israel

	Priests	**Prophets**	**Sages**
Who is or may become a member of the group?			
What are their primary concerns?			
What is the source of their information?			
What biblical books are associated with this group?			
What groups or individuals today are most similar to this group?			

The Prophets

The second group mentioned by Jeremiah's opponents are the prophets. Unlike the priests, the role of a prophet was not restricted by heritage, sex, or age. God called prophets from every family group or tribe of Israel; most appear to be male but not all (e.g., Miriam, Deborah, and Huldah). And as for age, Jeremiah complains that he is too young, just a boy, when God summons him to work (Jer. 1:4–8), and he continues his work well past the time others have been taken into Babylonian captivity (Jer. 39–45), a ministry of at least forty-one years.

God called prophets for a different purpose than priests, and they viewed life with God through a different lens. They may be compared to attorneys for the prosecution, on behalf of God, making the case against God's people for breaking the covenant and its fundamental concerns, especially the two greatest commandments: the first—place no other gods above or ahead of the Lord, and the second—love others, especially the vulnerable widows, orphans, and immigrants. The book of Isaiah, for example, begins with Isaiah accusing the nation of rebelling against their God (Isa. 1:2–4), calling the heavens and earth as witnesses and jury and spelling out the indictment: the Israelites have broken covenant while believing that as long as they brought the right sacrifices and went through the motions of worship, nothing else mattered (1:11–15). Isaiah emphasizes basic covenant ideas:

> *cease to do evil,*
> *learn to do good;*
> *seek justice,*
> *rescue the oppressed,*
> *defend the orphan,*
> *plead for the widow.* (Isa. 1:16d–17)

Elsewhere, other prophets emphasize similar themes:

> *He has told you, O mortal, what is good;*
> *and what does the LORD require of you*
> *but to do justice, and to love kindness,*
> *and to walk humbly with your God?* (Mic. 6:8)

> *But let justice roll down like waters,*
> *and righteousness like an ever-flowing stream.* (Amos 5:24)

> *For I desire steadfast love and not sacrifice,*
> *the knowledge of God rather than burnt offerings.* (Hos. 6:6)

Like the priests, the prophets spoke freely of God's history with his people. They appealed to the Lord's actions in history to motivate the people to be faithful to the Lord: what the Lord had done in the past, the Lord would do again in the future. Unlike the priests, however, the prophets did not derive their message from study of the *Torah*. Instead, they claimed to receive messages directly from God through visions, dreams, or the voice of God himself.

As a result, prophets often began their speeches with claims such as, "This is what the Lord says" or "Thus says the Lord."

The books associated with the prophets bear the name of a prophet from whom the book is derived or connected to in some way, for example Isaiah, Jeremiah, Ezekiel, Hosea, and Amos. The question, *who is most like a prophet today?* leads to additional, clarifying questions. Must a person see visions or hear the voice of God speaking directly to them in order to be a prophet? Or is a prophet today anyone who adopts the primary concerns of the prophets? If so, modern examples would include any person or group who intervenes and seeks justice for those on the fringes of society: the poor, the oppressed, or immigrants desperate for life, or others who take up different themes from the prophetic literature of the Bible.

The Sages

Finally, standing alongside the priests and prophets are the sages or wise women and men. The contrast between the sages and the prophets and priests is bold. Prophets and priests often spoke about Israel, God's chosen people, the covenants, and the history of God's relationship to Israel. Priests also spoke about holiness, purity, and worship, while prophets also spoke about love for God, the rights of the oppressed, and broken covenants. The sages, however, rarely if ever spoke about these topics. Nor did they appeal to the *Torah* for information or authority, like the priests. And they did not claim to have direct revelation through visions or words God spoke to them, like the prophets. Sages do not say, "Thus says the Lord" or "The Law of Moses says." This does not mean that the sages disagreed with the prophets or priests, or thought their witness less important. The sages simply operated from a different outlook on life from a source other than *Torah* or the prophets. The wisdom book Ecclesiastes provides the clues we need to determine the sage's source of information (all emphases are mine):

> *Moreover* I saw *under the sun that in the place of justice, wickedness was there, and in the place of righteousness, wickedness was there as well.* (3:16)
>
> *Again* I saw *all the oppressions that are practiced under the sun. Look, the tears of the oppressed—with no one to comfort them!* (4:1a)
>
> *Then* I saw *that all toil and all skill in work come from one person's envy of another.* (4:4a)

> *Again,* I saw *vanity under the sun: the case of solitary individuals, without sons or brothers; yet there is no end to all their toil . . .* (4:7–8a)

> If you see *in a province the oppression of the poor and the violation of justice and right, do not be amazed . . .* (5:8a)

> *There is a grievous ill that* I have seen *under the sun: riches were kept by their owners to their hurt . . .* (5:13)

> *This is what* I have seen *to be good: it is fitting to eat and drink and find enjoyment in all the toil . . .* (5:18a)

> *There is an evil that* I have seen *under the sun, and it lies heavy upon humankind . . .* (6:1)

What is the source of a sage's wisdom? Unlike prophets or priests, sages derive their understanding of God and life with God *from what they see or experience*, as well as what others have seen and experienced. They accept these insights as normative or God-given, just as a prophet regards a vision or a priest regards *Torah* to be God's message.

The nature of a sage's insight opens the door for anyone to become a sage, or as we will see, anyone may walk in the path of wisdom: male, female, old, young, rich, poor, royalty, or servant (Prov. 1:20–21; 8:1–5; 9:1–6). Because wisdom is a matter of human observation, wisdom also stretches across national boundaries to include non-Israelites (see 30:1; 31:1). And in harmony with this source of knowledge and understanding, the object of concern for a sage, as opposed to prophets and priests, is common life—daily living when we are away from worship and life beyond or outside the guidance of the covenant. What priests and prophets overlook is the target for wisdom literature—navigating life topics such as friendship, poverty and wealth, diligence and laziness, speech (e.g., gossip, slander, or truth-telling), marriage, and family—all aspects of daily life lived before God or, in other words, how to live a life that is good.

Intermission: A Working Definition of Wisdom

In the Old Testament, the Hebrew word *hokmah*, translated "wisdom," has two related levels of meaning, and the first level forms a foundation for the second.

The first level means any special skill or expertise. For example, Jeremiah calls for professional mourners to come weep at the funeral for Judah, because the nation is as good as dead.

> *Consider, and call for the mourning women to come;*
> *send for the skilled* (hokmah) *women to come;*
> *let them quickly raise a dirge over us,*
> *so that our eyes may run down with tears,*
> *and our eyelids flow with water.* (Jer. 9:17–18)

In the same way, Ezekiel composes a dirge for the coastal city-state of Tyre, describing them as a beautiful ship. In the process, he refers to the oarsmen and the "*skilled* (*hokmah*) men" who pilot the ship (Ezek. 27:8). In these two texts, the word *hokmah* is an adjective that describes the excellence with which the women sing and the skill with which the men pilot their ship; they are both *wise* or very good at what they do. The same is true for Bezalel and Oholiab, lead craftsmen for constructing the tabernacle. The Lord called Bezalel and gave him *ability* (*hokmah*) to work and also appointed Oholiab (Exod. 31:2–4). Then in reference to both men and others, the Lord explains: "I have given *skill* to all the *skillful*, so that they may make all that I have commanded you" (31:6). If we use the term "wisdom" with the same meaning today, we might identify *excellent* teachers (wise teachers) or *effective* public speakers (wise speakers). On this first level, the Hebrew term *hokmah* carries no mystical, esoteric, or special religious meaning. It simply means to be especially good at doing something.

The second level of the meaning of *hokmah* builds on the first level. On one hand, it expands the first meaning to include living life as a whole with expertise, to live a life that is good. Proverbs frequently uses *hokmah* with this idea:

> *Then you will understand righteousness and justice*
> *and equity, every good path;*
> *for wisdom* (hokmah) *will come into your heart,*
> *and knowledge will be pleasant to your soul;*
> *prudence will watch over you;*
> *and understanding will guard you.* (2:9–11)

> *My child, do not let these escape from your sight:*
> *keep sound wisdom* (hokmah) *and prudence,*
> *and they will be life for your soul*

and adornment for your neck.
Then you will walk on your way securely
and your foot will not stumble.
If you sit down, you will not be afraid;
when you lie down, your sleep will be sweet. (3:21–24)

This wisdom is a gift of God (2:6–7), given to those who ask for and strenuously seek wisdom (2:1–5) and who retain this gift only through constant attentiveness (8:32–36). The book of Proverbs also describes wisdom as a path or trail on which we walk (2:9, 20; 4:11), rather than a destination to which we arrive and proclaim ourselves wise, which is an act of pride (3:7; 11:2). Others may lead us onto this path, helping us learn how to walk in the way of wisdom (4:10–12). At first, we may find the path to be hazy, like the light at dawn. But the longer we stay on the path, the brighter the sun shines, illuminating our way so that we don't stumble or fall (4:18).

Precisely what it means or looks like to walk on the path of wisdom or to live a life that is good requires the remainder of this book to describe, and even then we will come up short. For now we can say that those who walk the path of wisdom live a self-reflective lifestyle, attentive to the insights they gain from experience (16:21), receptive to advice (12:15; 13:10; 20:18), and open to the wisdom of others (25:12). As the sages walk, they continually pay attention to what they see and listen to advice, adding both to their life knowledge (18:15; 24:5). They continually integrate what they learn into their understanding and practice of life (3:13; 10:13, 23; 14:6, 8, 33; 19:8; 24:3). And they are continually receptive to instruction (21:11; 23:23), obedient to commandments (10:8; 28:7), and willing to share their knowledge with others (15:2, 7).

As a result, those who live a wise lifestyle, according to Proverbs, not only gain benefits *naturally derived* from their lifestyle, for example understanding where they are going (14:8), finding a future (24:14), and obtaining life itself (16:22). In fact, they also gain benefits or blessings directly from the Lord:

For the L*ORD gives wisdom . . .*
he stores up sound wisdom for the upright:
he is a shield to those who walk blamelessly,
guarding the paths of justice
and preserving the way of his faithful ones. (2:6a, 7–8)

The Lord watches over and guards the path of those to whom he gives wisdom. So it is little surprise that another proverb claims:

To get wisdom is to love oneself;
to keep understanding is to prosper. (19:8)

I admit that this description of wisdom is vague, primarily because I have given examples from Proverbs that speak about wisdom with broad, sweeping terms. In the chapters to come, we will select one or more related topics—for example poverty and wealth, speech, friendship—and study them in as much depth as possible in order to understand what it means to be wise in each aspect of life—for example to be wise with our wealth, to be wise with our speech, or to be wise in our friendships.

The Sages (continued)

The books commonly associated with wisdom include Proverbs, Job, and Ecclesiastes in Protestant Bibles, and some also include the Song of Songs. Catholic Bibles include two additional wisdom books, the Wisdom of Solomon and Sirach, also called Ecclesiasticus. Researchers identify texts in other Old Testament books that have been heavily influenced by wisdom or perhaps even written by sages. Examples include the Joseph story in Genesis 37–50 and a few psalms such as 19 and 119.

Who are most like Israel's sages, wise men and women today? We may be tempted to think only of those who are older and have more life experience—and indeed, those who have been walking on the path of wisdom for many years may have much to teach us. Wisdom, however, does not discriminate on the basis of age. For example, one group that leaps to my mind are counselors and therapists who listen, ask questions, and help us with the most personal and practical aspects of our lives; thus, they are sages. Because sages learn or acquire knowledge through firsthand experience, as well as studying what others have discovered through firsthand experience, another large group fits the definition: scientists. Contemporary scientists of all types, for example biologists, chemists, and physicists, learn by conducting experiments that confirm or deny their hypotheses. These groups also have a body of knowledge built of years of observation and passed down from one generation to the next in textbooks and handbooks. Consequently, their conclusions and recommendations are determined both on the basis of their personal experience and on their accumulated knowledge of their field of study. Just as in ancient Israel, our sages are able to reliably instruct others because of their attentiveness to how the world works, while at the same time remaining open to new studies that might disprove old ideas or advance their understanding even more.

Before we go further into our study, I need to raise one more question—a question that haunted Job's friends and that I suspect only a few today have seriously considered: *What is the validity of experience in theological discussion?* What role, if any, should reflection on life experience (wisdom) play in church doctrine? I grew up in a church who loved me and encouraged me to be a preacher, but it was a conservative church in which the Bible and only the Bible was relevant in matters pertaining to God and Christianity. For every question we turned to the Bible for an answer and dismissed any recent experience as inadmissible evidence in the court of Christian belief and practice.

Job and his friends argue this point throughout the book of Job. His friends have a closed theological system, much like my early faith experience. For Job's friends, everything is determined by the wisdom of their ancestors, just as in my church Scripture—and only Scripture—determined everything. So it doesn't matter what Job claims about his experience that God is hurting him even though he is innocent. Job's friends cannot accept his claim into their equation because their ancestors (also sages) settled what they believe about suffering long ago. They have been taught and have believed all their lives that people suffer at a level equal to their sins: sin a little—suffer a little, sin a lot—suffer a lot. So if they decide to accept Job's experience and his testimony, *it will turn their entire world upside down*. But if Job is right, that he has not sinned very much but is suffering so much it is indescribable, and they accept his claim—*everything changes*. The friends will never be able to feel safe or secure again, because if Job is innocent and still suffers, *suffering could happen to anyone for no reason at all—including to them*. So they double-down on their accusations: Job must be hiding something; he must have done something wrong (see the accusations of Eliphaz in Job 22). Instead of being open to new ideas, they protect their doctrine and defend the God enclosed within their system of belief. They must, or the foundation of their theology will crack wide open, and the earth will swallow their security. The possibility that Job could be correct terrifies them.

So where does wisdom, learning from experience, belong in our theology—our understanding of God and the life of faith? What role do our sages, with their accumulated experience and understanding, have in our churches? Do sages even have a voice today? Or to reimagine the question: *If the sages behind Proverbs showed up on our church steps, what would we do with them?* Would we toss them aside as secular and irrelevant advocates of situational ethics? Or would we welcome them to the table?

I regret to inform you that *Proverbs will not let this question go unanswered.* For some, it will be easy to accept the sages. For most, however, I suspect we will hesitate because we belong to a Protestant faith tradition that looks only to the Bible for guidance. For us, like Job's friends, to begin listening to the voice of our sages is terrifying because our assured answers are no longer so assured—including our positions on some of the most important issues of our time, for example same-sex attraction. Simply put, *inviting sages to the discussion table may frighten the wisdom out of us*, at least until we begin to understand the sages and grow comfortable with their perspective.

To wrap up our brief introduction to the priests, prophets, and sages in ancient Israel, I need to stress that despite their differences, true, godly priests, prophets, and sages were not at odds with each other, nor did they argue. In some ways they "had each other's back," correcting misperceptions drawn from each other's teaching. For example, Isaiah, Micah, and Hosea correct a misunderstanding of priestly sacrifice (Isa. 1:12–17; Micah 6:6–8; Hosea 6:4–6; cf. Deut. 12:31; 18:9–10; Lev. 18:21, 20:2–5; see also Deut. 10:12–21). And some from the priestly tribe or family were prophets, including Jeremiah and Ezekiel, and some priests were also sages or influenced by sages (scholars frequently identify wisdom themes in the Joseph story of Gen. 37–50), just as some prophets were sages or influenced by sages (consider Hosea 14:10 and Isa. 11:2; 28:29; 40:14, 21, 28). The prophets, priests, and sages of Israel all served the same God. The Lord simply used them to provide a more robust theology, a fuller picture of the life of faith, and a sharper image of the God who is larger than any one portrait.

In the Beginning: The Prologue of Proverbs

As we turn to the book of Proverbs, it seems wise to first check our bearings and the direction in which Proverbs will take us in order to avoid confusion farther down the road. In other words, it seems wise to listen to what the sages have to say about their own book and their purpose for writing and their primary audience in the prologue (Prov. 1:1–7). The following translation of the prologue and its formatting and emphases are my own.

1 *The proverbs of Solomon, son of David, king of Israel.*
2 ***For** learning wisdom and discipline,*
***for** understanding words of insight,*
3 ***for** gaining instruction about wise dealing:*
righteousness, justice, and equity,

[4]**for** *helping the naïve become mature,*
for *[helping] a young man [with] knowledge and good sense—*
[5]*Let the wise listen and learn more,*
and a man of understanding acquire skill.
[6]**for** *understanding a proverb and difficult sayings,*
the words of the wise and their riddles.

[7]*The fear of the Lord is the beginning of knowledge,*
fools despise wisdom and discipline. (1:1–7)

The first verse establishes the title of the book, "the proverbs of Solomon," Solomon's lineage "son of David," and Solomon's title, "king of Israel." But before we get ahead of ourselves with twenty-first century assumptions about the authorship of this ancient Near Eastern document, we need to notice that several other texts in Proverbs explicitly attribute authorship to other writers or sources: to anonymous sages (22:17; 24:23), to Agur (30:1), and to Lemuel and his mother (31:1). The book also testifies to a date of composition that is at least two hundred years after Solomon: the heading in 25:1 attributes the arrangement to King Hezekiah's scribes. Consequently, it may be that references to Solomon (1:1; 10:1; 25:1) function less as the identification of the author and more as dedication pages to the patron of the wisdom movement in Israel, or perhaps even the one who initially financed the project of collecting and arranging Israel's proverbs. In the ancient Near East, scribes did not think of authorship as an individual accomplishment like we do today. Instead, the composition of a book was typically a group effort that took place over time. This is not at all to deny statements about Solomon's wisdom (1 Kgs. 10:23–24) or the possibility that some of his words might be in Proverbs. It is simply an effort to read what Proverbs says and does not say.[3]

What remains in the prologue is the purpose statement for this collection, arranged in a series of five Hebrew infinitives, translated above as "for," that solidify into two major ideas and an underlying foundation. First, the book of Proverbs has a set of intellectual goals for the reader: to acquire the content of wisdom (1:2a, 4b) and to understand this content, developing good sense and becoming more mature (1:2b, 4, 6). Becoming wise requires us to learn both a body of information and the ability to comprehend this information.

Second, Proverbs has an explicitly practical goal: to "gain instruction" in how

3. The frequent address to "my son" throughout the book may denote a familial relationship, especially the instructions from the father *and* mother (Prov. 1:8, 6:20), or it may indicate a teacher/student relationship as in Eccl. 12:12.

to live wisely or in "wise dealing" (1:3a). The writer clarifies this goal with three key words for ideas that weave throughout the Old Testament in the *Torah*, the prophets, and now in wisdom literature. Wise living is defined as doing what is right, doing what is just, and treating others with equity (1:3). If only knowing what is right, what is just, and what is equitable were as easy as it sounds!

The sages recognized that the foundation of their teaching—of wisdom—is being in relationship with the Lord: "the fear of the Lord is the beginning of knowledge" (1:7a). This expression, which we will study in detail in chapter five, is how sages expressed their understanding of a proper relationship with the Lord: a relationship of awe and reverence and a close union comparable to the unity and intimacy of a wife and husband in marriage. Human observation and experience of life may promote wisdom. But ultimately, the wisdom offered by Israel's sages begins and ends with relationship to God.

With these primary ideas in place, all that remains is to remind those who have been walking on this path for some time, "the wise" and "man of understanding" (1:5), that they could still benefit from instruction to "learn more" and "acquire [more] skill." As we will see, the life of wisdom is a journey, not a destination. So no matter how wise we may be or how old we may become, we can always benefit from additional instruction.

One last, important word before we leave the prologue. The opening verses provide the clues necessary—clear and strong in Hebrew, if not in English—to the identity of the target audience of the book: young men (1:4b), with older men a secondary objective (1:5). We cannot dodge this conclusion easily. The book of Proverbs comes from a culture far removed from our own and the distance between us and especially what the sages say about women will be all the more difficult to traverse if we don't acknowledge the obvious and the challenges it brings. The sages have much to say *about* women and wives, but unless the ode to the wise woman in 31:10–31 is for women (see ch. 2), the book of Proverbs *never speaks directly to women*.[4] The prologue explains why—the sages are primarily speaking to men—and this may explain why we find such negative statements about quarrelsome and nagging wives (see 21:9, 19; 25:24; 27:15–16), but not a single word about quarrelsome or nagging husbands (certainly a problem of equal prominence). Only with this said may we add that the principles of wisdom are no different for women than men. Reading Proverbs

4. In chapters 1–7, some versions translate the Hebrew word *ben* as "child" or "children" instead of its standard meaning: "son" or "sons." For "child" see the CEV and NRSV; for "son" see the NIV, CEB, and NASB. Several speeches are clearly to a son or sons, not daughters (5:7–20; 6:20–35; 7:1–27).

as women, however, is *on occasion* much like Ginger Rogers dancing with Fred Astaire. She did everything he did—only backwards and in high heels. So we too will be *occasionally* challenged to listen to wisdom from Proverbs that is slanted toward men—we must listen and then turn the idea around to hear its wisdom for women, an unfortunate but necessary hermeneutic (interpretative move) due to our separation from Proverbs in time and in place.

A Brief Tour of the House of Wisdom: Proverbs 1–9

The book of Proverbs consists of the prologue (1:1–7) and a conclusion (31:10–31), with two major collections of material (chs. 1–9 and 10:1–31:9), each edited or fashioned to serve a specific role in the book. Here we introduce the first collection of the book, chapters 1–9, and leave chapters 10–31 for chapter three. After the prologue, chapters 1–9 is composed of the following (see fig. 1.2):

- Ten speeches from a "father" or "father and mother" to a son or sons
- Three interludes from or about a woman named Wisdom
- A short collection of miscellaneous wisdom teachings
- A conclusion that features a final invitation from Woman Wisdom and an appearance by her nemesis, Woman Folly

Structure of Proverbs 1–9

Prologue (1:1–7)			
	Speech #1 (1:8–19)		
		Wisdom Interlude #1 (1:20–33)	
	Speech #2 (2:1–22)		
	Speech #3 (3:1–12)		
		Wisdom Interlude #2 (3:13–20)	
	Speech #4 (3:21–35)		
	Speech #5 (4:1–9)		
	Speech #6 (4:10–19)		
	Speech #7 (4:20–27)		
	Speech #8 (5:1–23)		
			Miscellaneous teachings (6:1–19)
	Speech #9 (6:20–35)		
	Speech #10 (7:1–27)		
		Wisdom Interlude #3 (8:1–36)	
Conclusion (9:1–18)			

Three primary themes run through these introductory chapters, interwoven strands that together create an enormous appeal for choosing wisdom. First, Proverbs 1–9 emphasizes the importance of wisdom. The theme is so prominent that the words "wise" or "wisdom" (*hokmah*) occur over thirty times in these chapters. The father and Woman Wisdom consistently urge the reader to get, acquire, or keep wisdom (e.g., 1:20–21; 2:2; 4:5, 7), and they motivate this action by describing the benefits of wisdom or a wise lifestyle. Wisdom will exalt and honor the reader (4:8–9), add length to life (4:10), heal the body (4:22), and provide protection and security (4:6). In essence, their message is that wisdom is the way to a life that is good, as opposed to a life that merely goes through the motions of being alive but is more like the living dead—the so-called "good life."

The second thematic element in Proverbs 1–9 is the path or trail that represents the nature of wisdom as a journey, not a destination. Wisdom is a practice or way of life, not a possession or achievement. These texts create stories in which the father and Woman Wisdom warn against taking the wrong path, the path of folly (e.g., 4:14–15; 5:6; 7:8, 22), while describing the path of wisdom as good and righteous and a path of justice (2:20; 4:11; 8:20). They encourage the reader to walk this trail with resolve (2:20; 4:25–27) and obedience (4:20), refusing to be side tracked onto the path of evil (1:14–15). They also assure those on the path of wisdom that they will discover many benefits for their decision and determination. The path is straight so that they may walk unhindered, even run and not stumble (4:12). God will protect them (2:6–8) and enable them to discern "every good course" or direction to take when they approach a fork in the road (2:9). Woman Wisdom will provide for them (8:20–21), and they will find the path to be pleasant and peaceful (3:17). The person who walks with her will be happy (8:32). And even if readers find themselves on the wrong path, wisdom will rescue them (2:12). Corrective teaching is also a path that leads to life (6:23). Or to look from a slightly different perspective, if the readers will "know God" in all their ways (3:6) and hold on to sound judgment and discretion (3:21), the Lord will keep their paths straight (3:6), and they will walk safely, without stumbling (3:23).

The third theme or thread weaving through Proverbs 1–9 is the necessity for the reader to decide to obey the father and decide for wisdom—*and decide now*. This theme begins with a simple call to listen and act. On one hand, it is the nature of a speech to call for the audience to listen. On the other hand, when we look at each speech and then all ten speeches together, the emphasis on ideas related to listening and not forgetting is overwhelming. If you are up to a little challenge, read this summary aloud:

> Listen (1:8), don't neglect your mother's teaching (1:8), accept my words (2:1), store up my commands (2:1), don't forget (3:1), guard my commands (3:1), don't reject the Lord's correction (3:11a), don't despise the Lord's instruction (3:11b), hold on to good judgment (3:21). Hear (4:1), pay attention (4:1), don't abandon my teaching (4:2), hold onto my words (4:4), keep my commands (4:4), don't forget and turn away from my words (4:5). Listen (4:10), take in my speech (4:10), hold onto instruction, don't slack off (4:13), protect wisdom (4:13), pay attention to my words (4:20). Listen to my speech (4:20), don't let my words slip from sight (4:21), guard my words (4:21), pay attention (5:1). Listen to what I know (5:1), listen to me (5:7), don't deviate from my words (5:7), keep my counsel (6:20), don't abandon your mother's instruction (6:20), bind and fasten them on you (6:21). Keep my commands (7:1), store up my commands (7:2), guard or protect my instruction—like the pupil of your eye (7:2), bind them on your fingers (7:3), write them on your heart (7:3). Listen to me (7:24), pay attention (7:24).

If you accepted my challenge, I think you will agree that it's difficult not to come away with the impression that for some reason listening, paying attention, and remembering are *major issues* for the sages. It's obvious, but why?

Why such a major emphasis on the common ideas of listening and accepting wisdom? One answer comes in the first speech (1:8–19, a detailed study will come later) that acknowledges the presence of another group who are also speaking to the son, "the sinners" (1:10). This group, the other voice in the room, wants the son to come with them: get crazy with their fun (1:11–12), get rich quick (1:13), and become an equal in their group (1:14). In other words, there is another way and another voice describing the path to "the good life," and it sounds exciting, easy, and fun. The parents know about this path and this voice. In addition, they are also aware of another woman (or women) on the prowl for young victims. Like "the sinners," this woman has a persuasive voice: a flattering tongue (6:24), lips that drip with honey along with speech that is smoother than oil (5:3), and slick words (2:16) that seduce the unsuspecting, naïve youth (7:21) with promises of "the good life" that in fact lead to *living death*. So not only do the parents realize that they are not the only ones speaking to the son; they know the other voices are intensely persuasive. And their son still lacks the wisdom to recognize the danger in the other path. But they see the risk, and they know that *the son's life depends on persuading him to listen to their voice, not others.*

Another answer comes from Woman Wisdom, a figure we will examine more closely in chapter two. In her first appearance, she works to be heard above the noise of the crowd (1:20–21) and is dumbfounded by the young men's refusal to listen to her (1:22–25). She knows that their decision is a matter of life and death (1:31–32). And like the parents, Woman Wisdom also recognizes the threat of a counter voice, Woman Folly, who must be refused if the youth is to live (9:13–18). As a result, Proverbs 1–9 is no serene, quiet text but a battleground of fighting with words for the son's attention—*for the sake of his life.*

These three themes constitute the message of Proverbs 1–9: the importance of wisdom, which is life over death; the nature of wisdom as a path to walk, not a destination at which we arrive; and the emphatic appeal to make a decision for wisdom and decide now to listen to the voices of wisdom rather than the voices promising "the good life." In this war of words and ideas, a battle over how we view the world and how we live, every reader must make a clear choice. And we must decide, because anything less is by default falling to the alternative voices. The path of wisdom demands a decision and commitment because it is the more difficult, strenuous way of life. Without this decision and commitment, the son will slide into the arms of "the good life" and *death.*

Conclusion

An open discussion about writers, their objectives, target audiences, and chapter summaries can have all the appeal of a root canal. Yet to skip over or minimize this information would severely weaken our ability to read and understand the book of Proverbs. So we have traveled a significant distance in this chapter, both back in time and toward the path of wisdom. In the process, we have heard multiple voices speaking for and about God, like a grand choir performing together: the prophets are sopranos, the priests tenors, and the sages altos. Each group sings a distinct range of notes, occasionally sharing notes and singing in unison with one another. But in most cases, their greatest musical achievement and richest testimony for the Lord come when each group and all of their individual singers engage their full range of voices in harmony—and occasionally in dissonance.

The sages have described the purposes and the persons for whom they wrote Proverbs. They wrote primarily for naïve young men who stand at a point in life when they must begin to take more responsibility for themselves and their decisions. With a non-negotiable foundation, the sages of Proverbs set out their agenda in two parts: 1) intellectual goals to help the youths secure the content of wisdom and learn how to understand this content, and

2) practical goals to provide instruction in how to live wisely in relationships with other people—doing what is right, acting in and for justice, and treating others with equity. To be wise, the youth must engage these practices within a proper relationship with the Lord, the foundation of wisdom: *the fear of the Lord.* The sages reject outright the possibility of genuine wisdom without this foundation of commitment to the Lord.

We've also found a woven tapestry in Proverbs 1–9, a composition made from primary colors of thread: yellow for the importance of wisdom; blue to represent wisdom as a way or path (not a destination); and red for the necessity of making a decision and committing to a wise lifestyle *now*. These primary colors are beautifully woven together in Proverbs 1–9 to create a tapestry that makes a massive appeal to the reader to listen and accept wisdom. To this tapestry and its rainbow of colors we turn in chapter two.

DISCUSSION QUESTIONS

1. Based on the assigned reading (see #3 above), how would you define wisdom? What types of things does a wise person do or not do? Describe what a wise person looks like. How does your definition compare to my description of wisdom?
2. Identify modern people or groups who are most like Israel's priests, prophets, and sages. Share and explain your selections. Does your faith tradition accept multiple perspectives on God and the life of faith? Which voices are accepted? Which are rejected? Explain.
3. What is the source of a sage's insight into God and life? On a scale of 1 to 10 (with 1 = no, unlikely, very uncomfortable and 10 = yes, very comfortable), how likely are you to accept someone's experience as a legitimate or authoritative witness to God and faith life? What factors influence your decision?
4. According to the prologue (1:1–7), what are the major goals or ideas in the book of Proverbs? How would you organize this set of goals or objectives?
5. What are the three major themes in Proverbs 1–9 described in this chapter? What larger message emerges from the combination of these individual themes? How does Proverbs 1–9 and its themes relate to the remainder of Proverbs, 10–31?

PROJECT CHALLENGE

If we accept that scientists are much like Israel's sages in their search for truth through the experience of experimentation, how does this view change the dynamic between science and religion? What place does (or should) the work of other sciences, for example psychology, sociology, or anthropology, have in religion? Are some faith traditions more accepting of these voices than other traditions? If so, please identify them and explain why they are more accepting.

CHAPTER 2

The Women of Proverbs and Proverbs 1–9

Here's all you have to know about men and women:
women are crazy, men are stupid.
And the main reason women are crazy is that men are stupid.

—George Carlin

Ginger Rogers did everything that Fred Astaire did.
She just did it backwards and in high heels.

—Ann Richards

TO PREPARE FOR READING THIS CHAPTER

Read either #1 or #2:

1. Proverbs 1–9
2. Proverbs 1:20–33; 3:13–18; 4:1–9; 5:1–23; 6:20–35; 9:1–18

I grew up in a hub for the Sante Fe Railroad, a business in existence to transport goods from manufacturers to consumers. Because we lived on one side of the rails and attended a church on the other side, it was not unusual for us to get stuck on the road when a train came rushing through. Or much worse, to wait as a slow yard engine pushed cars back and forth on the side rails, carefully creating the next big train from cars designed specifically for their cargo: *tank cars* filled with crude oil or milk; *refrigerated cars* for fruits and veggies; *hopper trucks* with trap doors for unloading coal, grain, or sand; *reefer cars* with solid sides and roof for anything that can be put in a box or crate; along with *flatbeds, stock cars, passenger cars,* and many others.

Proverbs 1–9 has its own "freight" to move and deliver. Its "bill of lading," a list of goods carried, consists of the three major themes: 1) the importance of wisdom for living a life that is good; 2) the nature of wisdom as a path or way of living, not a destination at which we may arrive and declare ourselves wise; and 3) the absolute necessity for youth, and all readers, to make a choice for wisdom—and to decide now—or by default choose to live foolishly. Proverbs 1–9 carries these three interwoven themes for delivery primarily to young men (1:4) and other sages for their continued growth (1:5).

If we were the writers and our audience consisted of young men, naïve and inexperienced as they stepped out to face new decisions, *what would we use to haul the freight?* What set of images would be most effective in convincing the youth to accept wisdom? What will best hold his attention? The editors/writers of Proverbs 1–9 do not hesitate to lay all their cards on the table in the first chapter. They choose the object of fascination, mystery, and desire for young men: women. Please forgive me for the images now racing through your mind; comparing women to freight trains is not exactly flattering. I'm reminded of a young pastor on Mother's Day Sunday who took Proverbs 31:10–31 as his text. Since his church was near the Gulf of Mexico, he decided to compare the "worthy woman" to a tugboat. He had good intentions, but poor execution. This is not to excuse my reference to freight trains, but an opportunity to point out that all metaphors only go so far before they begin to break down, just as my comparison of women to a loaded train breaks down before the caboose clears the station.

Women do carry a load in Proverbs 1–9: twice the young man's mother speaks alongside his father (1:8–9; 6:20); five lectures extensively develop one or more female figures (2:16–19; 4:5–9; 5:3–23; 6:20–35; 7:1–27); the first three interludes feature Woman Wisdom (1:20–33; 3:13–20, 8:1–36); and the conclusion sets Woman Wisdom against Woman Folly (9:1–18). Over half of Proverbs 1–9 is placed in the mouths or hands of women.[1] The strategy is logical: in a culture lacking movies, magazines, and photographs, the next best thing for anyone trying to get young men's attention is to speak to them about women. Describe various kinds of women and encourage them to pursue one kind of woman and stay away from others. In simple terms, use their raging hormones to help them make a wise decision.

As we move ahead, we will see on the one hand that the sages cast some women into roles that are nothing less than remarkable: mothers who speak to their sons and the personification of wisdom as a woman. These are wel-

1. Of 256 verses in Proverbs 1–9, 132 specifically mention or speak about women (1:8, 20–33; 2:16–19; 3:13–18; 4:5–9; 5:3–20; 6:24–35; 7:4–27; 8:1–36; 9:1–6, 13–18). In addition, another seventeen verses either introduce these texts or draw conclusions from them (2:20–22; 3:19–20; 4:1–4; 5:1–2, 21–23; 7:1–3), increasing the total to 148 of 256 verses, or 58 percent of Proverbs 1–9.

come moves in a society marked by patriarchy and misogyny. On the other hand, the sages also type cast women as predators on the prowl to take advantage of naïve young men: the "other woman" who is eager to lure a young man into her bed and Woman Folly who is loud and ignorant. When compared, the positive roles of women in chapters 1–9 outpace the negative type casting at the rate of sixty percent to forty percent. That said, before we move forward we need to address valid concerns raised by these texts.

First to men: I do not believe it is possible for us to fully realize the burden imposed on women by misogynistic type casting. It's all too easy for male readers to say these women are just literary personifications created to encourage us to concentrate on the principles or the positive images of women and to ignore any negative emotional response to these texts—to our own harm. Since Adam and Eve in the garden, men have been blaming women for their own lack of self-control and failure. My teenage years lacked no shortage of classes and youth sermons aimed straight at young women on their responsibility to dress modestly so they do not cause the boys to sin. I don't remember much aimed at me regarding self-control. Men, please do not dismiss or treat this matter flippantly.

Second to women: I can never fully understand the struggles and feelings created by these texts, and too many others. It's true that as long as men have been in charge of writing and reading texts, women have been objectified, used to carry male blame, and/or disregarded for most things other than being a sex object. At least in recent years new breezes have begun to provide fresh air and fresh interpretations that bring attention to figures such as Woman Wisdom. Still, we have these texts with their stereotypical language about women, their bodies, and their ability to seduce. I know some feminist interpretations dismiss these texts outright on the principle that a man's God controlling a woman's body contains no gospel. I am unable to go to such an extreme, and I will assume for now that you are also unable to set these texts aside. But what are we to do?

Women and men, all I know to do is to read carefully, listen attentively to one another, be sensitive to the emotions dredged up by these images, and give one another much grace. And alongside the troublesome texts, watch for remarkable claims made by or about women in these chapters. These assertions will not erase other problematic texts, but what we find will do nothing less than challenge every assumption we've made about women in Israel—and perhaps about women today.

Now to the plan. An easy way to "get at" this material about and from women is to identify the cast of women in Proverbs 1–9, explore the texts about each group of women, and trace their efforts to persuade the young men. These women include 1) the young man's mother, 2) the young man's wife, 3) any woman other than the young man's wife, 4) Woman Wisdom, and 5) Woman Folly.

The Young Man's Mother

The first woman in Proverbs appears alongside the father as a coauthor and speaker of the first (1:8–19) and ninth speeches (6:20–35). In both cases, she and the father warn against the seductive speech of a group posing a dangerous threat to the son. In the first speech, the "sinners" invite the son to join their gang for a life filled with excitement (1:11–12), fast money (1:13), and immediate recognition as an equal (1:14)—as opposed to the path of wisdom that does not feature cheap thrills at the expense of others. Together, the son's parents expose the truth behind the alternative rhetoric: they are a bloodthirsty gang in such a frenzy to steal and kill that they run into their own ambush and kill themselves (1:15–19).

In the ninth speech, the parents' instruction is all that stands between their son and married women who flatter (6:24) and use their bodies to seduce their son (6:25). Unlike the first speech, we do not hear a recreation of the words these women speak. Instead, without interruption or objection, the parents develop an argument that stresses two related points: 1) the high cost of adultery and 2) the certainty of payment. For example, a prostitute's fee is minimal in comparison to the price for fooling around with another man's wife: your life (6:26).[2] This warning is for all those who believe they will get away with their infidelity and that others having an affair may get caught, but not them. The parents stress the certainty of getting caught with two illustrations: a person cannot carry fire in their robe without catching fire (6:27), and a person cannot walk on hot coals without burning their feet (6:28). Everyone who has an affair with another person's spouse will be caught.

2. Proverbs 6:26 does not condone or approve of prostitution, but only uses the cost of prostitution as a point of comparison for the much higher cost of adultery. Prostitution often comes as the result of a lack of other options for women living on the margins of society or has to do with pagan fertility rites. So while the Old Testament may not explicitly outlaw prostitution as such, it does condemn sacred prostitution (men and women) associated with the temple (1 Kgs. 14:24; 15:12; 22:46; 2 Kgs. 23:7) and implicitly passes judgment on societies who leave (or force) women into such circumstances (cf. Gen. 38, in which Judah is ready to execute Tamar for "playing the whore" [v.24] until he realizes he was the one who slept with her).

In addition to their counter claim against the son's belief that he will not get caught, the parents also emphasize that his punishment will be severe. Think about it, the parents say; people feel sorry for a man who steals to feed his family, yet he will still be punished in full (Prov. 6:30–31). So what will happen to a man caught with another man's wife? *No one in the community* will feel sorry for him—he most certainly will pay in full! If people think otherwise, they are only fooling themselves. He will be wounded, disgraced, and dishonored. He will destroy himself (6:32–33). *And then he must face the woman's husband.* If the son is wealthy and thinks he will be able to pay off his lover's husband, once again he only fools himself (6:35). The woman's enraged husband will demand his revenge. Nothing will get the son off the hook: not his money nor mercy from his lover's husband. However, all of this is avoidable if only the son will listen to his mother and his father. Their wisdom can help him see through bogus invitations, sense the true nature of a situation before it grows out of control, and stay alive.

The Young Man's Wife

The young man's wife appears in only the eighth lecture (5:1–23), as a counter point to the "other" woman who attempts to seduce the young man with her smooth words (5:3). The father first identifies the true nature of her speech and ways: her sweet words leave a bitter aftertaste and cut like a double-edged sword (5:4); her "feet"[3] lead to death (5:5); and she hasn't a clue as to where she is going or what she is doing (5:6). Once again, the father urges the son to stay away from this other woman (5:8) by emphasizing the true cost of following her: he will lose his honor and years to the merciless (5:9); strangers will take all he has worked for (5:10); and eventually he will reach a point of "utter ruin" in the community (5:14).

The father presents the young man's wife as an alternative to the other woman. He encourages the son to "Drink water from your own cistern" (5:15), a thinly veiled reference to sex or making love (see the Song 4:12, 15 for similar language). He asks the son, would he want his springs "scattered" or flowing into the streets? Again, this is a thinly disguised reference to the son's wife and means, "Would you want your wife to spread her sexual favors to others in the

3. Terms such as "feet" sometimes denote sexual organs, for example Exod. 4:25, 1 Sam. 24:3 (lit. "to cover his feet"), 2 Sam. 11:8. In Proverbs 5:5, the word may carry a double entendre, following where her feet go and having sex with her.

same way that you are taking water from other men?" The question assumes the reply: "No, I want to keep my water for myself." So the father urges the son to find complete satisfaction in his spring, his wife, and to be completely intoxicated by her love (Prov. 5:19). Why would he ever want to let another woman get him drunk (5:20)? Familiar themes conclude this speech: God does see what we do (5:21), and it is our own actions that ultimately ensnare and trip us (5:22).

The "Other" Woman

In four speeches, the father (and mother) describe the "other" woman with two unflattering adjectives: 1) *zarah* (2:16a; 5:3a, 20a; 7:5); and 2) *nokriyah* (2:16b; 5:20b; 6:24b; 7:5b). Figure 2.1 provides a summary of *zarah* in four major translations.

The Translation of *Zarah* in Proverbs 1–9

Zarah	NRSV	ERV	NIV	ESV
2:16a	loose woman	that other woman	adulterous woman	mysterious woman
5:3a	loose woman	other woman	adulterous woman	mysterious woman
5:20a	another woman	another man's wife	another man's wife	mysterious woman
7:5a	loose woman	other woman	adulterous woman	mysterious woman

The translation of *nokriyah* in the same four translations of Proverbs 2:16b; 5:20b; 6:24b; 7:5b is as follows: NRSV and ESV "adulterous"; NIV "wayward woman"; and ERV "another man's wife," "another woman," or "the other man's wife."

These two terms suggest the basic idea of *otherness* or *not belonging in this place* regardless of her specific identity. She is foreign or off limits to the young man. Why she is off limits, however, not only varies from one speech to another, it is sufficiently vague in some speeches to evoke multiple identities as our perspective changes. The use of labeling, calling this woman loose, foreign, or strange, is a powerful way to strip her of identity or dehumanize her, an aggressive literary strategy—and a serious problem in our twenty-first century culture. Once we identify and label someone or some group, often those who are opposed to me or my group, we find it much easier to speak about them and treat them as if they were less than human. We erase their human face—God's image—so we call them *Tea Partyers, Liberals, Democrats, Republicans,* or *Jews.*

In the second speech (2:1–22), the woman may be an unfaithful wife who has broken her sacred marriage vows and left her husband (2:16–17). Or "the covenant" may refer to God's basic covenant with Israel (Exod. 20–24). If so, she is an Israelite who has broken faith and left her God. In speech eight (Prov. 5:1–23), the NIV indicates its conclusion by translating *zarah* as "adulteress" (5:3). But the speech actually says nothing about her marital status. She is "strange," one meaning of *zarah,* or a "foreigner," one meaning of *nokriyah* (5:20b CEB: "Why . . . embrace the breasts of a foreign female?"). This translation suggests a different reason why she is off limits: she is a non-Israelite who will lead the young man to worship her gods. In the ninth speech (6:20–35), the language strongly indicates that the woman is married (6:26, 29, 32, 34–35).[4] The same is true for the tenth speech (7:1–27). The woman may appear "decked out *like* a prostitute" (7:10, emphasis mine). But the speaker is abundantly clear that she is in fact married: her husband is away on business and will not be home for many days (7:19–20).

These multiple possibilities may leave us a bit confused, but we are very near the crucial idea. Throughout the various texts one truth holds constant about the identity of this woman: *she is a woman other than the young man's wife, or an "other" woman.* And any woman *other than* the son's wife is strictly off limits.

We have already examined the eighth (5:1–23) and ninth speeches (6:20–35) above. Here, I give brief attention to the "other" woman's role in the second (2:1–22) and tenth speeches (7:1–27). In the second speech, the "other" woman plays a small role (2:16–19) among the evil people (2:12–15). Wisdom will save the youth from terrible people who not only twist their words (2:12) and exchange the path of integrity for dark paths (2:15). Wisdom will also save the young man from the woman who has turned her back on her husband and her sacred marriage vows (2:17). She is an "adulteress" whose most dangerous weapon is her words (2:16).

One way that wisdom will save the young man is if he follows the father's advice at the beginning of the tenth lecture and *marries wisdom*: "Say

4. In 6:24a, the Hebrew text reads *ra,* "evil woman" (as in the CEB). The NRSV and NIV, however, emend the Hebrew to read *re'a,* and translate "wife of another" (NRSV) or "neighbor's wife" (NIV).

to wisdom, 'You are my sister,' and call insight your intimate friend" (7:4). I admit that this phrase is unlikely to strike many as romantic. So to be clear, the father does not expect the son to marry his sister or treat his wife as if she was his sister. Instead, "You are my sister" is simply an expression of intimacy between a husband and wife in their culture. For example, the same image appears in the love poetry of the Song of Songs:

> *You have captured my heart, my sister, my bride!* (Song 4:9a CEB)
> *How beautiful is your loving, my sister, my bride!* (Song 4:10a CEB)

Marriage to the right woman (Wisdom), the father suggests, will keep the son safe from the wrong woman and prevent what the father witnesses when day turns to night.

From his window, the father saw an episode play out one night (Prov. 7:6–23). We might conclude that this young man got too close; he should have stayed a safer distance away (7:7–8). But in reality, this woman is everywhere (7:11–12), so distance will not change the story. Wherever the son might go, he must be prepared to meet this woman and see through her words. It is in fact her words that are so dangerous (7:21). She speaks as if she were devoted to God (7:14). Even more, she makes the young man feel special, declaring that she has been out looking just for him (7:15).

Now that she has found him, her seduction shifts into high gear. She speaks of her bed and describes the delicate and erotic preparations waiting at home (7:16–17). Then she comes to the point: "Come, let us take our fill of love until morning; let us delight ourselves with love" (7:18). She calms his anxiety by anticipating and answering his unspoken questions (see 7:19–20):

> Where is your husband? *"My husband is not at home."*
> Where did he go? *"He has gone on a long journey."*
> How long will he be gone? *"He took a bag of money with him."*
> So when will he be back? *"He will not come home until the full moon."*

Her answers persuade the youth to follow her "like an ox to slaughter" (7:21–23). Her house is the portal to death itself: those who enter never leave. For fellow children of the sixties and seventies, it's like checking into the "Hotel California."

> *You can check out any time you like,*
> *but you can never leave!* (The Eagles)

Like in the other speeches in Proverbs, path imagery dominates in both the second and the tenth lecture. The wisdom offered by the father is critical for the youth to be able to differentiate folly and wisdom, thereby saving his life. Again, the son must decide now what he believes and how he will live.

Woman Wisdom

The fourth woman is one of the most provocative yet overlooked figures in the Old Testament, the mysterious woman named Wisdom. Five texts in Proverbs feature this woman (1:20–33; 3:13–20; 8:1–36; 9:1–6; 31:10–31), with passing references elsewhere (e.g., 4:5–9; 7:4). We treat the first two and last of these texts here (1:20–33; 3:13–18; 31:10–31) and the third in chapter five (8:1–36). The fourth is included below in our discussion of Woman Folly (9:1–6, 13–18).

Introduction to Woman Wisdom: Proverbs 1:20–33

The book of Proverbs quickly introduces the figure of Wisdom after the parent's first speech (1:8–19). Here, as elsewhere, Wisdom not only comes to life but takes the shape of a woman (not a man): *she* raises her voice (1:20b); *she* cries out (21a); and *she* speaks (21b). With a little imagination, we may follow her movement. She speaks everywhere: in the street, in the squares (1:20), at the busiest corner, and in the city gate (1:21). In other words, Wisdom is available everywhere—the youth must only recognize her voice. As we overhear her words, it is difficult not to notice a thick accent of favorite words and phrases: she "cries out" (1:20a, 21a), "raises her voice" (1:20b), and asks, "How long?" (1:22a, b). Her words sound much like the prophets who also asked, "How long?": Moses (Exod. 10:3), Elijah (1 Kgs. 18:21), Isaiah (Isa. 6:11), Hosea (Hosea 8:5), Habakkuk (Hab. 1:2; 2:6), Zechariah (Zech. 1:12), and especially Jeremiah (Jer. 4:14, 21; 12:4; 13:27; 23:26; 31:22; 47:5–6). In other words, not only is Wisdom depicted as a woman, she is also cast as a powerful prophet.

Woman Wisdom, an exasperated prophet, addresses young men (Prov. 1:22–23). She has done everything possible to get their attention so that they will listen to her. But they have refused to respond and accept any of her counsel or correction (1:24–25). So in a bold move, she tells the young men that when disaster hits them, she will laugh and mock them, apparently just as they have responded to her (1:26–27).

A slight but significant shift in pronouns occurs between Proverbs 1:27 and 1:28. In 1:20–27, Wisdom calls to the young men using the second person plural pronoun "you." But in 1:28 and afterward, she refers to the young men with the third person plural pronoun "they." This shift denotes that her audience has changed. She no longer speaks to the young men but explains and defends her behavior to another audience and uses the young men who would not listen as an object lesson. She tells the new audience that she will ignore the young men when they call to her in crisis (1:28) because they hate knowledge and did not choose "the fear of the Lord"—a proper relationship with God (1:29; see ch. 3). They have rejected everything she has tried to teach them (1:30). So now they get what they wanted: their "waywardness" and "complacency" will destroy them (1:31). But Wisdom assures this second audience that those who listen to her voice will be secure and have no reason to fear disaster (1:33).

About Woman Wisdom: Proverbs 3:13–20

The second text featuring Woman Wisdom is a bold contrast to her first appearance. The writer speaks about Woman Wisdom; she does not speak. The ominous threatening tone of the first speech is also replaced with a text of high praise. She is better than wealth (3:14), jewels (3:15a), and any other desire (3:15b). She holds long life in one hand, a full and genuine life that is good (3:16a). And in her other hand she holds wealth and honor (3:16b). The paths she travels, and implicitly invites the reader to walk with her, are all pleasant and peaceful (3:17). Then comes a surprise: Wisdom is also "a tree of life" (3:18a), which sends our thoughts racing back to the tree of life forever lost to humans (Gen. 3:22–24). Wisdom provides the life God has always intended for humanity. The catch? The young man and others must "find wisdom" and "get understanding" (Prov. 3:13). Even more, they must "lay hold of her" and never let go (3:18), an idea that leads to the proposal in 7:4—where the father arranges and proposes a marriage between the son and Woman Wisdom.

Woman Wisdom as the Capable Wife: Proverbs 31:10–31

The fifth text featuring Woman Wisdom comes in the final chapter of Proverbs: the ode to the "capable wife" or the "wife of noble character" (NIV), an apt conclusion for a book that begins with Woman Wisdom. The ode itself is an acrostic consisting of twenty-two lines or verses in which each line begins with the next successive letter of the Hebrew alphabet. A comparable poem in English would begin line one with the letter A; line two would begin with B, line three with C, and so forth all the way through X, Y, and Z. It is unlikely the poet used this literary form as a memory aid. Much more likely, he used it to create a beautiful poem in which everything is said that can be said about this woman—everything from Aleph to Tav in Hebrew—or as we would say, "Everything from A to Z."

Like other texts in Proverbs, the ode to the worthy woman was most likely adopted by the sages and brought into the book of Proverbs as a whole. In other words, it is not an original composition by the sages explicitly for the final chapter. In its original setting, I expect that the poet spoke in praise of wives who guided their homes and businesses with great skill or excellence (recall the first or primary meaning of wisdom; see ch. 1). It's not difficult to see or read the poem with this meaning. The sages, however, appear to take this poem and place it at the end of their collection for a different purpose: to summon Woman Wisdom to a final appearance, a curtain call of sorts. Two factors support this reading:

- It seems unlikely that a book that has not directly spoken to women would suddenly speak to them at the last minute. In scattered verses, the sages have spoken about women or wives that make a husband's life miserable (12:4b; 19:13b; 21:9, 19; 27:15–16) and women who bless their husbands and families (12:4a; 14:19; 18:22; 19:14). Of course it is possible the sages would want to provide another example of an excellent wife, but the imbalance created (22 sustained verses for the excellent wife versus a few scattered verses for the bad wife) and the placement of this poem at the end of the book make me suspicious that something else is going on.
- The more closely we examine what this woman does, the more echoes we hear of Woman Wisdom from chapters 1–9. Recall that in these earlier chapters Woman Wisdom was the one the father encouraged the son to love, hold on to, prize, honor (4:5–9), *and marry* (7:4). Notice the correlation between what the father says Woman Wisdom will do if the son accepts her (Prov. 1–9) and the description of this woman who (later) will have blessed the son's life.

Woman Wisdom in Proverbs 1–9 and the Worthy Woman in Proverbs 31

	Statements or Promises in Proverbs 1–9	Outcomes of Marrying Woman Wisdom in Proverbs 31
#1	Wisdom is the woman the young man should love and embrace (4:6, 8), lay hold of her and never let go (3:18), and say to her, "You are my sister" (7:4): *he should marry her.* She even invites him into her home (9:4–6).	"A capable wife who can find?" (31:10a), but he has clearly found her, married her, and now enjoys a lifetime of benefits from living with Woman Wisdom.
#2	Wisdom promises riches and honor (3:16b; 8:18), and endows with wealth (8:21).	She brings wealth and honor to her family through the many things she does. She is a hardworking, successful businesswoman (31:16, 18a, 24) who also works with her own hands (31:13, 17, 19), never stopping to rest (31:15a, 18b, 27b). She clothes herself and the family with luxurious, expensive clothing (31:21–22) and because of her, he has no lack of gain or wealth (31:11b).
#3	Wisdom is more precious than jewels (3:15; 8:11).	She is more precious than jewels (31:10b).
#4	Wisdom cries out in the streets and city squares to teach others (1:20–21; 8:1–9, 14; 9:4–6).	"She opens her mouth with wisdom" (31:26).
#5	Her paths are ways of pleasantness and peace (3:17).	She does her husband good, not harm (31:12).
#6	She is trustworthy: she gives good advice, sound wisdom, insight, and strength (8:14).	Her husband trusts in her and lacks nothing (31:11). She is clothed with dignity (31:25a).
#7	Those who trust Woman Wisdom will be secure with no dread of disaster (1:33).	She is not afraid of the future for her household (31:21) and "laughs at the time to come" (31:25b).
#8	By her kings reign, "rulers decree what is just," nobles govern rightly (8:15–16); she walks in the paths of righteousness and justice (8:20).	Because of her, her husband is able to sit in the city gate, where court cases are heard and justice dispensed (31:23).
#9	Wisdom has prepared luxurious food, meat and wine (9:2).	She provides food for her household (31:15b), and purchases food from far away (31:14).

#10	"Wisdom has built her house" (9:1); she gives house servants their tasks (9:3).	She supervises the home, directing servants (31:15c) and managing household affairs (31:27).
#11	The foundation and essence of Wisdom is the fear of the Lord (1:7; 9:10).	She fears the Lord (31:30).
#12	She is incomparable (3:15b; 8:11b); her income is better than silver and gold (3:14; 8:19).	Her husband praises her (31:28b) and says she surpasses all women (31:29). He calls for her work to publicly praise her (31:31).
#13	The one who finds her finds life and favor from the Lord (8:35).	This man/husband has definitely found life with her.
#14	Those who find Wisdom are happy (3:13a); those who listen to her and follow her ways are happy (8:32, 34).	If the man married to this woman is not happy, not only will he never be happy, nothing could ever make him happy.

The parallels between Woman Wisdom in chapters 1–9 and the worthy woman in chapter 31 are striking. At points the similarity is uncanny (e.g., #3), and in other points the similarity bears a family-like resemblance (e.g., #2). This mirror-like image is no accident or happenstance, but the very reason the sages employ this poem to conclude the book: to make one final appeal for accepting Woman Wisdom because of what she will do for our lives.

Note: Just as earlier collections have occasionally included the same proverb and been included as they stand (with the proverb already included earlier), so the final poem retains the shadow of its original self (aspects that may not precisely fit the earlier description of Woman Wisdom, e.g., the presence of children in 31:28) and may still be read as an ode to a worthy woman/wife (not Woman Wisdom).[5] In fact, this shadow from the poem's original purpose is insightful into the extent of women's activities in ancient Israel (when the poem was written):

- organizing and supervising household business (31:13–15, 19, 21)
- purchasing and developing real estate (31:16)

5. We find the same usage of poems elsewhere, where writers have incorporated a poem that works in its new context but does not fit in all its precise details. See the prayer of Hannah (1 Sam. 2:1–10): especially notice statements in vv. 5b ("the barren has borne seven") and 10b ("he will give strength to his king, and exalt the power of his anointed") that do not correlate to her present circumstances.

- running a profitable business (31:18, 24)
- looking after the poor (31:20)
- teaching others wisdom (31:26)

And for all these activities her husband and children are to praise her (31:28–29).

This leaves us with two reading or interpretive possibilities for the ode to the worthy woman:

- To read this poem in praise of ideal wives and mothers and as an example for women to follow
- To read this poem within the context of the book of Proverbs as a final appearance of Woman Wisdom, a familiar friend, guide, and spouse reaffirming the benefits promised to those who pursue a relationship with her

Woman Folly

The final chapter of Proverbs 1–9 permits Woman Wisdom and her nemesis, Woman Folly, another personification, to make their final appeals to the son and the reader. Wisdom presents her case first in the form of an invitation to a marvelous feast. She has made all her preparations and sent her servants to invite the young:

> *"You that are simple, turn in here!"*
> *To those without sense she says,*
> *"Come, eat of my bread*
> *and drink of the wine I have mixed.*
> *Lay aside immaturity, and live,*
> *and walk in the way of insight."* (9:4–6)

Woman Folly is given an equal opportunity to make her claims. Unlike Woman Wisdom, Folly is loud, a trait born of ignorance. Woman Folly sits outside the door of her house or on a perch at the highest places in town (9:14) and calls to those who pass by: "You who are simple, turn in here!" (9:16a).

If her invitation sounds familiar, it should: her opening invitation is identical to that of Woman Wisdom (see 9:4). A warning to the son and reader: discerning who to listen to, who is wise and who is a fool, may not always be easy. Woman Folly proposes illicit thrills just like the gang in Proverbs 1: eating bread in secret and enjoying stolen water (9:17). Recall 5:15–19, the advice to the young husband to drink from his own well, and the sexual innuendo involved. If this youth does not remember anything his mother, father, or Woman Wisdom have taught him throughout Proverbs 1–9, he will fall for Woman Folly's invitation and join her prior guests in the grave, Sheol (9:18).

Conclusion: Listening to Women

The speeches about and from women establish the primary themes of Proverbs 1–9, identified in chapter 1: the importance of wisdom for genuine life; wisdom as a path or way of life, a journey, not a destination; and the necessity of a firm decision and commitment to a wise lifestyle. Each of the speeches, as we've pointed out above, speaks to these themes—and even more, the speeches also expose cultural values that stand behind the attitudes and actions mentioned in the speeches. As we close this chapter, I want to suggest the types of attitudes that will lead to the problems confronted by the parents and Woman Wisdom in the text, *and I want to suggest that these attitudes from ancient Israel are also prevalent in our contemporary culture.*

- We want to be happy and fulfilled, to have "the good life" that comes from wealth, possessions, and position in society.
- We are an impatient society, demanding fast results and often taking foolish shortcuts. Whatever we want, *we want it now*: sexual pleasure, wealth, and positions of respect. The long path of wisdom has all the attraction of a cutting-edge computer from 1995.
- We avoid commitments, especially long term commitments that tie us down. In our minds, success requires flexibility—keeping our options open just in case a better opportunity comes along.
- We are certain that we are smarter and wiser than others, especially others who are trying to teach us. We will never be discovered in bed with someone other than our spouse or be caught ambushing and killing innocent people. We are too wise and sophisticated to be caught or to pay for the consequences of our lifestyle.
- Our world revolves around us: our well-being, our desires, and our happiness. Other people are merely a way to get what we want—a means to an end.

- Our goal is "the good life:" a life that is filled with excitement of all types, money, and happiness, the more of all the better. And we are convinced that the way to the good life is by making ourselves happy—whatever it takes.

The Israelites' world, the world that produced Proverbs 1–9, may be far away and long ago. But their cultural values are little different from our own. The specific cultural expressions of these values may differ from our own, but they are still recognizable—and they still destroy us. In response, the father and mother along with Woman Wisdom look the youth in the eye and say, "Don't be a fool. The path to the so-called good life does not lead to a good life, but to a living death."

Instead, the voices in Proverbs 1–9 urge us, "Make a decision for wisdom and a life that is good." A life in which we are committed to walking with wisdom and doing what is right, just, and equitable. A life in which we are married to wisdom, trusting that the Lord and Woman Wisdom will bring more blessing than we will ever find in "the good life." That life begins with a proper relationship with the Lord. All that comes in Proverbs 10–31 depends on this prior decision, and if we refuse to make it, we have little sense to continue. The sages have pushed us to the edge; now it's up to us to decide which life we will pursue: "the good life" or "the life that is good."

DISCUSSION QUESTIONS

1. Read through Proverbs 1–9 again and make a few notes. What impresses you as the most important ideas in Proverbs 1–9? In what way does the text indicate or show that these are the most important ideas? Explain each idea or concept.
2. Why do you think the writers choose to personify wisdom as a woman? In Hebrew, all nouns and adjectives are masculine or feminine; *hokmah*, translated "wisdom," is feminine. What advantages do the writers gain by personifying wisdom as a woman? Does this choice surprise you in any way?
3. What is the most effective weapon of the "other woman" in Proverbs 1–9? Why is it so effective? Would this weapon be the most effective today, or would the most effective weapon be different? What if the concern was about "other men?" What is their most effective weapon for persuading women?

4. How do you feel about the descriptions of the "other woman"? How do these descriptions compare to the evil or wicked men in Proverbs 1–9? How has this difference in describing men and women influenced or impacted your life? What most concerns you, if anything?
5. Does the recognition of Proverb's primary audience as young males change the way you now respond to question #4? Had you noticed this specific claim before? In your opinion, who is the woman in Proverbs 31:10–31? Is this a normal human wife and example to follow, or is this Woman Wisdom? How does your answer change the message of the chapter?
6. Proverbs primarily addresses young men who are beginning to make life decisions and who are becoming more responsible for their lives. At what age(s) or point(s) does this shift occur in your culture? What happens at these points in life?

PROJECT CHALLENGE

Proverbs 1–9 features three speeches from Woman Wisdom that encourage people to accept her words, live in her path, and ultimately marry her. *Reimagine these speeches.* What if the primary audience consisted of young women and that instead of Woman Wisdom, the sages selected *Mr. Wisdom*? Write a speech from Mr. Wisdom to a young woman. What dangers face a young woman today? What are the "other" or "strange" men like? How can a young woman recognize and avoid them? Share your speech with the group.

CHAPTER 3

The Proverb and Proverbs 10–31

Stick to the wicket
and the runs will come.

—Anonymous

I came to a fork in the road
and I took it.

—Yogi Berra

Mokopi o na le marago a malele
(A beggar has a long bottom [must be willing to wait])

—Botswana

TO PREPARE FOR READING THIS CHAPTER

Read the proverbs in either #1 or #2:

1. Read Proverbs 10 and 26 with special attention to possible connections between the proverbs. For example, do you see a connection between 26:1 and 26:2? Also pay attention to what the sages say about the nature of a proverb. For example, are proverbs true in every situation?
2. Read Proverbs 13:8; 14:20; 15:27; 17:8, 23; 18:8; 19:4; 20:16; 21:14; 22:6, 7; 27:13

How we communicate with one another is at the heart of the 2014 movie, *The Imitation Game*, a loose adaptation of historical events surrounding the breaking of the German Enigma code machine during World War II. As a young boy, the lead character, Alan Turing, speaks about the similarity between oral human communication and codes and code breaking. He grieves his inability to understand what people say because they always use codes, saying one thing when they mean something else. For example later in the movie, Turing confuses his colleagues when they say, "We are going to lunch," and he makes no response. Then they are flustered when they ask if he heard what they said, and Turing replies, "Yes." Only after labored repetition and clarification are they able to help Turing understand that they are inviting him to lunch, which he turns down because he does not like sandwiches. Turing's mind is simply incapable of deciphering common human codes as they are used in contexts or particular situations. However his insight that language is essentially *communication in code* helps him understand the only way to beat the German Enigma code.

Turing struggled with what communication specialists now call "pragmatics." He was unable to see or understand the way in which context, a social situation, contributes to the meaning of words. Here I want to make a loose comparison to another language feature that frequently contributes to misunderstanding: "genre." Genre is a form or type of oral or written speech with its own set of rules for interpretation, called the conventions of the genre. In fact, all communication has a genre, such as a literal report, a conversation, a formal speech, a sermon, a fable, a myth, a novel, a historical report, a parable, and a short, two- to three-line proverb. It is somewhat easy to see the importance of recognizing the genre of a written text. After all, we don't read *Moby Dick* as a historical report of a fishing expedition, or the Warren Commission's findings regarding the assassination of President Kennedy as a novel. Raised within American/Western culture, we have become accustomed to the genres of our culture and how they work. Consequently, in most situations we automatically recognize the genre we are listening to, for example political commentary, a talk show, or the news, or reading, for example different genres in a newspaper: front page stories, opinion columns, want ads, obituaries, and comic strips. Once we identify the genre, subconsciously in most cases, we adjust our interpretation to fit the genre.

But what comes so easily from growing up in our own culture isn't so easy when we read the Bible, a text from the ancient Near East with literary forms and genres that fit an ancient Near Eastern mindset or philosophy. This is a particular problem when we are reading and trying to understand proverbs. Consequently, our first task in this chapter is to unpack the challenges involved in understanding the genre of proverbs. Though understanding proverbs may seem simple, the challenges are far more complex than we may imagine them to be. Second, we will take a brief tour of Proverbs 10–31 and set the stage for the study to come.

The Question of Genre

Challenge #1: Absolute versus Conditional Meaning

Whenever I taught Proverbs 10–31 and had extra time, I distributed 3 x 5 cards and asked the students or seminar participants to write down proverbs or short sayings that they recalled hearing while they were growing up, and not necessarily proverbs from the Bible. After a few minutes, I asked students to share their most memorable sayings and their source. Among my favorites, some from traditional American wisdom and others shared by permission, are the following:

The early bird gets the worm.

Too many cooks spoil the stew.

People won't care what you look like,
but they'll remember you coming late.
(I'll let you guess the gender of the man who said this.)

A penny saved is a penny earned.

Never put off until tomorrow
what you can do today.

Next I would ask, "Are these proverbs always true? Can you think of other proverbs that contradict these sayings?" It would not take long for proverbs to be flying back and forth across the room, and the class would be having a good time.

The early bird may get the worm,
but the second rat gets the cheese.

Look before you leap,
but he who hesitates is lost.

Too many cooks may spoil the stew,
but two heads are better than one,
and many hands make light work.

People won't care what you look like,
but they'll remember you coming late.
(a grandfather's perspective)

People won't care if you come late,
but they'll remember what you look like.
(a grandmother's perspective)

A penny saved is a penny earned,
but don't be penny wise and pound foolish.

Never put off until tomorrow
what you can do today;
but learn to stop and smell the roses.

What this means for reading the proverbs in the book of Proverbs is more than significant: it turns on the reading lamp. As a rule, proverbs are not one-size-fits-all statements of absolute truth. They are observations about life from limited perspectives and specific circumstances. This is true for the genre of proverbs that are outside and inside the Bible. Take for example the second and third proverbs in Proverbs chapter 10:

The LORD does not let the righteous go hungry,
but he thwarts the craving of the wicked. (10:3)

A slack hand causes poverty,
but the hand of the diligent makes rich. (10:4)

If we misread the genre of these claims and take them as flat assertions of absolute truth, because they are in the Bible, we are in trouble. For example, with the greatest of sarcasm I assert that the first proverb confirms what I have always thought of the apostle Paul: he was a terrible man. After all in 2 Corinthians when he describes his hardships, he admits that he had been hungry and thirsty many times and often without food (2 Cor. 11:27). Paul isn't fooling me for a minute. Even after he became a Christian, he must have been wicked because Proverbs 10:3 says the Lord won't let righteous people go hungry. That's what happens to the wicked—I say with great sarcasm. *See the problem?*

We find the same trouble with Proverbs 10:4, except now I ask us to draw from our experience and what we see in the world. Does diligence always make a person wealthy? What about the poor; are they always lazy and unproductive? Of course not. Many are born into wealth and never do anything productive. They have trust funds that ensure they will always be wealthy. Most of the world's wealthiest people did not start from square one without a dollar to their name. They began with money to invest. So when their investments paid off big and they became multi-millionaires, their fortune was less about long hours and hard work than about the advantage of starting life ahead—like on the fourth lap of a four-lap race. On the other hand, some of the most diligent workers in the world are in factories, hotels, fast food restaurants, and refugee camps. But these persistent, hardworking people are not exactly becoming wealthy.

The book of Proverbs also establishes the proverb as a non-absolute genre. In chapter 26 we read

> *Do not answer fools according to their folly,*
> *or you will be a fool yourself.* (26:4)

This proverb urges us to avoid correcting or arguing with fools because such an engagement is certain to make us look like a fool. Then we read

> *Answer fools according to their folly,*
> *or they will be wise in their own eyes.* (26:5)

This instruction is equally clear: we should reply to fools and put them in their place so that their pride, being "wise in their own eyes," does not continue to grow.

But just exactly what are we supposed to do with fools? Verse five tells us to respond and put them in their place, but verse four tells us not to respond at all, or we will look like or even become fools. So what gives? *To speak or not to speak, that is the question.* And the answer to our dilemma is simple: it all depends on the circumstances or situation. And even then, the only way to know is by wisdom.

The ability to memorize and quote proverbs is not the same as becoming wise. Any fool can quote a proverb, and many do. But their deployment of a saying may be useless and unhelpful.

> *The legs of a disabled person hang limp;*
> *so does a proverb in the mouth of a fool.* (26:7)

Or much worse, a fool can hurt others by quoting proverbs as absolute truth when the proverbs do not fit the situation:

Like a thornbush by the hand of a drunkard
is a proverb in the mouth of a fool. (26:9)

The image is graphic and violent—a drunkard flaying about with a thorny bush or large branch, such as a rose bush or branch off a mesquite tree with its long, sharp thorns. The fool swings wildly, indiscriminately hurting other people with his proverb branch, cutting into them with deep gashes. In the process, madly swinging a thornbush is likely to hurt the fool himself.

In the discussion questions, I challenge you to identify proverbs that you have heard misused as absolute statements of truth. As they come to mind, you might take a minute to write them down; sayings used like a thornbush to harm other people. For me, one proverb leaps to mind.

Train children in the right way,
and when old, they will not stray. (22:6)

I have seen two unfortunate uses of this proverb, both the result of misunderstanding the genre of a proverb. First, preachers have unleashed unjustified pain onto parents who did their best to raise their children "in the right way." But because their grown children have made their own decisions and left the church or lost their faith, "It is obvious," so say the preachers, "that the parents did not do their job. Just look at what the proverb says. If children are trained properly, they will not stray." So the parents catch the blame for decisions made by their adult children. What a foolish thing to say to parents who already beat themselves up and wonder what they could have done better.

The second misuse stemming from misunderstanding proverbs as absolute statements of truth comes in the commentaries and journal articles I've read that work intensely hard to make this proverb say something other than what it says so that it may still be read as an absolute. These interpretations include train a child in harmony with the child's nature; train a child appropriate to their developmental stage; or train a child in a trade or occupation that fits them, and they will do it all their life. What a terrible misuse of a proverb that by its genre only makes a general claim: when parents raise their children well, they usually, but not always, turn out well. That's all, folks. Proverbs are not grand promises with sweeping statements of absolute truth, and to read them as such is to misunderstand them.

Challenge #2: Translation and Culture

We return to the classroom to reveal the second challenge presented by the genre of proverbs. When my students shared their favorite proverbs, their university instincts kicked in to lead them to the funniest or catchiest sayings they could remember. So we shared proverbs and laughed until I noticed our international students. While we were having so much fun, they sat politely and quietly. They had no idea what was so funny about our proverbs. But when I invited them to share their proverbs, their faces grew broad smiles, and they laughed as they recited sayings from their homeland, first in their native language, as the American students sat quietly:

> *Mokopi o na le marago a malele.* (Botswana)

> *Allen Leuten recht getan*
> *ist eine Kunst die niemand kann.* (Germany)

> *Más sabe el diablo por viejo de que por diablo.* (South America)

> *Hecha la ley*
> *hecha la trampa.* (South American)

Although these students were fluent in English, when we asked for translations, they stumbled for the right words: "It means something like . . . but that's not exactly it . . . I don't know how to say it." Sometimes they even laughed as they tried to explain that back home, their proverb was really funny. Here are their best efforts at translation, in the same order:

> *A beggar has a long bottom.*
> (Meaning: A beggar must be willing to wait.) (Botswana)

> *Making it right for everyone is an art that no one can do.* (Germany)

> *The devil knows more because he is old,*
> *than because he is the devil.* (South America)

> *As soon as the law is made,*
> *the trick is made.*
> (Meaning: A way around the law is found.) (South America)

Never has the dictum "To translate is to lie" been so eloquently demonstrated. Spoken aloud by native speakers, each proverb had a rhythm or even rhyme; but when we hear a translation, we are left cold. We lose the sound, and most of all we lack the cultural awareness that makes a proverb work. The magic is gone.

So to our observation that the proverbs in the book of Proverbs are the outgrowth of a particular place and its culture, we add two footnotes. First, we may be equally separated from these proverbs because they come from a culture other than our own. Here is an example to illustrate:

Stick to the wicket
and the runs will come.

This saying comes from a part of the United Kingdom where people speak English and play cricket. Its meaning, however, befuddled me and others at a conference in the States because we knew nothing of the game cricket. A friend and former editor told me about another proverb that has different meanings in different cultures. In American culture, the saying "A rolling stone gathers no moss" suggests that motion is a good thing: a person should stay busy. But the same proverb in England suggests a negative image: while a moss-covered rock in a brook is a beautiful thing, a rolling stone will never acquire such beauty.

Second, proverbs are not only the outgrowth of a culture; they also come from a particular time in a culture's development. Consequently, even proverbs from North America in English are subject to confusion. For example, a colleague at a conference contributed the following:

A whistling woman and a cackling hen
come to no good end.

The rhyme is catchy, but why a whistling woman should meet the fate of a cackling hen and the precise nature of that fate is part of American culture that predates my time. A variant of the saying suggests the idea:

A whistling woman will never marry.

I suspect this second version is a later attempt to update the proverb for an audience removed from cackling hens. It explains the enigma of the proverb, but in the process loses much of the original appeal.

Not all proverbs are so embedded in a culture or a native language that they are impossible to translate or whose meaning cannot travel to a new place. Even so, in the best of circumstances, our translations and interpretations will suffer some slippage in meaning and persuasiveness. However, I am not at all ready to throw my hands up in surrender to these problems. Quite the opposite, I am eager to dig into Israel's proverbs—but we need to do so with full awareness of the challenges that culture, language, and time present to our work.

Challenge #3: Enigma

Other examples I have gathered raise a third observation and corresponding challenge: proverbs often convey their message in enigmatic ways to capture the hearer's imagination. Humor or a striking image might stir reflection, or maybe a powerful truth expressed in such a memorable way that the proverb evokes internalization. Here are a few examples from the graphic to the sublime:

He who sweats in peace
will not bleed in war. (Asia)

You cannot wake one who pretends to be sleeping. (Navajo)

Whether proverbs cause us to laugh so hard we cannot catch our breath or are breathtaking in their simplicity and insight, often the key idea relies on the hearer catching and understanding *what is not said between the lines*—or the precise relationship between lines. Some call this feature the "gap" between the lines of the proverb. Our challenge is to read the gap by asking the question, what connecting idea links line A to line B? But however we may describe it, like a joke or parable, if a speaker has to explain the enigma, then the proverb has lost its power. For example if our hearer does not understand that "sweating in peace" denotes the incredibly difficult work of maintaining peace between two or more factions or nations, the first proverb above will be senseless. Or if we fail to realize that a person who is pretending to be asleep will continue pretending no matter what we do, we will miss the point that you cannot wake such a person—or make anyone do something they do not want to do. Proverbs are like jokes. Whenever we must stop to explain a joke, it is no longer funny. The moment we must explain a proverb, it loses much of its power or punch.

Challenge #4: Descriptions or Prescriptions

The fourth challenge in reading Proverbs 10–31 is recognizing when a proverb describes an action or activity observed to be true and when a proverb prescribes an action to take. A descriptive proverb explains the way the world works, what people do and why, without passing judgment. A prescriptive proverb, however, names a situation and/or diagnoses a condition and directs a person toward a wise response.

Descriptive Proverbs

Descriptive proverbs are common in the book of Proverbs and our own cultural stock of sayings. Two examples from our culture may be helpful:

Money talks.

It's not what you know,
but who you know that counts.

Both proverbs make a claim about the way things work in our culture. The first, like it or not, communicates how money often speaks louder than words; money is persuasive and powerful. The second also acknowledges what we know: more often than not, knowing the right people gives us access to a better job or preferential treatment. *Neither proverb necessarily endorses the truth it expresses.* They simply state what they see to be true about their world—right or wrong, like it or not.

The book of Proverbs includes many descriptive or observational proverbs that lack ethical judgment and directions for what the reader should do:

The poor are disliked even by their neighbors,
but the rich have many friends. (14:20)

Wealth brings many friends,
but the poor are left friendless. (19:4)

A bribe is like a magic stone in the eyes of those who give it;
wherever they turn they prosper. (17:8)

A gift in secret averts anger;
and a concealed bribe in the bosom, strong wrath. (21:14)

The first two proverbs (14:20; 19:4) state a plain truth we don't like to hear: wealth attracts friends. Is this statement generally true? My students and I say yes. We only need to look around; for example, who is on the guest list and who isn't? But my students have also argued, correctly I believe, that these friends are likely to be shallow and quick to leave when the money runs out. In many places, the poor have the richest quality circle of friends of anyone in the world. Still, the fact remains that people want to be friends with those who are wealthy.

The second set of proverbs (17:8; 21:14) expresses the simple fact that bribes are effective. A bribe is like a "magic stone" that brings favor or the desired outcome (17:8). And a bribe or secret gift can placate or calm someone who is very angry (21:14). We may not like what these proverbs say, but neither can we claim that they are incorrect about Israel's culture or our own. At the same time, it is crucial that we realize these proverbs do not endorse bribery.

Prescriptive Proverbs

I suspect that because the book of Proverbs is in the Bible, we expect most (or all) proverbs to identify what is good or right, condemn what is wrong, and direct the reader toward wise living. In other words, we expect to find prescriptive proverbs. Of course such proverbs are common in the book Proverbs and in our own cultural sayings. We begin with our sayings:

Give a pig and a boy everything they want,
and you'll end up with a good pig,
and a bad boy.

You can't win a pukin' contest with a buzzard.

Whether you think you can
or you think you can't,
you are probably right.

The first proverb vividly warns against spoiling children by giving them everything they want. This is a good formula for raising a pig to slaughter, but it is a terrible way to raise a child. The prescription is implied: stop giving in to a child's every desire and learn when and how to say no. The second proverb is straightforward and even more vivid than the first. The turkey vulture (the buzzard) defends itself by hurling its vomit toward an enemy as far as ten feet away. It also defecates all over its bare legs and feet, leaving a terrific aroma. So on a literal level, no one stands a chance of out puking a buzzard. The proverb, of course, employs the buzzard as a metaphor for fools who love to argue and are never willing to reconsider their position. We had just as well find a buzzard and have a pukin' contest: it is useless to argue with some people, so don't do it. The third proverb is more reflective but equally direct in its counsel. If you think you can, you are probably right; and if you think can't, you are probably right. The message is clear: set a positive attitude that will give you a better chance of success.

We find the same type of prescriptive sayings that give direct orders or imply the right course of action throughout the book of Proverbs. Since we brought up the topic of bribes above, we pick up this topic again.

> *Those who are greedy for unjust gain make trouble for their households,*
> *but those who hate bribes will live.* (15:27)

> *The wicked accept a concealed bribe*
> *to pervert the ways of justice.* (17:23)

The first proverb diagnoses one factor that may lead to bribery, greed, and one symptom of the disease, a troubled family, before offering a contrast: the benefit of hating bribes is life. The unstated but clear prescription is to refuse bribes and live! The second proverb describes a situation in the first line, accepting a bribe in secret, and passes ethical judgment in the second. This judgment passes an unspoken prescription or implied direction to the reader: do not pervert justice with bribes.

Descriptive or Prescriptive?

Examples of prescriptive and descriptive proverbs could be multiplied, but these are enough to establish our challenge. The book of Proverbs requires readers to continually ask, is this proverb an explicit or implicit prescription for wise living, or is this proverb only describing the world for the sake of awareness? Make no mistake: the difference between these two types of proverbs is enormous. For example, we could misread the texts about bribery as an implied approval and do terrible things. While it may be easy to determine the nature of the proverbs cited in this section, our task is not always so simple. Two examples will suffice, staying with our earlier theme of wealth:

> *The wealth of the rich is their fortress;*
> *the poverty of the poor is their ruin.* (10:15)
>
> *Wealth is a ransom for a person's life,*
> *but the poor get no threats.* (13:8)

What is the purpose of these proverbs, to merely observe or to direct? The first describes the security that wealth brings to a person's life, and is perhaps even truer today. Wealth gives us access to the best doctors, the best schools and universities, the best automobiles, and the best lawyers to keep us out of jail. But poverty ruins the poor for lack of access. So is the purpose of this proverb to imply that a person should work hard to acquire wealth, the ticket to life? Or is the proverb simply telling it like it is without implying anything? The second text may be a little easier to understand: a wealthy person who is threatened or taken hostage is able to pay their way out of trouble. But the poor person is not threatened or taken hostage because there is no payoff to be gained. So is the proverb making the point that the poor are better off than the wealthy, therefore a person should not invest so much energy in becoming rich? Or is it only making an observation about the upside and the downside to having wealth with no further implication?

Challenge #5: The Bible Factor

Recently, I read a book that presented itself in a way that caused me to think I was reading a memoir. It was written in first person and referred to real places and events. And the memoir was really good: I was underlining important passages, writing in the margins, and eager to find out how the author's life came back together. Until the book suddenly ended with more loose threads than a teenager's new pair of jeans (the style these days). Only when speaking to my wife did I discover the book was a novel. I was more than a little frustrated—I felt led on to believe something that wasn't true at all. I was angry—and I wasn't even reading the Bible.

The fifth and final challenge of reading Proverbs is the Bible factor. Most of us do not read Proverbs like every other book because for us, the Bible is

Holy Scripture, God's word, inspired in some way, and authoritative in some way for faith. So suddenly, the identification of the genre of a text that is over three thousand years old and how we read this text involves a volatile set of decisions. And many of us were raised in traditions that had a default setting for all Scripture, a literal reading. For example we heard,

> *The Bible says it, I believe it, and that settles it.*
> *The Bible says what it means and means what it says.*
> *Amen and Hallelujah, anyone can read the Bible and understand it.*

I was immersed in this way of reading the Bible when I first came to faith and affirmed by my grandfather when I came home on visits from college. For him the Bible only had one basic genre, historical report, with other similar forms, letters and books that contained accurate historical information about past events and instructions.

To his credit, my grandfather came a long way in his understanding of Scripture. Even so, he is about to do a triple flip with a half twist in his grave for what I am about to suggest. Reading the Bible and identifying its different genres is far more complicated than a one-size-fits-all approach. And negotiating the genres of the Bible can be threatening to many believers who have never considered the Bible to be anything other than absolute truth. So the first brave soul to suggest that proverbs express general truths that depend on circumstances risks a church fight that will make Luther look like a conformist—a fight sure to be remembered accurately for years—unless we exercise due caution and much wisdom in helping others recognize the Bible factor. Only then, with respect and patience, do I believe it is possible to help believers not only come to a better understanding of Proverbs, but also a better understanding of the Bible as a whole. But this is only possible if we read with full recognition of the Bible factor.

A Brief Tour of Proverbs 10–31

The prologue of Proverbs (chs. 1–9) makes the argument for why readers should follow the path of wisdom: 1) the importance of wisdom cannot be exaggerated; it brings genuine life—a life that is good. 2) Wisdom is a path or trail on which we walk, not a destination to which we arrive and can consider ourselves to be wise. 3) The young man or reader must actively, purposefully choose to walk the path of wisdom—and they must decide now. Anything less than a commitment to walk with wisdom is by default a decision to walk the path of folly.

The persuasion in chapters 1–9 is designed to lead the reader to chapter 10 with a new or renewed commitment to the path of wisdom, but to this point, the sages have not said much about the actual content of wisdom. This is the purpose in chapters 10–31: to present the content of wisdom for the reader to read, absorb, and make part of their life. This is practical wisdom for the whole of daily living, including speech, justice and mercy, wealth and poverty, leadership, friendship, and the family. These topics are representative of the practical nature of wisdom presented in Proverbs 10–31. The two parts of Proverbs, then, work closely together to persuade the reader to choose wisdom (chs. 1–9) and then present to the reader the content of wisdom (chs. 10–31).

The Collections of Proverbs 10–31

Like chapters 1–9, Proverbs 10–31 is a collection of earlier collections and documents, with perhaps only a few new proverbs written by the editors to connect the units and lines and to give credit to the person or group responsible for the earlier work.

The Proverbs of Solomon

The first and longest collection, "The Proverbs of Solomon" (10:1–22:16), sometimes referred to as the first Solomon collection, or Solomon I, consists of 375 proverbs. Recent research has attempted to demonstrate some type of organization in these chapters, but for the most part, their results have been unconvincing. There does not appear to be any overarching organization, only the use of key words or ideas that link one proverb to the next. For example notice the ideas in 10:13–17: wisdom/wise, lips/babbling (vv. 13–14), ruin/ruin (vv. 14–15), wealth/gain (vv. 15–16), and life/life (vv. 16–17). Most likely, as discussed in chapter 1, the heading "Proverbs of Solomon" does not denote authorship but some association such as sponsoring the collection or the wisdom movement in Israel.

The Words of the Wise

The second collection is entitled "The Words of the Wise" (22:17–24:22), or "The Sayings of the Sages" (my translation). The most noteworthy feature of this collection from anonymous sages is its similarity to the Egyptian collection "Instruction of Amenemope," which is available in English translation.[1] The general consensus from interpreters is that the Israelite sages used this Egyptian collection as a source while composing Proverbs 22:17–24:22. Of course, since wisdom by nature comes from careful observation of the world, sages in Egypt are able to contribute to the stock of wisdom in the world. The Israelite sages apparently took the Egyptian sayings and filtered them through the lens of relationship with the Lord.[2]

The third collection is only of twelve verses and is also attributed to anonymous sages (24:23–34). Both collections include proverbs and sayings that are longer than the two-line proverbs of "The first Proverbs of Solomon" collection.

Proverbs of Solomon Copied by Hezekiah's Men

The second collection associated with Solomon comes next (25:1–29:27). This collection is attributed to the work of the scribes of King Hezekiah, a king who lived approximately two hundred years after Solomon. This collection is composed of the short, two-line proverb featured in Solomon I. In addition, there is evidence here of an attempt to organize some sections according to theme, for example the king (25:2–7b), the court (25:7c–10), words (25:11–15), and actions that cause pain (25:18–20).

The Words of Agur

Another collection with foreign influence titled "The Words of Agur" (30:1–33) is attributed to "Agur son of Jakeh. An oracle," also translated, "The words of Agur, Jakeh's son, from Massa" (30:1 CEB). The term "Massa" can be trans-

1. See William Kelly Simpson, trans., "The Instruction of Amenemope," *A Reader of Ancient Near Eastern Texts*, ed. Michael Coogan (New York: Oxford University Press, 2013), 191–93.

2. See Michael Fox for the editorial procedure used by Israel's sages: *Proverbs 10–31*, Anchor Bible 18B (New Haven: Yale University Press, 2009), 753–67.

lated as "oracle" or taken as the name of a nation or state. Either way, Agur was no Israelite or Hebrew, but a man who loved to collect or write lists. He especially liked to use the formula three plus one, for example, "Three things are too wonderful for me; four I do not understand" (30:18; cf. 21, 24, 29). This formula may mean "there are four things" in this list, or it is possible, but less likely, that the formula draws special attention to the fourth item in the list.

The Words of King Lemuel

The final collection is initially attributed to King Lemuel (31:1–31), but then confesses that he is not the origin of the material: "The words of King Lemuel. An oracle that his mother taught him" (31:1). Again, international wisdom makes a strong impression on Israel's sages. The only issue in this collection is its ending point. Do Lemuel's words stop in 31:9 or 31:31? The style of 31:1–9 compared to 31:10–31 makes it most likely that Lemuel's words stop in 31:9. The sages who put the book together either wrote or used an existing poem for 31:10–31 (see ch. 2).

Why a Collection of Collections?

What difference does it make that Proverbs is a collection of collections? How does that information aid our ability to read the book? First, I think it helps us make sense of the shift in the nature of material from one section to another, for example the short proverbs in Solomon I, to longer speeches in the Sayings of the Wise. Second, recognizing the nature of the book helps us understand why some proverbs are repeated: they are in different subcollections. See for example 21:9 and 25:24; 18:8 and 26:22; and 20:16 and 27:13. Apparently, these proverbs in two different collections were kept intact when the collection was made part of the larger book. Third, we are reminded of the international nature of wisdom by the inclusion of non-Israelite material—we see that wisdom is not limited to one place and time but is a trajectory on which sages continue to observe the world, reflect, and add new insights.

Conclusion

Wisdom does not come easily, as if we could pour the contents of Proverbs into our lives, stir well, let the mixture interact and rise for a year, maybe two, and we are done. Proverbs makes us work for wisdom, teaching us through a genre that is not popular today and a type of writing that requires us to reset our manner of reading. We recognize that proverbs are limited statements of conditional, not absolute, meaning that are sometimes descriptive and other times prescriptive. We are also aware that as we read the book of Proverbs, we are one or two steps removed from the original text and experience a slippage of meaning caused by translation and the differences of culture. At the same time, by nature proverbs are often enigmatic, relying on clever word plays and cultural references, and challenge the reader's ability to see and solve the question of how one poetic line connects or relates to the next. No, our task is not easy. The path of wisdom calls for our consistent willingness to study the text with patience and walk a more difficult path than the one chosen by the crowd. When the inevitable happens and we lose our way, wisdom only requires us to look for our people—the wise—to reset our course and to step back onto the way of living a life that is good.

With renewed awareness of our task and a basic understanding of how the text unfolds, we are now prepared to begin examining key themes in Proverbs. We begin with major concepts: the idea of folly and how a person becomes a fool, God's presence and God's relationship to wisdom in the book of Proverbs, and the emphasis on justice and the search for mercy. Make no mistake, these concepts are not theoretical or esoteric reflections separated from life. Quite the opposite. In the book of Proverbs, each of these ideas is worked out in practical terms with practical implications. Next, we turn to specific topics and relationships, asking what it means to live with wisdom in our speech, use of money, practice of leadership, friendships, and families. In each case, I gather all the material on the topic. A complete list is available in item #1 under the heading "To Prepare for Reading the Chapter" at the beginning of each chapter.

As we will discuss soon, the proverbs we study come from the Bible, a set of documents long recognized by diverse faith communities as authoritative in some way for the life of faith. Or as Paul states, "inspired by God" (2 Tim. 3:16). As we have seen in this chapter, this "inspiration" does not erase the genre of the proverbs and make them into statements of absolute truth. The proverbs we read are still proverbs. In coming chapters, my organization of these proverbs is in fact only my organization—one way of seeing a single topic and making sense of it. We will discuss this issue as it relates to the book of Proverbs just ahead in chapter 4.

DISCUSSION QUESTIONS

1. Take a few minutes to write proverbs you recall from grandparents, parents, teachers, coaches, or others. Biblical proverbs are okay, but nonbiblical proverbs may work better for this discussion. Share your proverbs with one another and tell who taught you these sayings. Consider your proverbs: What makes a good proverb? What gives a proverb its authority or strength?
2. Examine the proverbs you have written: are they descriptive or prescriptive? Share examples of descriptive and prescriptive proverbs. Does anyone have a proverb that is not easily categorized? Why not?
3. Based on the various features of proverbs noted in the chapter, write a one sentence definition of a proverb. Read these definitions aloud in your discussion group, and work together to write a definition that is no longer than two sentences.
4. Can you think of any proverbs that have been used or applied foolishly? Describe the situation (without names), and explain how the proverb was misused. Did unfortunate consequences occur as a result?
5. What initial impression or response, if any, do you have to the foreign influence on Proverbs? What does this foreign influence teach us about wisdom?
6. Based on the nature of Proverbs as a collection of collections and the minimum length of time it took to create this book—based on 25:1, at least 200 years—how would you describe God's involvement in the production of the book of Proverbs? Does the compilation of this book challenge your prior view of inspiration or the authority of Scripture? In what ways might God's work through many people, in many places, and over a long period of time make you even more appreciative of Scripture?

PROJECT CHALLENGE

First, make a list of the features that create a good proverb and provide a brief explanation of each feature. Second, with these features in mind, create three to five original proverbs. If you need an extra challenge, make all of your new proverbs address a common theme.

PART TWO

Major Concepts in Wisdom

CHAPTER 4

Deforming Character: How to Become a Fool

Never wrestle with a pig—
you will only get dirty, and the pig will like it.

—Anonymous

A foolish person ruins his way,
but his heart rages against the Lord.

—Proverbs 19:3 (my translation)

I have great faith in fools
—self-confidence my friends will call it.

—Edgar Allen Poe, *Marginalia*

There are no foolish questions
and no man becomes a fool
until he has stopped asking questions.

—Charles Proteus Steinmetz

TO PREPARE FOR READING THE CHAPTER

Read the proverbs in either #1 or #2:

1. Proverbs 1:7, 22, 32; 2:1–5; 3:35; 9:13; 10:1, 8, 14, 18, 21, 23; 11:29; 12:15–16, 23; 13:1, 16, 19–20; 14:1, 3, 7–9, 16–18, 24, 29, 33; 15:2, 5, 7, 14, 20–21; 16:22; 17:7, 10, 12, 16, 21, 24–25, 28; 18:2, 6–7, 13; 19:1, 3, 10, 13, 29; 20:1, 3; 22:15; 23:9; 24:7; 26:1, 3–12; 27:3, 22; 28:26; 29:9, 11, 20; Matthew 5:21–22; Titus 3:3–7
2. Proverbs 10:1–23; 14:1–9, 16–18; 15:2–7; 17:7–28; 26:1–12; 29:9, 11, 20; Matthew 5:21–22; Titus 3:3–7

Mention the term "fool" to anyone under the age of thirty, and they will likely envision Lloyd Christmas and Harry Dunne from the movie *Dumb and Dumber* and its sequel, *Dumb and Dumber To*; Wayne and Garth from *Wayne's World*; Tommy Boy from *Tommy Boy*; or for Anglophiles, Mr. Bean. The more mature among us may think of Barney Fife from *Andy Griffith*, Gilligan from *Gilligan's Island*, Inspector Clouseau from *The Pink Panther* movies, or perhaps Lucy and Ethel from *I Love Lucy*. For some the word "fool" conjures proverbial descriptions such as the lights are on, but no one is home; he's not the sharpest knife in the drawer; her elevator doesn't go all the way to the top; or he is a few bricks shy of a load. Depending on our geographic location, we may also think of lighthearted "Aggie jokes" or politically incorrect "Polack jokes." Regardless of our age or location, the foolish woman with blonde hair is a staple of our culture, as powerfully demonstrated and reversed by Reese Witherspoon in the movie *Legally Blonde*.

Our typical image of a fool is that of an inept yet lucky, gullible but sincere, blundering but lovable person. They are slow witted, lack intellectual savvy, and are most likely toward the lower end of the IQ scale. It's not an image to which any aspire: "Pity the fool," Mr. T advises, and we do. Even so in our world being a fool is not a tragic flaw, and certainly not an ethical failure or moral catastrophe. As a result, Jesus's warning from the Sermon on the Mount sounds like nonsense to our generation:

> *I say to you that if you are angry with a brother or sister, you will be liable to judgment; and if you insult a brother or sister, you will be liable to the council; and if you say, "You fool," you will be liable to the hell of fire.* (Matt. 5:22)

We can understand Jesus's concern for anger and insults, but his claim about calling someone a fool, at least in our culture, is not logical. Jesus doesn't seem to be speaking our language and certainly doesn't share our image of a fool. We may use the same English word, but we have in mind two very different things. We think of the gullible, inept but lovable person; Jesus speaks of a moral category or lacking quality of character. We call a person a fool as a joke or slight insult; but for Jesus, calling a person a fool is a vicious, brutal act of character assassination because his understanding of a fool ultimately derives from Israel's sages and the book of Proverbs.

Our first task in this chapter is to define the difference between our understanding of a fool and what the sages and Jesus recognize by composing a picture of a fool as described in the book of Proverbs. As our sketch develops, the image will help us understand why Jesus considers calling a person a fool to be an offense deserving "the hell of fire." Our sketch will also provide a skeleton for us to flesh out as we study themes from Proverbs 10–31 in coming chapters. When we finish our work, we will have our own *Frankenstein Fool who lives!* And by that time we will not only understand the fool better, but we will see the stark contrast between our frightening creation and the life of wisdom. In fact, our model may appear so lifelike and dangerous that we are motivated to pick up our own pitchfork or ax and join others in the city who are chasing away the monster lurking within each of us.

The second objective of this chapter is to map the deformation of character from the time a person steps innocently onto the path of folly until they are a complete fool leading the parade of fools-in-the-making down the path of folly. We want to understand what creates fools: How did they begin? What lured them to this lifestyle? What shaped or formed them? In simple terms, how does a person become a fool? This chapter takes on this challenge of mapping a fool's life by identifying four stages in a fool's character deformation, stages that naturally overlap and merge subtly one into the other.

In order to achieve this goal, I have collected and arranged the proverbs that mention the fool or foolish behavior. My arrangement of this material is the result of my own study and effort to present the subject in a way that makes sense to me. The book of Proverbs itself lacks such organization. Other than small clusters on the same topic, Proverbs has defied all efforts to find a detailed and meaningful organizational strategy, for example the organization of proverbs in chapter 10. Consequently, as I lift proverbs from their places in the book, gather, and arrange them, I recognize that I am imposing an organization onto text that does not exist in Proverbs. Ideally, I agree with Ellen Davis and others who point out that the frustrating lack of arrangement in Proverbs is in fact purposeful. Davis argues that the sages did not collect and arrange the proverbs according to subject so that,

> it is impossible to "look up the answer" to the problem at hand. The only way to learn from the Proverbs is by living with the book for a long time, dipping in and out with regularity, or (ideally) working through it, proverb by proverb, even over years. Then one discovers that progress through the book is movement along a spiral. The same relatively few themes recur, but each time we are looking at them from a different angle.[1]

I agree with Davis and also advocate the practice she describes. Practically speaking, however, it is at best very difficult, if not impossible, to introduce

1. Ellen Davis, *Proverbs, Ecclesiastes, and the Song of Songs*, Westminster Bible Companion (Louisville: Westminster John Knox, 2000), 21.

the message of Proverbs or to study Proverbs in Bible classes, small groups, or through sermons without organizing what we find into meaningful units of thought. This is my purpose here and in the chapters to follow. By no means should my work substitute for your own reading and analysis of the proverbs, listed in the reading assignments. Nor should our study stop your own reading of Proverbs as Davis describes it. Actually, my hope is that this introduction to the message of Proverbs will create greater interest in this book so that you will be more motivated to read Proverbs in the years to come.

In simple terms, the proverbs are biblical, and my organization in this chapter and those that follow is not. So I invite you to enter these chapters as a dialogue partner. Take my claims and organization of the texts and consider whether or not I have captured the sages' ideas and the spirit of their teaching in a reasonable manner. Where necessary, make changes to my outline to express what you see. If nothing else, this chapter provides the raw material for any study of fools or folly.

Becoming a Fool

No one wakes up in the morning and while yawning decides, "I think I will become a fool. I have always wanted to become a fool!" Instead, the progression is slow and perhaps even invisible at first. Then over time, folly sells a person a series of lies about themselves and the world, leading them further and further down the road of folly. I believe we can fish out this progression from the various proverbs about fools and folly, just as we fish out other theologies from other biblical books. For our own well-being, we need to learn what happens to people as they travel this path, moving closer and closer to becoming stubborn fools walking toward a tragic end.

One final preface. As we walk along this path following a person who is becoming a fool, we will recognize people we know. At least this has been my experience and that of my students as we have studied this material together. Before we begin, however, we agree to change the names and camouflage the identities of our examples—especially if our example is sitting in the seat beside us. More important, in a moment of clarity, we may see ourselves somewhere along the path. An old saying suggests that if we find ourselves in a hole, the first thing we should do is stop digging. In other words, if we find ourselves on the wrong path, the first step in the right direction is to stop walking in the wrong direction and take the time to reevaluate the trajectory of our lives.

Stage One: Foolish Actions

The first stage of character deformation is when a person occasionally or randomly does something foolish. I cringe when I recall some of the foolish things I've done. One time I walked off a job in self-righteous anger because my supervisor and owner of the company took an extra day off during the holidays, but asked employees to work. I still marvel that he didn't give me a lot of days off by firing me. Then there was the time I took on the role of Grand Inquisitor, Defender of the Faith in a conversation with a young friend while he visited home between semesters at college. He wasn't going to the Right Church, otherwise known as my denomination, so I went after him like stink following a skunk. I still pray that God has repaired the damage I did in a matter of hours. With a double shot of brutal self-honesty, we can all remember similar moments in our lives that are best described as a loss of self-control that we would prefer to forget. In the first instance, I lost control in a moment swollen with self-righteous pride and foolishly walked off the job. In the second, I lost control of my mouth—along with humility, compassion, and the discipline to listen, the perfect trifecta—with a sudden foolish compulsion to win an argument of orthodoxy no matter the cost.

The book of Proverbs bolsters support for my claim that we all lose self-control from time to time and do foolish things, if for no other reason than we have all been young and naïve, two overlapping groups who by nature are prone to lose control and do foolish things:

> *Folly is bound up in the heart of a boy* (*naar* in Hebrew, 22:15a)
>
> *The simple (pethayim* in Hebrew*) are adorned with folly* (14:18a)[2]

As we look at our own world, we see that the claim still rings true. We see young people in high school and college on spring break having fun on the beach, at least until they begin to lose control because of too much alcohol.

The sages in Proverbs identify many foolish activities that are the result of a loss of self-control:

- expressing a quick temper (12:16; 14:17, 29)
- drinking too much (20:1)

2. The book of Proverbs is addressed to these two groups. See the goal in Prov. 1:4: "to teach shrewdness to the *simple* (or *naïve, from pethayim*), *knowledge and prudence to the young* (or *youth*, from *naar*)."

- being reckless or acting as if we are indestructible (14:16)
- burning through our salary (21:20)
- trusting in ourselves (12:15; 28:26)

By far the most obvious indicator in Proverbs of an inability to maintain self-control has to do with what people say or how they speak:

- failing to limit or stop speaking (10:14; 12:23; 15:2; 18:2)
- speaking hastily (29:20) or without listening (18:13)
- chattering away in ignorance (14:7; 15:7, 14)
- agitating or inciting others (27:3)
- speaking dishonestly (19:1)

The sages attribute a person's collapse or demise to their foolish, uncontrolled speech. It's the "babbling fool" who comes to ruin (10:8) or brings ruin near (10:14). A fool's mouth destroys their life: their lips set a trap, which they walk in to (18:7). The lips of a fool call for trouble and beg for someone to beat them: "A fool's lips bring strife, and a fool's mouth invites a flogging" (18:6; 14:3; cf. 29:20). The obvious remedy for all this foolish speech is to speak less and listen more (10:19) or to think just a little more before speaking (15:28; 21:23). But this is as unlikely as Buford, my basset hound, not begging for food. The impossible dream, the sages claim, is for a fool to stop talking long enough that others believe he is a sage (17:28)—but it's never going to happen because a fool lacks the self-control required to stop talking.

An initial reading of the texts cited above appears to suggest that if I ever fail to listen to advice, then I must be a fool (12:15), or if I talk too much, I must be a fool (18:2). Before jumping off the cliff to this conclusion, however, remember: 1) the sages often paint with broad brush strokes in order to make a point (see ch. 3), and 2) not listening to advice and talking too much are the types of things fools do, but an occasional failure in these areas does not make a person a fool. *Thank God, or we would all be in trouble.* If I spoke too much instead of listening to my friend, I did something foolish. But isolated foolish actions do not make a person a fool any more than an isolated act of wisdom makes a person a sage. Like wisdom, folly is a path or way of life that shapes a person's character over time into a fool.

This does not mean, however, that we should not be concerned about doing something foolish. Quite the opposite: the best time for shaping character is during this stage. Here we may learn from our mistakes and become wiser—not simply because we learn from experience—but because we reflect on our experiences and learn. Proverbs 10–31 has much to say about shaping of character, a theme Dave Bland has taken up in his work. Just as the sages regard wisdom as a path or way of living, Bland defines character development in Proverbs as a process by which virtues form into habits as by-products of a relationship with God and others.[3] Bland also employs Lawrence Kohlberg's theory of moral development as a descriptive lens for character development in Proverbs, a lens that appears to be well suited for this book.[4] Kohlberg identifies three stages of moral development or personal growth:

- *Preconventional.* Individuals interpret right and wrong on the basis of the physical and emotional consequences of actions.
- *Conventional.* Individuals learn to conform to the social order including family and cultural expectations regardless of physical consequences.
- *Postconventional* or *principled*. Individuals make decisions on the basis of justice, regardless of family or cultural reactions.[5]

As Bland demonstrates, the sages in Proverbs envision a similar process along the path of wisdom. The sages place the responsibility for the initial character formation of a child firmly in the hands of the parents and encourage them to begin the process of teaching and discipline early, Kohlberg's first stage, before it is too late, and their child is so far away on the path of folly that almost all hope is lost.

Discipline your children while there is hope;
do not set your heart on their destruction. (19:18)

Do not withhold discipline from your children;
if you beat them with a rod, they will not die.
If you beat them with the rod,
you will save their lives from Sheol. (23:13–14)

Because of the paramount role of the parent in character formation, several proverbs promise parents that if they will attend to their child's moral and spiritual development, their child will become a joy and a blessing to them.

3. Dave Bland, *Proverbs and the Formation of Character* (Eugene, OR: Cascade Books, 2015), 3.

4. Lawrence Kohlberg, *The Psychology of Moral Development: The Nature and Validity of Moral Stages, Essays on Moral Development* 2 (San Francisco: Harper & Row, 1984), 172–76.

5. Bland, *Proverbs and the Formation of Character,* 31–39.

Train children in the right way,
and when old, they will not stray. (22:6)

Discipline your children, and they will give you rest;
they will give delight to your heart. (29:17)

Conversely, the sages warn the parents of the shame to come if they fail to keep their responsibility.

A wise child, his father rejoices;
a foolish child, his mother's grief. (10:1, my translation)

The vexation of his father: a foolish son,
and bitterness to the one who bore him. (17:25, my translation)

The one who begets a fool gets trouble;
the parent of a fool has no joy. (17:21; see also 15:20; 19:13; 29:15)

These proverbs raise thorny problems regarding physical or corporeal punishment, a topic we will return to in chapter 11. For now it is enough to establish that parents must not be lax in their efforts to lead their children on the right path. Instead, their primary responsibility is to shape their children's character into the image of God and correct foolish actions before it is too late and a fool begins to emerge, every parent's worst nightmare. It is now, not later, that parents must be about their task.

Stage Two: Stepping onto the Path of Folly

In stage two, a person passes three safety barriers—three decisive hurdles that transform a person who acts foolishly on occasion into a person walking the way of folly. First, young people who not only reject but also rebel against the instruction and correction of their parents cross a protective boundary intended to keep them safely away from the path of folly. As we have seen, parents have some responsibility to help form their children's character, but they are not completely responsible. Each child, whether age ten, fifteen, or thirty, ultimately decides the course of his or her own life. Ideally, wise children will listen and respond to discipline (13:1). But foolish children will go beyond typical teenage rebellion to loathing parental instruction (15:5). They may even "do violence to their father and chase away their mother" (19:26) and curse their parents (30:11).

By extension, the same hurdle exists for young people in our culture who have other adults in their lives who care about them: friends, coaches, teachers, youth pastors, anyone who loves young people. When we deliberately, consistently, and flagrantly disregard the guidance of parents and others who care about us, we push past a barrier on the path to becoming a fool.

Second, as we mentioned earlier, foolish actions do not make a person a fool. Only when a person repeats foolish behavior do they place both feet firmly on the path. Or as a favorite proverb explains: "Like a dog that returns to its vomit, a fool repeats his folly" (26:11, my translation). Though the folly or foolish behavior is grotesque and repulsive, like dogs eating their vomit, in this second stage the fool will eat what makes him ill, vomit, then eat it again, *and then repeat the cycle*. Or from another perspective, when asked, what is the worst, most unimaginable thing you can think of doing? A fool will answer, "To stop doing the terrible, horrible things I have already done and will do again" (see 13:19b).

The difference between isolated actions and recurring activity is also a safety barrier, much like a runaway truck ramp in the mountains. Should truck drivers overuse and overheat their brakes on long downhill slopes—ultimately losing their brakes entirely—they still have hope. They can use a runaway truck ramp, a straight road attached to the highway that goes up at a sharp angle and has a soft roadbed to slow down and stop their truck. This safeguard, however, is not automatic. Drivers must recognize the situation, take the danger seriously, and deliberately steer the truck up the ramp in order to save their life and the truck.

Finally, the third barrier in stage two is a crucial change in attitude: the foolish things a person has been repeating become fun, even exciting to do, which explains why they have already begun repeating the behavior. A dispositional shift is the only explanation for claims such as, "Folly is a joy to one who has no sense" (Prov. 15:21a), and "Doing wrong is like sport to a fool" (10:23a). The foolish activity has become a game, a challenge that stimulates and excites.

A good example of what happens in stage two is in the first parent/son speech of Proverbs 1–9. Literally, the speech is to "my son" (1:8, 10). Theologically, however, the speech addresses any young person coming of age and taking more and more responsibility for their decisions and lives. Here, the parent reconstructs an invitation the son may receive from "sinners" to entice him.

If they say, "Come with us, let us lie in wait for blood;
let us wantonly ambush the innocent;
like Sheol let us swallow them alive
and whole, like those who go down to the Pit.
We shall find all kinds of costly things;
we shall fill our houses with booty.
Throw in your lot among us;
we will all have one purse." (1:11–14)

What's so appealing or enticing about this invitation? Why would any youth want to join this gang? First, this gang promises excitement, the antidote to "all we ever do is work" or "I'm so bored." They will take the young man into the suspense of lying in ambush for people and killing an unknown, innocent person (1:11–12). They also promise fast money, the remedy for "I want this, I want that." The new friends invite him to strip the dead of valuables (1:13). Finally, this gang commits to a communal purse in which everyone shares and shares alike (1:14), a response to the stiff hierarchy within families.[6]

Put together, the sinners' invitation stands in contrast to the young man's present way of life at home and the path of wisdom, both of which offer a fair profit, wealth or wisdom, through sustained hard work and a supportive community in which everyone has their place. It's not so difficult to see why the invitation would be attractive. They offer excitement, fast money, and a community of equals—all here and all now, "the good life." But their invitation threatens to take the youth from doing the occasional foolish thing to walking on the path of folly. The invitation looks good, at least until the parents flip the switch and name reality: these "sinners" may set a trap and wait in ambush, but it's only to catch and kill themselves (1:15–18). Even more revealing, the parents claim this is the story of all those who are greedy: greed will take your life (1:19).

Stage Three: The Hardening

Concrete is a good image to describe what happens in stage three. Concrete consists of simple elements, sand, small pebbles, and cement, that when mixed together with water and given time to set up become as hard as rock.

6. If the reality behind the words of the gang is a bit too obvious to us, keep in mind that the parents have control of this speech, rewriting the words of the sinners through their own perspective.

In a similar way, the longer people walk the path of folly, the more they begin to harden: to stiffen their attitudes, their resolve, and their heart against God. As a result, hope for breaking through and changing their lives grows slimmer by the day. Though again it is good to remember that by nature, proverbs are not absolutes.

The book of Proverbs identifies two ingredients that contribute directly to a fool's hardening. The first is *a refusal to listen*, normally because they are confident that they already know everything (12:15). As a result, they not only babble on and on spouting their so-called knowledge (18:2), they trust completely in self (28:26). Should an opportunity to acquire wisdom fall in their lap like a present on Christmas day, they wouldn't open it (17:16). As they grow harder, they loathe instruction (1:7), and they hate knowledge (1:22). If a wise person brings a law suit against a fool, there will only be "ranting and ridicule without relief" (29:9). No one can win an argument, legal or otherwise, with a fool: a fool has far more experience arguing with others, is always right, will never listen, and will certainly never admit being wrong. Such an extreme case of a closed mind is captured in two other proverbs:

> *Do you see persons wise in their own eyes?*
> *There is more hope for fools than them.* (26:12)
>
> *Do you see someone who is hasty in speech?*
> *There is more hope for a fool than for anyone like that.* (29:20)

Both proverbs are hyperbolic, statements that go beyond the most extreme idea to make a point. In the first, the point is that a fool would have more hope than someone who is wise in his own eyes, a proud know-it-all. But in fact, the fool is also wise in his own eyes and as a result, really has no hope. The same idea holds in the second proverb. A person who speaks before they think has more hope than a fool, but in fact, a fool is also hasty in speech because they do not listen and as a result, have no hope.

The second ingredient that causes fools to grow hard is easily overlooked. All their life, when they have come to a fork in the road, they have consistently taken the path of least resistance, whatever was the easiest thing to do. We see this feature in the first parent/son lecture in the invitation to take the easy path to wealth and success (see above). Another speech describes the invitation of a woman who was not only ready and willing, she acted as if she had been out looking for just this young man (7:15). This woman offered the easy path to self-gratification. She had already made all the preparations, including exotic and erotic bed coverings as well as a luxurious meal. All waiting for the young man if he will just say yes (7:16–21; see also 5:3–6).

In comparison to the path of wisdom that demands strenuous effort, crying out for understanding, and searching for wisdom like a lost treasure (2:1–5), walking on the path of folly is simple. Just do whatever comes easily, naturally. Take the path of least resistance to whatever you want: sex, money, thrills. The hardness emerges when a person has lived for years under the banner, "Take the Easy Way Out." Now to change course and walk the path of wisdom requires an about face, a 180-degree turn to embrace the difficult—the one thing they have avoided all their lives. Consequently, the demand is more than most of us could ever imagine, like an addict trying to beat their addiction. In fact, what is needed is the same change as that represented in many twelve-step programs:

- Admit we are powerless over __________ (fill in the blank), and that our lives have become unmanageable.
- Come to believe that a Power greater than ourselves could restore us to sanity.
- Make a decision to turn our will and our lives over to the care of God, as we understand God.
- Conduct a fearless moral inventory of our lives.
- Admit to God, to ourselves, and to another human being the exact nature of our wrongs.
- We are ready to have God remove all these defects of character (see the son's confession in 5:11–14).

However the sages confess that at this point, not only is a fool unlikely to change, but there is also little anyone else can do to help (26:3; 27:22).

One final observation is necessary as we near the final stage on this long path: as their character deforms even more, fools are likely to become a menace or danger to society. For this reason, the sages urge their listeners to avoid companionship with fools (13:20; 14:7) and not try to correct them (9:7). It is natural to want to help, but our real opportunity to help was back in stages one or two, not stage three. Now it is becoming too dangerous.

Imagine these word pictures from the sages:

- **Picture #1**: You have accidentally made the mistake of getting between a she-bear and her cubs, and she perceives you as a threat to her little ones. A grizzly picture will confront the coroner who comes to pronounce dead whatever is left of your body. But the sages say your odds are still better with the she-bear than with a fool (17:12).

- **Picture #2**: A person who depends on or hires a fool would do just as well to take out their bow and begin shooting arrows randomly at people (26:10). Or when we hire a fool, we would do as well or better if we cut off our feet and drank poison (26:6). This is what happens when we hire a fool—we hurt others and kill ourselves.
- **Picture #3**: Fools, however, do not recognize the nature or genre or proverbs (see ch. 3). So at best, a proverb may hang like an unlit cigarette out of a fool's mouth (26:7). Worse, a fool swings a proverb like the branch of a thornbush (26:9). Blood drips from the fool's hands from the damage he does to himself, and others have gashes and long open wounds from the attack of the thorn bush—all because a fool lacks the wisdom to use proverbs well.

At this point, the sages cannot see much hope for fools. They have moved beyond the most drastic efforts to help them and have become hard to the core of their character:

- They are over-confident in their knowledge. They know everything and are always right and never wrong.
- They have taken the easy way for so long that taking the difficult path is an Everest-sized challenge.

As much as we would like to be optimistic, it is difficult to see much good coming from this situation.

Stage Four: Collapse and Rage

According to the sages, even more certain than death and taxes is the tragic end that awaits fools: to utterly lose their way, be lost, and die—literally or metaphorically in a living death (5:23, 10:21; see also 10:14; 11:29). Above all, the book of Proverbs stresses that what brings the fool to such a tragic end is nothing other than the fool himself:

The lips of a fool bring strife,
his mouth calls out for blows.
The mouth of a fool is his ruin
and his lips are a trap for his life. (18:6–7, my translation)

Because they hated knowledge
and did not choose the fear of the Lord,
would have none of my [Woman Wisdom's] counsel,
and despised all my reproof,
therefore they shall eat the fruit of their way
and be sated with their own devices.
For waywardness kills the simple,
and the complacency of fools destroys them;
but those who listen to me will be secure
and will live at ease, without dread of disaster. (1:29–32)

In sum, fools destroy their own life and the lives of those close to them (14:1). Then, in a final climactic statement that sets fools apart from all others, instead of turning to the Lord in penitence (14:9), fools blame the Lord for their downfall:

A foolish person ruins his way,
but his heart rages against the Lord. (19:3, my translation)

Fools self-destruct and hold God responsible for all their problems. In fact, nothing is ever their fault. Family, friends, society, and God are to blame for the disarray of their life.

Conclusion

In coming chapters, we will examine what wisdom and folly look like in regard to specific topics such as speech, money, family, and friends. Here, however, in an attempt to deal with the diversity of material about the fool in Proverbs, our study has discerned four primary stages of character deformation and important warning signs that people pass on their way to becoming a fool:

- **Stage One**: An occasional act of folly that we identify and correct is a normal state, even for those walking the path of wisdom.
- **Stage Two**: Acts of folly become habitual when people blast through three protective barriers: they no longer listen to voices they should trust; they intentionally repeat foolish actions; and they have begun to enjoy what they are doing.

- **Stage Three**: The heart and attitudes of fools grow harder and harder because they believe they know everything and have no need of counsel. And because they have taken the easy path for so long, a change of direction to trek up the difficult path of wisdom is most unlikely.
- **Stage Four**: As their own actions tear their lives apart, fools rant and rave at everyone who has "failed" them—including God.

A path with these four markers is not the only way to map or arrange this material, or to envision how a person becomes a hardened fool. The book of Proverbs does, however, require us to deal with these texts and what they suggest about a long process of development in becoming a fool.

Paramount in the sages' understanding of the fool's character development is that unlike becoming wise, becoming a fool requires no decision and no action at all. A person who does not actively decide for and seek wisdom in time and by default will become a fool. In the same way, parents or a community who do not deliberately work to shape a child's character will in time become the parents and associates of a fool. As a result, what the sages say about the character formation of a fool strikes in two directions.

First, the sages urge parents and communities to embrace their responsibility for the character formation of the next generation. Or in the words of an African proverb, "It takes a village to raise a child." Proverbs urges the older and wiser reader to see that failure to correct the folly of youths while correction is still possible leads to dire consequences for the entire community. Parents should not fool themselves into thinking they may be inattentive or lax during the crucial formative years of a child and expect a good outcome. Left alone, Proverbs warns, a child will become a fool, and once that happens, it will be difficult to reclaim what has been lost. Thus the description of character deformation in Proverbs is a clarion call for parents and the community to take up their roles now.

Second, the sages speak directly to the youths and older readers who may be slipping down the path to becoming a fool. No one decides to become a fool. The process is slow, gradual, subtle, and seductively dangerous. Perhaps this is why the sages portray fools in so many different ways or with such a broad range of images. Their descriptions provide a master pictorial guide so a reader can take a "selfie" photo and compare it with the character sketches in Proverbs. In some cases, we may recognize how far we have slid down the path of becoming a fool.[7] In all cases, the sages through their proverbs challenge

7. R. R. Wyse comes to a similar conclusion regarding the use of character types in coun-

readers to face or be responsible for their own character development. Don't fool yourself, Proverbs warns. And don't become a fool.

Before we end this chapter, we must pause for a moment to raise a central issue for wisdom as it relates to this particular topic. Sages gain wisdom by careful observation of the world and how the world works, not by dreams, visions, or special inspiration. Consequently, we have come to the point at which we must ask, what have we learned about this topic on the basis of our experience or what our ancestors taught? Then, if not before, we must determine what value our experience and observation of the world have for theological reflection and the life of faith. Does our insight have any value, or does what Proverbs or another biblical text say limit us? Two examples might help clarify what's at stake with these questions.

- **Example #1**: What role does physiology or physical condition play in the potential development of a fool? Might some foolish behavior be the result of depression, addiction, manic/depressive cycles, or some other physical trouble beyond our control, for example a serious accident, stroke, or dementia? If so, how do we add these new threads to the tapestry?
- **Example #2**: Studies have also shown that attachment disorders develop when orphaned babies have no significant touch or human interaction. Later, these children and youths may display behaviors consistent with that of a fool. But are they fools? What do we do with these studies?

These two examples are merely suggested places to begin a conversation that will continue through the end of this book. What have you seen? What have you learned that is relevant to the subject at hand? Does your understanding of wisdom and the life of faith accept these new insights as valid for the discussion? Or does your community acknowledge good ideas, but dismiss them because they are not from the text of the Bible?

Finally, despite all the negativity associated with the fool, we bring good news. We began with Jesus's words from Matthew 5, and we conclude with words from the Letter to Titus:

---

seling: "With regard to the character-type of 'the foolish', one may come to see that he or she is displaying foolish tendencies; in relating to people, in dealing with relational pain, or in one's relationship to God (our present, inside or deep stories). In this recognition of foolishness in oneself, the hope is then that one can move beyond such by choosing the way of wisdom, and thus to move into more of the breadth of life's fullness." "The Proverbial Fool: The Book of Proverbs and 'Biblical' Counseling," *Skrif en Kerk* 17 (1996): 252.

> For we ourselves were once foolish, *disobedient, led astray, slaves to various passions and pleasures, passing our days in malice and envy, despicable, hating one another. But when the goodness and loving kindness of God our Savior appeared, he saved us, not because of any works of righteousness that we had done, but according to his mercy, through the water of rebirth and renewal by the Holy Spirit. This Spirit he poured out on us richly through Jesus Christ our Savior, so that, having been justified by his grace, we might become heirs according to the hope of eternal life.* (Titus 3:3–7, emphasis mine)

We were once foolish—doing everything Proverbs associates with foolish behavior. And we still found hope, or better said, *hope still found us*. Our God saved us, not for anything we had or could do, but through his mercy expressed by the Spirit and Jesus Christ, our Savior. That is indeed good news.

DISCUSSION QUESTIONS

1. Define in your own words what it means to be or to become a fool. Do you see different degrees of fools, one worse than another? How does your definition fit with the words of Jesus in Matthew 5:21–22? How does your definition differ from commonplace use of the term "fool"?
2. As you discuss the four stages to becoming a fool, do you think of people you know or have known? Describe these people (without using their names) and where they are within the four stages. Do you see yourself in one of these stages?
3. Is the progression toward becoming a fool described in this chapter correct? Would you say that one or more stages have been left off the list? Describe these stages. Or should any of the stages described in the chapter be split into two or even three stages? Please explain.
4. What causes a person to become a "hardened fool," a person with no intention of changing the course of their lives? This chapter identifies two hardening ingredients. What other factors might be involved in changing people into hardened fools? Is there any hope for these people? What can be done to help them?
5. Does your faith tradition accept insights from contemporary wisdom as legitimate for theological reflection—discussing the life of faith? Explain. What fresh insights do you have on the process of a person becoming a fool? How do these ideas fit with what we find in the book of Proverbs?

PROJECT CHALLENGE

Update and change the description of a fool in Proverbs to fit your own time and culture. You may accomplish this task by selecting ten to fifteen proverbs and rewriting them in your cultural language and writing three to five new proverbs to cover situations not envisioned by the book of Proverbs. Then summarize what fools look like today. What are their habits? Where do they like to go? What do they like to do? Do you see other important traits? Please explain.

CHAPTER 5

What's God Got to Do with It? Searching for God in Proverbs

The fear of the Lord *is the beginning of wisdom,*
and the knowledge of the Holy One is insight.

—Proverbs 9:10

You can safely assume you've created God
in your own image when it turns out that
God hates all the same people you do.

—Anne Lamott

God is a comedian playing to an audience
that is too afraid to laugh.

—Voltaire

TO PREPARE FOR READING THIS CHAPTER

Read the proverbs in either #1 or #2:

1. Explicit References:
    a. *Yahweh* (the Lord): 1:7, 29; 2:1–6; 3:5, 7, 9, 11, 12, 19, 26, 32–33; 5:21; 6:16–19; 8:13, 22, 35; 9:10; 10:3, 22, 27, 29; 11:1, 20; 12:2, 22; 14:2, 26, 27; 15:3, 8, 9, 11, 16, 25, 26, 29, 33; 16:1–7, 9, 11, 20, 33; 17:3, 15; 18:10, 22; 19:3, 14, 17, 21, 23; 20:10, 12, 22–24, 27; 21:1–3, 30, 31; 22:2, 4, 12, 14, 17–19, 22–23; 23:17; 24:17–18, 21; 25:21–22; 28:5, 25; 29:13, 25, 26; 30:7–9; 31:30
    b. *Elohim* (God): 2:5–6, 17; 3:4; 25:2; 30:5, 8–9
2. Select Topics:
    a. The Fear of the Lord: 1:7, 29; 2:5–6; 3:7; 8:13; 9:10; 10:27; 14:2, 26, 27; 15:16, 33; 16:6; 19:23; 22:4; 23:17–18; 24:21; 31:30
    b. Woman Wisdom: Proverbs 8:1–31
    c. Creation in Proverbs: 3:19–20; 8:22–31; 14:31; 16:4; 17:5; 20:12; 22:2; 29:13; 30:4

As odd as it may seem, at points in Proverbs we might begin to wonder, "Where has God gone?" or "Is this book really promoting what it appears to be saying about our world and God?"

After the introduction, does God disappear, like the clockmaker who set the gears in motion and walked away? And is the book of Proverbs really about my personal happiness, a manual for finding and living the good life? I would leave both questions in the capable hands of academics if not for the likelihood that our reading will require us to deal with these issues. I would also skip these questions if not for the "me first" focus of North American culture and the all-too-often complicit role in it of North American Christianity. Scratch the paint off the surface of our own spiritual practices—our worship, our ministries, our branding, and the campuses under our control, our facilities, and our programs—everything. Now look closely: Do we see authentic faith? Does each practice have the support of a well-thought-out theology? Do we find God or the same secular purposes of other groups in town: a set of practices motivated not by faith but by "what makes me happy," "the good life," or "what's in it for me"?

The wise course here, it seems to me, is to take a little time to familiarize ourselves with these two closely related questions. Not as an academic exercise, but so we may approach both with care, aware of the potential dangers—and optimistic for what we may find that will enrich our understanding of Proverbs and its testimony about God and the way of wisdom. The first question on God's role in the book of Proverbs carries a formal name with an ominous ring: "the deed-consequence nexus." The question here is the nexus or connection between God and the stated outcome of a proverb. To be specific, when a proverb does not mention God, does it assume God to be at work in the outcome of events? Or in these cases, do the sages assume that human actions carry their own consequences, like seeds that contain the necessary DNA to guide the action of planting seeds to its natural outcome, a new plant? Klaus Koch, a leading figure in this discussion, answers yes: the sages saw that actions and consequences go hand in hand. The Lord has no need to be involved in dealing out rewards and punishments. Instead, God is more like a "midwife who assists at birth" by "facilitating the completion of something which previous human action has already set in motion."[1]

To get a feel for this claim, consider the following proverbs and ask, "where is God?" and "what is God doing?"

1. Klaus Koch, "Is There a Doctrine of Retribution in the Old Testament?" in *Theodicy in the Old Testament*, ed. James Crenshaw (Philadelphia: Fortress, 1983), 60–61.

Like somebody who takes a passing dog by the ears
is one who meddles in the quarrel of another. (26:17)

A fool's lips bring strife,
and a fool's mouth invites a flogging. (18:6)

Neither of these texts refers to God. Instead, each proverb offers a vivid picture of what will happen should a person act as described. In the first text, as the owner of a basset hound named Buford Hercules, I can assure you that pulling his ears will earn you a massive slobbery mouth clamped down on your arm. So don't meddle—don't intrude into arguments that are not your own, or you will be the one with bite marks and basset drool on your arm. In the second text, the mouth of fools not only gets them into constant trouble, but at times it seems like they are deliberately trying to antagonize others, pushing and pushing until the other person has had all they can stand and can't take any more. Fools underestimate the power of their negative words and fail to see how they have begged another person to beat them up. Where is God in the space between these actions and their consequences? Is God absent, uninvolved in human affairs? Or is more happening in these proverbs than meets the eye?

Second, although the book of Proverbs looks religious, according to some readers it has only a façade of God's presence and religious values. Scrape off the surface like a lottery ticket, and we will be disappointed by what we find beneath Proverb's ultrathin surface, or rather what we don't find: *God*. Both on and below the surface, Proverbs appears to promote a secular agenda: how to succeed in life, to be happy, and most of all, how to get what you want, when you want it, and how you want it. It is all about us and how we can live the good life!

William McKane provides strong support in favor of reading Proverbs as *originally* a secular work. A man of his times, McKane proposes a developmental view of Proverbs in which the first and thickest layer of Proverbs is secular. The second and next thickest layer involves community and society, but nonetheless still looks to individual success in these contexts. The final and thinnest layer features God or spiritual language, but only as the result of editing material from the first category that was originally secular.[2] In other words scratch off "the corrections" or God language, and we are back to the old secular outlook.

2. William McKane, *Proverbs: A New Approach*, Old Testament Library (London: SCM, 1970), 10–22.

In most instances, McKane's explanation of this process is complicated. One set of texts, however, provides a simple example of spiritual reinterpretation by means of word substitution. Proverbs 13:14 is an example of the older secular material:

The teaching of the wise is a fountain of life,
so that one may avoid the snares of death.

This proverb mentions nothing about God or the Lord, only the guidance of the sages for attaining a full life. In contrast, Proverbs 14:27 provides what appears to be a reinterpretation or rewritten version of the original proverb:

The fear of the LORD *is a fountain of life,*
so that one may avoid the snares of death.

Now, instead of the "teaching of the wise" it is the "fear of the LORD" that promises life. According to McKane, this type of development is evident throughout Proverbs.[3] In truth, I'm not sure that McKane's hypothesis is necessary to file a charge against the sages for promoting a secular lifestyle. But his work, if accepted, slams the door shut on the case against secularism.

A Map for the Journey Ahead

Now that we are aware of the sinkholes, let's think over the best course for moving forward. Whether or not we find God or authentic faith in the book of Proverbs depends on whether or not we decide to accept the book as it now stands in Scripture and to study this text rather than earlier conjectural forms. McKane could be correct about the earlier forms of some proverbs, but ultimately it is the final shape of this material that faith communities have accepted as a reliable witness to the way of wisdom for those who fear the Lord. So, we are ready to begin exploration of what Proverbs says about God. First, we turn to explicit references, texts that include the terms "God" or "Lord." Within this first step emerges a second: what is the meaning of the motto "the fear of the LORD" (1:7), and how does this phrase shape the book of Proverbs?

Third, at this point on our journey we may be surprised to meet Woman Wisdom, who has much to say about God and human life. Once again, we

3. McKane, *Proverbs*, 18.

need to meet this woman, get to know her, and understand her contribution to our perception of the Lord and wisdom. Finally, as we work through steps one to three, we will notice texts that mention or speak at length of the connection between wisdom and creation. So our fourth and last step will venture into these texts: What do the sages say about the relationship between creation and wisdom? And how does this relationship define God's presence or place in the world? So with a deep breath for courage, we step onto the path leading toward an understanding of God's relationship to wisdom.

Explicit God-Talk

A study of what Proverbs teaches about God begins by identifying the primary texts: the verses that use either the Hebrew word *Elohim* / *elohim* for God / gods or the specific name of Israel's deity, *Yahweh*, translated as "the LORD," a substitution for the Hebrew name. Although Hebrew does not use capital letters, most English Old Testaments use "LORD" to distinguish the divine name from other words that mean "master" or "lord" (e.g., Ps. 8:1). In this chapter and those that follow, I use "the Lord" or "Lord" for the divine name.

Uses of *Elohim* in Proverbs are rare—only seven verses use the full form (2:5, 17; 3:4; 25:2; 30:5, 9). However clear cut this information might appear to be, comparison of five common English Bibles—NASB, NRSV, NIV, CEB, CEV—reveals different translation practices. All five translations use the word "God" in the seven verses where *Elohim* occurs, with two exceptions: 1) Instead of "covenant of her God" (2:17 NASB), the NRSV and CEV omit the word "God" and translate "her sacred covenant" (NRSV) and "her wedding vows" (CEV). 2) Instead of "name of my God" (30:9 NRSV), the CEV reads "disgrace your name."

A suffix *-el* occurs twice in Proverbs 30:1. The suffix appears to be a shortened form of *Elohim*, but the term's ambiguity has led to a diversity of translations: a) both lines translated as "God" (NRSV); b) both transliterated as the human name "Ithiel" (NASB); c) the first transliterated as "Ithiel" and the second translated "God" (NIV); and d) either line one or line two regarded as a duplication and removed, leaving only one phrase: "Someone cries out to God" (CEV).

Greater confusion, however, waits to pounce upon the unsuspecting reader as their translation wrestles with questions of interpretation and clarity. For example, should a translator add the word "God" when *Elohim* is not present in a verse, but the verse clearly, according to the translator, includes God? Translations answer this question in different ways. The NASB answers with a strict *no* (with no exceptions), as does the NRSV and CEB with one exception each. The NRSV adds "God" in Proverbs 14:9, and the CEB adds "God" in 8:26. The NIV makes a modest six exceptions, adding "God" in 5:14; 11:26; 14:31, 32; 17:11; 28:14, one of which, 14:32, may be due to a conflict in ancient manuscripts and/or a theological concern to not suggest that people can save themselves. Finally, the CEV follows its translation philosophy, to make the underlying point clear, and adds "God" in a few dozen verses in which *Elohim* does not occur.[4]

As opposed to the rarity of the word *Elohim*, the divine name *Yahweh*, "the LORD," occurs eighty-seven times in Proverbs, often in small clusters: nine times in 3:5–33; eighteen times in 15:3–16:11; nine times in 20:10–21:3; and eight times in 21:30–22:23, which account for forty-four of the eighty-seven instances or 51 percent of the uses of "the LORD" in Proverbs. Several chapters do not include the divine name at all (chs. 4, 7, 13, 26, 27) or include the divine name only once (chs. 5, 6, 9, 23, 25, 31), a total of eleven chapters with only one or no inclusion of the name *Yahweh*.[5] And either as a strange coincidence or intentionally, the seven uses of *Elohim* occur in the same chapters that use *Yahweh* (chs. 2, 3, 25, 30).[6]

Analysis

Texts that include *Elohim* or *Yahweh* emphasize three themes, each foundational for what Proverbs teaches about the Lord. First, the Lord is a source of blessing. The Lord hears the prayers of the righteous (15:29, implying a positive answer; cf. Pss. 17:6; 66:19). The Lord meets basic needs (Prov. 10:3), grants favor (12:2), and sometimes gives wealth or riches (10:22; 28:25, see also 16:20; 19:17), and provides a good spouse (19:14). The Lord causes our enemies to be at peace with us (16:7), corrects us when needed (3:12), and above all, promises life itself (10:27).

4. Proverbs 2:7, 8; 3:13; 8:26; 9:10; 10:3, 25; 11:4, 11, 21, 28; 12:7; 13:13, 22; 14:9, 19, 21; 16:6, 17, 20; 20:7, 25, 28; 21:12, 18, 26; 23:11; 24:12; 28:7, 9, 13, 20, 28; 29:13, 18; 30:3, 6.

5. The five chapters without *Yahweh* also lack *Elohim* (chs. 4, 7, 13, 26, 27), and in the six chapters that include the divine name only once each (chs. 5, 6, 9, 23, 25, 31), *Elohim* occurs in only one chapter (25).

6. Both names occur in Proverbs 2 (*Yahweh* in 2:5, 6; *Elohim* in 2:5, 17); chapter 3 (*Yahweh* in 3:5, 7, 9, 11, 12, 19, 26, 32, 33; *Elohim* in 3:4); chapter 25 (*Yahweh* in 25:22; *Elohim* in 25:2); and chapter 30 (*Yahweh* in 30:9; *Elohim* in 30:9, and a variant *Eloah* in 30:5 and the suffix *El* for God twice in 30:1).

Second, the Lord has the ability to control all things, from the outcome of cast lots (16:33) to the outcome of war (21:31). We want to believe we are in control, that we call the shots and make things happen. But in fact it is the Lord who directs and controls the outcome of human plans (16:1, 9; cf. 16:3; 21:1, 30). The Lord has this power in part because the Lord made the world (3:19). A reminder of what we learned earlier provides an important caution here: proverbs are not absolute guarantees, but depend on and are limited by context or life setting. Consequently, just because a proverb says that the Lord controls the casting of lots (16:33) or that the Lord's purpose "will be established" (19:21) does not mean the Lord controls every detail of life. Such a conclusion fails to recognize the genre of proverbs (see ch. 3).

Third, the Lord is committed to justice. The Lord watches human paths (5:21), and unlike human judges, he is able to see into a person's heart and test attitudes and intentions (15:11; 17:3; 20:27). The Egyptians believed that after death, Anubis the judge weighed a person's heart on a scale of justice with the feather of Maat, a goddess who represented order, morality, and justice, to see which weighed more. Perhaps drawing from this imagery, the sages say the Lord weighs the human heart (21:2) or spirit (16:2). The ability to see and test the heart enables the Lord to administer true justice (29:26), identifying the arrogant and destroying their property or house (15:25a). And though the Lord recognizes and rejects the wicked (3:33; 15:8; 22:12), he has special regard for those who are vulnerable (15:25b; 19:17) and who do not always receive fair treatment in the court held in the city gate (22:22–23). On the bottom line, the sages claim that justice belongs to the Lord (29:26).

In addition to these three major themes, other proverbs identify the attitudes and behaviors the Lord loves and hates. On the positive side, the Lord loves, enjoys, or favors those who pray (15:8), conduct fair business with accurate scales (11:1), live with integrity (11:20), always try to do the right thing (15:9b; see also 21:3), and are faithful to their friends and their God (12:22). On the other side, the Lord hates certain attitudes and actions, many designated as "abominations": unfair business practices (11:1a; 20:10); devious or crooked minds who plan wicked schemes (3:32; 6:18; 11:20; 12:2); lying lips (6:19; 12:22a); arrogance (6:16–17; 8:13; 16:5); injustice (17:15); the wicked way of life (15:9a); and those who act in these ways and come to worship by offering sacrifices as if God can be fooled (15:8).

The Fear of the Lord

One key phrase that distinguishes the book of Proverbs from collections of advice for "the good life" at local bookstores is: "the fear of the LORD." This phrase occurs eighteen times in Proverbs, most notably along the major seams of the book, the beginnings and ends of smaller collections (see analysis below). It is like a golden thread holding Proverbs together.

Proverbs associates only a few generic virtues with the fear of the Lord. On the negative side, those who fear the Lord hate and avoid evil (8:13; 16:6) and refuse to envy sinners or their way of life (23:17). In Proverbs, the fear of the Lord does not mean to be terrified or afraid of God (as in 2 Chr. 14:14; 17:10). On the positive side, they do the right thing (Prov. 14:2), learn wisdom, and develop humility (3:7; 15:33). This said, in Proverbs the phrase appears to work at a higher conceptual level with two basic ideas.

- The object of our fear, the Lord, transforms the subject, us, so that we who fear God "stand in awe of him" (Ps. 33:8) or respect the Lord (24:21).
- Proverbs closely associates the fear of the Lord with the knowledge of God. Respect and awe for God is the point from which we start our quest for knowledge (Prov. 1:7; 9:10; see also Ps. 111:10). And fear of the Lord is also equated to the knowledge of God (Prov. 2:5; see Job 28:28).

A person who fears the Lord is the recipient of the Lord's blessings, the epitome of which is life (Prov. 10:27; 22:4), described as "a fountain of life" (14:27) or emphatically affirmed, "the fear of the LORD is life indeed" (19:23).

Analysis

With the phrase "the fear of the LORD," we have stumbled upon the way sages express their unique understanding of a proper relationship to God, which is required to really be wise. This relationship begins with awe and reverence for the Lord, but is not limited to mere respect or distant admiration. The sages pursue wisdom that culminates in the knowledge of God, not a set of data or information over which they may be tested but a bond, a union with God. Their knowledge of God—what they pursue and gain with wisdom in the fear of the Lord—is like the profound intimacy between a man and a woman first described in Genesis as "the man *knew* his wife Eve, and she conceived"

(Gen. 4:1, emphasis mine). To be wise means nothing less than knowing God intimately.

Proverbs 15:33 emphasizes two other related ideas:

> *The fear of the* L*ORD* *is instruction in wisdom* (NRSV)
>
> *The fear of the* L*ORD* *is wise instruction* (CEB)
>
> *Fear of the Lord teaches wisdom* (NLT)
>
> *Wisdom's instruction is to fear the* L*ORD* (NIV)

The ambiguity of the Hebrew may be unintentional, if so, it's difficult to know which of these translations is correct. But I wonder if the ambiguity is intentional. In other words, all the ideas expressed by these translations are on the mind of the writer. The fact that we could continue working through these texts about "the fear of the LORD" in Proverbs, arranging and rearranging them so that they emphasize first one idea and then another, is evidence not of confusion but of the presence of three interrelated concepts: the fear of the Lord, wisdom, and the knowledge of God. We can see at least one way they relate to one another: the fear of the Lord teaches wisdom (NRSV, CEB, NLT), and wisdom instructs us to fear the Lord (NIV).

These three ideas come as a set *and only a set* to express what is too marvelous for words: the wonder of an intimate relationship with the Lord in day-to-day life. The sages may use any one of these three concepts to evoke the whole idea of an individual living in proper relationship to the Lord. This rediscovery has the potential to change the way we read the book of Proverbs.

The sages make it clear at the outset that they expect the reader to enter this book with at least a least a minimal respect for the Lord (1:7) without which we need not continue, because *genuine wisdom comes only within a relationship to the Lord.* So that the reader does not forget, sentries stand guard at key positions throughout the book to remind us. For example, at the close of chapters 1–9, we read:

> *The fear of the* L*ORD* *is the beginning of wisdom,*
> *and the knowledge of the Holy One is insight.* (9:10)

In the midst of the first collection associated with Solomon (10:1–22:16) and again near the end are these reminders:

The fear of the LORD *is instruction in wisdom,*
and humility goes before honor. (15:33)

The reward for humility and fear of the LORD
is riches and honor and life. (22:4)

Close to the beginning of the first collection from the sages (22:17–24:22), a variation lacks the phrase "the fear of the LORD" but stresses *trust* in the Lord (22:19). The full phrase appears at the end of this collection:

My child, fear the LORD *and the king,*
and do not disobey either of them;
for disaster comes from them suddenly,
and who knows the ruin that both can bring? (24:21–22)

The next sentry stands at the end of the second collection associated with Solomon (25:1–29:27). Like 22:19, it lacks the specific phrase "the fear of the LORD," yet true to an emerging theme (see below), it contrasts fear of others with trust in the Lord, which is inseparable from fear of the Lord:

The fear of others lays a snare,
but one who trusts in the LORD *is secure.* (29:25)

And finally, the last verses of the book read:

Charm is deceitful, and beauty is vain,
but a woman who fears the LORD *is to be praised.*
Give her a share in the fruit of her hands,
and let her works praise her in the city gates. (31:30–31)

These sentries stand throughout the book of Proverbs to inform and remind us that the book is for those who have a proper relationship with the Lord, *and only those in relationship with the Lord.* This precondition is absolute: the entire content of wisdom is true and life giving, but only for those who fear, trust, and follow the Lord. From the outset, this precondition makes Proverbs different from books filled with advice for those wanting to live "the good life." Even if Proverbs may look like its secular counterparts, the sentries remind us that genuine wisdom comes only with acceptance of the Lord as God to be feared and trusted.

Outside of Proverbs

Outside of Proverbs, various expressions of "the fear of the LORD" occur in over seventy texts, providing further insight into the meaning of this phrase. In these texts, most often those who "fear the LORD" are eager to hear and obey the Lord's instructions (Deut. 6:2, 24; 13:4). Psalm 34 emphasizes this idea:

Come, O children, listen to me;
I will teach you the fear of the Lord.
Which of you desires life,
and covets many days to enjoy good?
Keep your tongue from evil,
and your lips from speaking deceit.
Depart from evil, and do good;
seek peace and pursue it. (Ps. 34:11–14)

Those who "fear the LORD" not only do what is good rather than evil; they also serve the Lord alone (Deut. 6:13) with their whole heart (Deut. 10:12; 1 Sam. 12:34; 2 Chron. 19:9), and they live their lives with integrity (Job 1:3; 2:3; Ps. 15:4; Neh. 5:15).

Those who "fear the LORD" believe in the Lord (Exod. 14:31), "stand in awe" of the Lord (Pss. 22:23; 33:8; cf. Isa. 8:13; Jer. 5:22), and naturally praise or worship the Lord (Pss. 22:23; 118:4; 135:20; Deut. 10:20). They also put their hope in the Lord.

Truly the eye of the LORD is on those who fear him,
on those who hope in his steadfast love. (Ps. 33:18; see also Ps. 147:11).

Ultimately, these individual ideas lead to a core value: those who "fear the LORD" put their trust in the Lord.

You who fear the LORD, trust in the LORD!
He is their hope and their shield. (Ps. 115:11)

Who among you fears the LORD
and obeys the voice of his servant,
who walks in darkness
and has no light,

yet trusts in the name of the L*ORD*
and relies upon his God? (Isa. 50:10; see also Ps. 40:3)

Because they fear and trust God, they have no reason to be afraid of others (Ps. 27:1; see also Ps. 118:6; Isa. 51:13; Jer. 46:28). The Lord delivers and protects them (Ps. 34:7, 9), blessing them in ways that lead to their well-being and happiness (Pss. 34:9; 112:1–4; 115:13; 128:1–4). The Lord extends his compassion to them (Ps. 103:13), and his steadfast love:

But the steadfast love of the LORD *is from everlasting to everlasting*
on those who fear him,
and his righteousness to children's children. (Ps. 103:17)

Let those who fear the LORD *say,*
"His steadfast love endures forever." (Ps. 118:4)

Even more, those who "fear the LORD" experience and live with the "friendship of the LORD" (Ps. 25:14), as the Lord "takes pleasure" in them (Ps. 147:11).

This data from the Old Testament reinforces and enhances what we have already seen in Proverbs. Those who fear the Lord believe in, stand in awe of, and obey the Lord's teachings. They see themselves properly (in humility) and trust the Lord to watch over them within a close relationship or friendship. And together, all these voices from Proverbs and the Old Testament express the blessings that come as a natural result of living in relationship to the Lord. The Lord gives them a fullness of life, joy or happiness, and in short—the life that is good.

Woman Wisdom

To the explicit claims about the fear of the Lord, we add Woman Wisdom. Earlier, we studied four of the five texts associated with this figure (1:20–33; 3:13–20; 9:1–6; 31:10–31; see ch. 2), leaving an examination of the fifth text (8:1–36) until now.

After Wisdom calls to readers for attention (8:1–3), she claims the trustworthy nature of her teaching; she speaks truth and righteousness in straightforward words (8:4–9). Woman Wisdom continues to bolster confidence in her words by explaining that she is the force that enables kings to rule, princes to order righteous decrees, rulers to govern, and judges to make right decisions (8:12–16). She loves those who love her and provides them with wealth, honor, and righteousness (8:17–18). In fact, what she gives is better than gold or silver (8:19). Woman Wisdom walks on the paths of justice and righteousness and provides for those who love and walk with her (8:20–21). What Woman Wisdom does overlaps with the primary purposes for Proverbs (1:3).

Next, Woman Wisdom reaches back to a memory before the beginning of time to describe her relationship to the Lord:

> *The* LORD *created* (qanah) *me at the beginning of his work,*
> *the first of his acts of long ago.*
> *Ages ago I was set up* (nasak),
> *at the first, before the beginning of the earth.*
> *When there were no depths I was brought forth* (hyl),
> *when there were no springs abounding with water.*
> *Before the mountains had been shaped,*
> *before the hills, I was brought forth* (hyl). (8:22–25)

Wisdom describes her relationship to the Lord with three remarkable Hebrew verbs. The first, *qanah,* appears in verse 22a. It has overtones of pregnancy or formation in the womb, similar to the meaning of *qanah* in Genesis 4 and Psalm 139.

> *I have produced* (qanah) *a man with the help of the* LORD. (Gen. 4:1)

> *For it was you who formed* (qanah) *my inward parts,*
> *you knit me together in my mother's womb.* (Ps. 139:13)[7]

The second term, *nasak* (8:23a), most likely means to "install" or "appoint" to an official position, as in Psalm 2 when the Lord says, "I have set (*nasak*) my king on Zion, my holy hill" (Ps. 2:6). The related noun, *nasik,* is often translated "ruler" or "prince" (see Josh. 13:21; Ps. 83:11; Ezek. 32:30; Mic. 5:5).[8]

The third term, from the root *hyl* (8:24a, 25b), has some connection to the pain of childbirth or childbirth itself (Deut. 32:18; Job 39:1; Isa. 26:17). Thus, English translations express the idea in Proverbs 8 by the phrase, "I

7. See God described as the one who "brought forth" or "gave birth" in Deut. 32:6; Job 15:7; Ps. 90:2. Other meanings of *qanah* include to purchase or acquire goods (Prov. 4:5), and what is won or acquired through battle (Ps. 78:54).

8. *Nasak* sometimes means to weave or woven cloth (Isa. 25:7), or to make an image or idol by pouring hot, liquefied metal into a form (Isa. 44:10). The noun (*nesek*) denotes an idol made by this process (Dan. 11:8).

was brought forth" (ASV, CEB, KJV, NASB, NRSV, RSV) or with more specific language, "when I was born . . . my birth" (CEV, ERV, NIV, HCSB).

Together these verbs express a unique relationship between the Lord and Woman Wisdom. Far before the creation of the world, the Lord created, brought forth, or gave birth to, and appointed Woman Wisdom. On one hand, the imagery is staggering: Wisdom claims some form of descent from the Lord. On the other hand, before our imaginations run away from us, we must remember that the sages are personifying Wisdom as a woman—or here as a child of the Lord, just as they personified Wisdom as a mighty prophet in Proverbs 1. Yes, the sages claim some sense of "divine birth" for Wisdom, but only as a vivid literary way of expressing the close relationship between wisdom and the Lord. Just as the Lord "founded the earth" by wisdom, wisdom is intimately related to the Lord, a divine attribute. And so Woman Wisdom implies that she is a child or daughter of the Lord—a way to say that wisdom originates from God.

The sages continue this personification of wisdom in Proverbs 8 with reference to creation in verses 30–31. Here, we encounter one of the greatest puzzles in the book of Proverbs: the translation of a single word, *amon*.

then I was beside him like ____________ (amon, 8:30a)

Scholars debate the origin and meaning of this term, typically coming to one of two conclusions.

1) The term *amon* derives from the Akkadian loan word *ummanu* (via Aramaic) and most likely means "artisan" or "master craftsman" (see Jer. 52:15):

   I was beside him as a master of crafts (CEB)

   I was beside him like a master worker (NRSV)

2) The word *amon* derives from the Hebrew root *'mn* (the same three consonants as in *amon*) and has the idea of a child being nurtured, or brought up (similar to Esth. 2:20):

   I grew up as a child by his side (ERV)

   I was like a child by his side (NCV)

A full discussion of the arguments for each meaning is beyond the scope of this study; a few observations and references must suffice.[9] The first option has held the field for many years. The second has been recently bolstered by the work of Michael Fox, a leading scholar in Proverbs and ancient Near Eastern wisdom. In my opinion, the context or the lines following *amon* tilt the scales in favor of "child," "infant," or "growing up"; the position held by Fox. Verses 30b–31 read:

and I was daily his delight,
rejoicing before him always,
rejoicing in his inhabited world
and delighting in the human race. (NRSV)

or

and I was his delight day by day,
frolicking before him at all times,
frolicking in his inhabitable world.
And my delight is in mankind. (Fox, *Proverbs 1–9*, 285–89)

In either translation, the description of Woman Wisdom is not what I would expect of an architect or master craftsman. Notice the repetition of two key terms: "his delight" or "delighting" (vv. 30a, 31b) and "rejoicing" or "frolicking" (vv. 30b, 31a). The first term (*shq*) is not typically used to describe someone doing serious work. Wisdom frolics, plays, or enjoys herself (see 1 Sam. 18:7; Judg. 16:25; Ps. 104:26). The second term, "delight" or "delighting" (*shashuim*) may denote the action of an adult (as in Ps. 119:24, 77, 92, 143, 174; Isa. 5:7) or may denote a parent's delight in a child: "Is Ephraim my dear son? Is he the child I delight (*shashuim*) in?" (Jer. 31:20). As a whole the evidence is not clear cut or overwhelming, but in my opinion, it is more suggestive of the picture of a young child rather than a master craftsman. I do admit that a case may be made in the opposite direction; thus, the question of *amon* and 8:30–31 remain without a conclusive resolution.

Accepting *amon* as a child, at least for a moment, allows a vivid personification of the Lord and wisdom to come into focus. Before creation, the sages

9. See the summaries by Michael Fox, *Proverbs 1–9*, Anchor Bible 18A (New York: Doubleday, 2000), 285–89; and Ernest Lucas, *Proverbs*, Two Horizons Old Testament Commentary (Grand Rapids: Eerdmans, 2015), 82–85.

inform us, the Lord created, brought forth, or gave birth to Wisdom and appointed her to her present position. Then, at creation, Wisdom was at the Lord's side frolicking, playing, or rejoicing. The Lord took pleasure in Wisdom and Wisdom took pleasure or delight in the human race. The picture implies something like the Lord participating in a special "take your child to work" program.

Again, the sages are employing vivid personification in order to capture the reader's imagination. Then they spring their literary trap. However one may translate the terms in verses 22–25 or verses 30–31, at issue is Woman Wisdom's presence at creation and her delight in humanity. Now she shares what she knows about how this world works from what she saw at creation with those who will listen (8:32–33). Whoever will listen to her will find life—the life that is good, true life (8:34–36).

With this relationship secured, eventually by marriage (Prov. 7:4; see ch. 2), the son is ready to listen to the words of Woman Wisdom. The task of chapters 1–9 is complete, and the book is ready to present the content of wisdom (chs. 10–31). We have not, however, heard the last from this woman or what life will be like if the son will marry her. As we saw in chapter 2, when Proverbs concludes, Woman Wisdom will make a final appearance to describe the blessings to be had in an intimate relationship with her and God (31:10–31).

Creation

Although not the first to see the connection, Walther Zimmerli noticed the relationship between creation, wisdom, and theology and declares, "Wisdom thinks resolutely within the framework of a theology of Creation."[10] In other words, the wisdom theology of Proverbs is inextricably tied to creation theology, a thesis taken up more recently by Leo Perdue.[11]

It is undeniable that Proverbs connects wisdom, creation, and God. After all, we have already seen the association between God, Woman Wisdom, and creation in Proverbs 8:22–36. We have also read the ode to Wisdom (3:13–18) in which the writer declares Woman Wisdom to be of greater value than anything else because she offers a long, full, pleasant, and peaceful life. The sages

10. Walther Zimmerli, "The Place and Limit of the Wisdom in the Framework of the Old Testament Theology," *Scottish Journal of Theology* 17 (1964): 148.

11. Leo Purdue, *Wisdom & Creation: The Theology of Wisdom Literature* (Nashville: Abingdon, 1994), and *Wisdom Literature: A Theological History* (Louisville: Westminster John Knox, 2007).

also refer to Woman Wisdom as "a tree of life" (3:18a), bringing to mind the tree of life lost in Eden (Gen. 3:22–24). But now this tree of life is available to those who will embrace and hold her (Prov. 3:18). To this the writer adds that it was by wisdom that the Lord founded the earth, established the sky, and took control of the chaotic waters (3:19–20).

Outside of the first nine chapters, only a few texts in Proverbs explicitly link the Lord to creation. In three proverbs, it is the Lord who makes ears that hear ear and eyes that see (20:12) and the rich and the poor (22:2; 29:13). In three others, the Lord is the "Maker" or Creator (14:31a; 16:4; 17:5; see also 30:4).

Conclusion

We began with two problematic features of the book of Proverbs: 1) the deed-consequence nexus which suggest that God is not significantly involved in human affairs, and 2) the claim that the original text of Proverbs presented nothing more than secular wisdom for the pursuit of the good life. And at most, the sages sprinkled spiritual or religious pixie dust over these texts to create the mirage of God's involvement and a religious outlook in Proverbs.

So what does the book of Proverbs have to say about God and the life of faith? In summary, what we have found is that the entire book is about God and the life of faith. Specifically, the explicit testimony of God language, the placement of the key phrase "the fear of the LORD" throughout the book, and the witness of Woman Wisdom and creation all support this claim in the following ways.

To begin, Proverbs testifies that God's nature is to bless: to hear and respond to the prayers of those trying to do what is right and to give everything from basic needs to great wealth. At the same time, the Lord is committed to justice and has a clear set of expectations about attitudes and actions that he hates and that he will punish. Because the Lord can see into a person's heart to know their intentions, he is able to exercise fair justice. He also has a heart for those who are vulnerable, like orphans and widows, and is able to protect them from those who try to take advantage of them in the court and life. So despite the Lord's preference to bless, the guilty will not be spared from the consequences of their actions. In this way, the deed-consequence nexus is swept up into a larger vision *and mystery* of the Lord's involvement in the world. The sages affirm that the Lord is present, involved, and committed to justice. But the sages also know that the Lord cannot be roped or shackled into enforcing a system. The Lord is free and autonomous, and he enters into world and personal affairs as he chooses.

The sages also make it clear at the beginning of the book that the wisdom of Proverbs stands on "the fear of the LORD" (1:7). In other words, genuine wisdom can be followed only within a proper relationship to the Lord that overcomes fear of other people and circumstances with trust in the Lord. This precondition is absolute: the entire content of wisdom is life-giving—but only for those who fear, trust, and follow the Lord. In addition, this precondition separates Proverbs from other "wisdom" books filled with advice for those who want to live "the good life." Proverbs may look like its secular counterparts from time to time because the nature of wisdom is careful observation of the order of life. Nonetheless, genuine wisdom comes only in relationship to the Lord as our God—to be feared and trusted.

The presence of Woman Wisdom at creation also distinguishes Proverbs from other books searching for the good life. She observed what God made and as a result knows how the world works. What she has seen and knows, she shares with those who will listen. This further vivid personification of wisdom emphasizes the inseparable nature of wisdom from the Lord. Wisdom belongs to and originates from the Lord; thus, what the Lord offers, Woman Wisdom also offers. But again, what Woman Wisdom has to offer only comes when people turn to her as a guide for life. Those who find Wisdom will discover that what she offers is better than wealth. She does not offer "the good life" but a long life that is *full and genuine*. In fact, she is no less than a tree of life. But Woman Wisdom will only come to the son if he pursues her as a lover, holds her close and does not let go, and marries her. Only then will the son enjoy all the blessings she will bring to his life.

So yes, the book of Proverbs offers wisdom that will help the reader negotiate life. But there are terms for what Proverbs has to offer, and these are the non-negotiable terms that include the Lord's presence from beginning to end. This is the God who is active in the world, watching over, sustaining, and intervening in his freedom to do so. We have seen more than enough evidence to support these conclusions. It is true that the sages do not explicitly refer to the Lord with great frequency, but in their defense, why should they mention the Lord's presence and activity when the presupposition of wisdom is a relationship to the Lord? The Lord's presence is taken as a given in a world created and ruled by the Lord. This is the world of the sages—not secular or selfish but immersed in the Lord's presence and advocating a life that is good.

DISCUSSION QUESTIONS

1. How does what we learn about God in this chapter challenge the two basic charges that a) the book of Proverbs appears to promote a deeds-consequence nexus that leaves out God, and b) Proverbs is a secular book, lacking and/or replacing concern for God with self-centered interests? In what specific ways do the claims about the Lord in Proverbs respond to these challenges?
2. Define the meaning of "the fear of the LORD" and "the knowledge of God," knowing God. How does each of these key phrases fit into the message of the book of Proverbs? On what basis or evidence do you reach your answer?
3. Have you ever heard sermons or Bible classes about the personification of Woman Wisdom? If so, what did you hear? If not, why do you think most sermons have bypassed this text? What benefits or insights into God do you gain from the texts about Woman Wisdom in Proverbs 1–9?
4. Some early Christians identified Woman Wisdom as the Holy Spirit or Jesus (see John 1:1–18). What stands for and against equating Woman Wisdom to Jesus? What is your conclusion, and why?
5. In what ways is creation an overarching concept for understanding God in Proverbs? How would you advance the argument in favor of this relationship?

PROJECT CHALLENGE

The sages used vivid literary images to describe the close relationship between the Lord and wisdom. What images or illustrations might you use in your culture or context to describe this relationship? In other words, use your imagination to complete this thought: the relationship of the Lord to wisdom is like the relationship between __________ and __________. Or complete this comparison: the Lord is to wisdom as __________ is to __________. What points or ideas do your illustrations stress about the relationship between the Lord and wisdom?

CHAPTER 6

Justice and Mercy: The Wisdom of Merciful Justice

The evil do not understand justice,
but those who seek the Lord *understand it completely.*

—Proverbs 28:5

I have always found that mercy bears richer fruits than strict justice.

—Abraham Lincoln

Justice will not come to Athens until those who are not injured
are as indignant as those who are injured.

—Thucydides

TO PREPARE FOR READING THIS CHAPTER

Read the proverbs in either #1 or #2:

1. Proverbs 1:1–3; 3:3–4; 8:15–16, 20; 10:12; 11:24–26; 12:5, 10; 13:23; 14:21, 31; 16:8, 10–11, 33; 17:9, 23; 18:5; 19:17, 28–29; 21:3, 7, 10, 13, 15, 26; 22:9, 16, 22–23; 23:10–11; 24:10–12, 23–24; 25:21–22; 28:5, 8, 13, 27; 29:4, 7, 26; 31:6–9
2. Proverbs 1:1–3, 20–33; 2:7–19; 3:21–35; 6:6–15; 11:24–26; 16:8–11; 21:10–15; 22:22–23; 23:10–11; 24:10–12, 23–24; 25:21–22; 31:6–9

Have you noticed how badly we want justice when we are at the receiving end of an injustice, for example an accident caused by the negligence of another person, a contractor who took our money and ran, a boss who treated us unfairly, or the hacker who stole our identity and drained our bank account? String 'em up, it'll teach them a lesson. Or do you recall the nation's state of mind after the attacks of September 11, 2001? Palpable feelings of rage lingered in the dust-filled air of the Twin Towers and a *demand* for justice that came from the nationwide perception of an unprovoked murder of innocent men, women, and children. It could only be a matter of time before our military invaded or bombed someone. We just didn't know who to blame, who should receive our national fury and demand for justice. We had a new national motto, "Remember 9/11," to add to the others: "Remember Pearl Harbor! Remember the Alamo!" and "Remember the kid who let his shopping cart scratch my car!"

Ah, but when the sandal is on the other foot and we have caused the pain, like skilled attorneys we rally to our defense: "It was just an accident, a terrible mistake." "Our child has never done anything like this before—it's not like her." "We promise it will never happen again." The words stumble and tumble over our lips: "I am so sorry, so sorry." And sometimes, we might let the truth slip out to a friend: "They had it coming."

Justice is everywhere in the book of Proverbs, rewards and punishments explicitly stated though far more often implicitly lurking in the shadows. Even a fast reading of the text will lead us to recognize that justice is not just one among many equally important principles in Proverbs. Justice is foundational to the composition of wisdom. It is the basis on which the sages composed and constructed their vision of the world, regardless of their status or place in society: peasant farmers (20:4, 24:27), mothers and fathers (1:8; 6:20), teachers (5:11–14), or royal clerks or aides to rulers (23:1–3). Each sage works from the assumption that justice is an underlying principle of world order. In fact, this commonality among the sages across centuries and the socioeconomic spectrum leads to a shared ethical outlook in Proverbs—a vista that imagines the world as it could and should be, while challenging the injustice of the present world. In this the sages share the prophetic vision: to "establish justice" (Amos 5:15) and for justice to "roll down like an ever-flowing stream" (Amos 5:24; see also Isa. 1:16–17).

In our reading of Proverbs, we also discover the theme of mercy. Defined in the simplest of terms, mercy is a generous response to need, a gift that is not earned or deserved, but given nonetheless. Whenever mercy is given, it is given despite the offense or actions that created the need for mercy. In other words, when we need mercy, we will never deserve mercy. If we did, it would not be mercy. Simple metaphors also fail to represent the interplay between these concepts. For example, justice and mercy are not balanced like two sides of a single coin—and they are also more interwoven than the sides of a coin. While justice leaps off the page, making its presence known and overwhelming us with examples, mercy has a tremendous potential to underwhelm us. To be sure, mercy is present in the book of Proverbs. But to see mercy, we will need to take our time and look between lines and under a few rocks.

In what follows, we pursue an understanding of both concepts. This task requires us to first isolate and develop the sages' teaching about each idea through their explicit use of the vocabulary of justice and mercy. It also requires us to pay careful attention to the implicit references to both concepts. We begin with justice followed by mercy, developing each in its own unique way. As we attend to these two steps, and especially the further we progress in our study, we need to watch for connections and congruities as well as collisions—the ways in which justice may run amok and threaten to swallow mercy whole, devouring the disenfranchised, the oppressed, and the poor. Or a lesser concern in Proverbs, the ways in which mercy may sugarcoat or weaken justice—actions that allow lawbreakers, criminals, and the violent to walk away undeterred from their way of life. The balance of justice and mercy requires more than just formulas and rules. It requires wisdom, even as we seek to become wiser. Of course Israel's sages had no interest in a sterile analysis or a balance of disembodied ideas, as if we were in white lab coats conducting experiments in petri dishes. Instead, our hope shared with them is for a clearer vision of how a life that is good may exist with these two forces settled in their proper places.

Justice in Proverbs

As we have seen, the first seven verses of Proverbs establish the book's primary objectives for its readers: to learn the content of wisdom, to understand this content, and to put this wisdom into action, all of which depends on a proper relationship to God, "the fear of the LORD" (1:7; see ch. 1). We begin our search for justice in Proverbs by returning to the sages' call to put wisdom into action and the three words that further describe "instruction in wise dealing" (1:3): to do what is right (*tsedeq*), to do what is just (*mishpat*), and to do what is fair or equitable (*mesharim*). If the book is consistent with its introduction, justice has a major role to play in Proverbs because enacting justice is an essential element of wise living.

Justice in Proverbs 1–9

The Hebrew word *mishpat*, translated "justice," or the related word *shopet* appear only five times in the overture to Proverbs, chapters 1–9.

- The first of these appearances comes in the prologue's statement of purpose for the book:

for gaining instruction in wise dealing,
righteousness, justice (mishpat), *and equity* (1:3b).

The father's second speech contains the next two references to justice. He advises the son that only a diligent search for wisdom that is like looking for a hidden treasure will succeed (2:1–4). Then, and only then:

- The seekers will understand the fear of the Lord (2:5) and the Lord will give wisdom to the upright (2:6–7). The Lord will shield these people, those who walk with integrity. And the Lord will guard "the paths of justice" (*mishpat*, 2:8a), the paths of these faithful followers (2:8b).
- The seekers will "understand righteousness and justice (*mishpat*) and equity" (2:9; cf. 1:3). Wisdom will enter their heart, and this God-given gift of wisdom will safely lead them (2:10–11).

As we have just seen in chapter 5, Woman Wisdom also establishes justice as a key credential that makes her a reliable source for successful leadership (8:4–9, 15) and life (8:18–19).

- It is by Wisdom that "*rulers rule, and nobles, all who govern* (mishpat) *rightly*" (8:16).

Wisdom also aligns her life with the fear of the Lord (8:12–13), including the way of righteousness and justice:

I walk in the way of righteousness,
along the paths of justice (mishpat, 8:20)

For chapters 1–9 to explicitly mention justice only five times would seem to suggest that the way of wisdom has little use for justice, a conclusion almost as true as the claim that Elvis was an alien who returned home. In fact, justice is an implicit theme throughout all of the speeches and interludes of Proverbs 1–9. Space and the sheer boredom of repetition advise against commenting about every instance—essentially every text in these chapters. So we turn to three examples: one parental speech, one speech from Woman Wisdom, and one text standing outside the speeches.

We begin with the father's speech to his son (3:21–35). The speech opens with a reminder not to let wisdom escape from sight, followed by a series of motivation clauses: wisdom will bring genuine life (3:22); wisdom will provide security (3:23); wisdom will enable them to sleep without fear (3:24); and wisdom will free them from fear of a sudden "storm" (3:25). All of this will happen because the Lord will be their "confidence" and keep them safe (3:26). Notice that the movement from "wisdom" (3:21) to the "Lord" (3:26) is seamless: it is wisdom (3:21–24) and the Lord who provide these benefits (3:25–26). The speech continues with a series of negative imperatives: do not withhold good when you have it to give (3:27–28), plan to harm your neighbor by filing a frivolous lawsuit (3:29–30), or "envy the violent" (3:31). Our special interest is in the final four verses of the speech (3:32–35): why shouldn't the son do these things? The answer does not include the word "justice" but does emphasize the Lord's response to people who act unjustly: they are an "abomination" (NRSV) or "detestable" (CEB) to the Lord (3:32a), and the Lord's curse is upon them (3:33a). The Lord treats them just as they treat others (3:34a), and finally, stubborn fools will inherit disgrace (3:35b). In other words, justice dealt out by the Lord will catch up to those who hurt others. At the same time, the Lord will bless the upright (3:32b), the righteous (3:33b), and the humble (3:34b), or in sum, the wise (3:35a). Wise or foolish, justice will be enforced.

In her first appearance, Woman Wisdom takes on the guise of a prophet and rapidly reviews what she has said to young men on a collision course with disaster (1:20–33). She has appealed and even begged them to listen to her and pay attention, but they have refused (1:22–25). So when disaster hits—justice is coming—Woman Wisdom will watch them with the same attitude they had toward her. She will laugh and silently speak those immortal words: "I told you so" (1:26–27). Then Wisdom will turn to speak to onlookers and explain the tragedy. She warned the young men, but they would not accept a relationship with God. So as a result, justice has come, and the young men have destroyed their own lives (1:29–32).

Finally, the text standing outside the framework of speeches also gives an implicit message on justice (6:6–15). Sluggards or lazy people will be ruined because unlike the industrious ants, they do not do the hard work of preparing for winter by planting summer crops (6:6–8). As a result, they will reap the justice of nothing to eat: poverty will assault the lazy person like a warrior or thief (6:10–11). Villains will also be ruined for all their efforts to cause trouble, devising secretive plans to ruin others and putting their plans into action with a wink or nod (6:12–14). Suddenly, however, and without warning, what they tried to do to others will backfire on them, and they will be ruined beyond repair (6:15). Justice will catch up to them.

Despite only five texts that explicitly mention justice, the overture to wisdom, Proverbs 1–9, is not only founded on justice, it also lays a foundation of justice for the chapters to come. What is not mentioned is nonetheless present—and obvious. It's as if at first the house of wisdom with all its weight appears to be floating above the ground. But when we investigate and attempt to pass our hand under the house like a magician's wand, we hit solid concrete—present but not explicit in the text. When we see the social and community principles, we realize that the sages have built their house on the bedrock of justice.

Justice in Proverbs 10–31

Terms for and related to justice occur twenty times in Proverbs 10–31. The verbal form translated "to judge" (*shapat*) occurs three times, the noun or adjective translated "justice" (*mishpat*) sixteen times, and the noun translated "judgment" (*shepet*) once.[1] In these explicit references, the sages articulate four distinct ideas, three of which continue from chapters 1–9.

First, justice is a characteristic of a person's relationship to God and is one aspect of wisdom or wise living—as we have seen in the prologue ("the fear of the LORD" is the starting point or foundation for a life of wisdom, 1:7; a life of learning about wisdom, 1:2; and gaining "insightful instruction" [CEB]—doing "righteousness, justice, and equity," 1:3) and in chapters 1–9.[2]

- When the righteous see justice (*mishpat*) enacted, they rejoice (21:15).
- "The thoughts of the righteous are just (*mishpat*)" (12:5a).
- To judge (*shapat*) righteously is synonymous with defending "the rights of the poor and needy" (31:9).
- To do what is right and just (*mishpat*) is "more acceptable to the LORD than sacrifice" (21:3).
- It is better to be righteous and have only a little, than have wealth without justice (*mishpat*) (16:8).

1. "To judge" (*shapat*): 29:9, 14; 31:9. "Justice" (*mishpat*): 1:3; 2:8, 9; 8:20; 12:3, 5; 13:23; 16:8, 10, 11, 33; 18:5; 24:23; 28:5; 29:4, 16. "Judgment" (*shepet*): 19:29.

2. "The fear of the LORD" is the starting point or foundation for a life of wisdom, 1:7; a life of learning about wisdom, 1:2; and gaining "insightful instruction" (CEB)—doing "righteousness, justice, and equity," 1:3.

The Hebrew word *mesharim*, meaning evenness, uprightness, or equity is also used in these chapters, but only once with a meaning relevant to our study. In a short speech resembling the speeches of chapters 1–7, a father says he will be glad if the son is wise (23:15); he will rejoice when the son speaks "what is right (*mesharim*)" (23:16); and he hopes the son will continue in the fear of the Lord (23:17). A phrase synonymous with equity is also used: "If a king judges (*mishpat*) the poor with equity, his throne will be established forever" (29:14).

Second, chapters 10–31 credit the Lord as the source of justice: a person does not get justice (*mishpat*) from rulers, but from the Lord (29:26). Just (*mishpat*) or honest scales belong to the Lord (16:11). And humans may cast "the lot," but the decision (*mishpat*) of the lots comes from the Lord (16:33; see examples of casting lots in Josh. 14:1–5; 1 Sam. 10:20–21; Acts 1:23–26).

Third, because injustice is such a problem to society, the sages have venom in their quills for anyone who dares to manipulate the court in their favor. In descriptive proverbs, the sages acknowledge the reality that the wicked accept bribes to pervert justice (*mishpat*, 17:23), and a worthless witness invents lies to mock justice (*mishpat*, 19:28). But in prescriptive proverbs, the sages instruct the reader not to favor the guilty and deny the innocent of justice (*mishpat*, 18:5). In fact, people will curse and hate those who show partiality (24:24).

Fourth, just as the prologue recognizes the presence of injustice—the attack of sinners on the innocent (1:11–14), the mistreatment of neighbors (3:27–30), and the violence of the wicked (4:14–17)—chapters 10–31 also live in the real world of what happens, not what is supposed to happen. The poor may work hard to plant and cultivate their fields, but those with power may take away or destroy their harvest or profits, literally "with no justice (*mishpat*)," a grievous act of "injustice" (13:23). But in time, the violent will be swept away "because they refuse to do what is just" (*mishpat*, 21:7).

Finally, one proverb captures the significance of justice for the sages:

> *The evil do not understand justice* (mishpat),
> *but those who seek the* LORD *understand it completely.* (28:5)

The only way to understand justice so we can live a just life, to uphold justice, and protect justice is to seek the Lord in relationship. Only those who seek and follow the Lord will grasp genuine justice because they alone know and understand the Lord, from whom justice derives.

The results of a concordance or online search for "justice" in Proverbs 10–31 seem to suggest that the sages have little use for justice. Though quick and easy, a concordance study or search of key words in an online Bible will lead theological investigation to the wrong conclusion almost every time. Instead, we must change our method of study to the radical, revolutionary, and fanatical: *we must read Proverbs 10–31.* We must read and reread, listen and listen again, and live with the book echoing in our mind. When we do, we will discover that the sages may have chosen to refer explicitly to justice in only twenty texts, but the Lord's justice is critical for understanding wisdom.

For example in Proverbs 10–31, the sages use two formulas over and over again:

> *If you want to receive X,*
> *then you must do Y.*
> or
> *If you want to avoid X,*
> *then you must not do Y.*

For the sages, the only reason these types of proverbs could be true as a general rule is because the Lord upholds justice in the world. It is the sage's unified theory of truth: this is how the ethical world works. Consequently, the explicit vocabulary of justice is optional for the sages. As long as the Lord reigns, they are confident that justice gives shape to our world.

To establish this claim, we can read almost any proverb that prescribes an attitude or action and ask why? The proverbs in chapter 10 serve our purposes as well as any:

> *The treasure of the wicked won't profit them,*
> *but righteousness rescues people from death.* (10:2 CEB)

> *The* LORD *does not let the righteous go hungry,*
> *but he thwarts the craving of the wicked.* (10:3)

> *Laziness brings poverty;*
> *hard work makes one rich.* (10:4 CEB)

How can these proverbs be true? Why will the wealth of the wicked not help them? Why will the righteous not go hungry? Why does laziness lead to poverty? At the danger of belaboring the obvious, the answer to each question depends on the unspoken force of justice. Why pursue righteousness over treasure (10:2)? Because justice prevails: right living provides a reward, not wickedness. Why be righteous (10:3)? Because justice prevails: the Lord will provide food to the righteous, but he will not provide what the wicked desire. Why be diligent in work (10:4)? Because the just penalty for laziness is poverty, and the just reward of diligent work is wealth.

Others have made the same observation, most notably Michael Fox, a preeminent specialist in wisdom literature and the book of Proverbs. With great sophistication, Fox explains that Proverbs is not a haphazard collection of sayings but a book unified by an underlying "system of assumptions about knowledge,"[3] and central to the system is harmony, which Fox defines as "the rule and the ideal in matters of justice."[4] However he prefers the idea of balance: what God seeks is "balance: good deeds balanced by good results . . . bad deeds by bad results . . . with divine correctives remedying any imbalance."[5] So for a person to be wise, "one must acquire a sense of harmony, a sensitivity to what is fitting and right, in all realms of attitude and behavior."[6] In other words, a person must understand and practice justice, especially when the power of wealth and the vulnerability of poverty threaten to undermine what is just. Fox writes, "counterbalancing these realities, the sages believe, is the force of justice. Its working is not always evident in the short run, but its certainty is asserted as a point of faith."[7]

Summary: Justice in Proverbs

From the opening notes (1:1–7) to the overture (chs. 1–9) to the symphony of wisdom (chs. 10–31), justice is an ever-present theme sung by dozens of voices in dozens of variations. Justice is the ethical focal point around which the sages construct life. They are not ignorant nor do they close their eyes to the presence of injustice. They see bribes, partiality in court, theft, and senseless destruction that takes away the hard work of a poor family—all the practices that call the justice of the Lord into question. They see and know all too well. But they do more than just recognize injustice; they call it by its true names: folly, wickedness, and sin. Despite all that they see, the sages can still hear the music of justice: their God setting things right and maintaining justice in a world hell bent on destroying itself with injustice.

3. Michael Fox, *Proverbs 10–31*, Anchor Bible 18B (New Haven: Yale University Press, 2009), 968.

4. Fox, *Proverbs 10–31*, 972.

5. Fox, *Proverbs 10–31*, 972.

6. Fox, *Proverbs 10–31*, 973.

7. Fox, *Proverbs 10–31*, 511.

Mercy in Proverbs

Since justice is an ever-present theme in Proverbs and central to the way of God in wisdom, what space, if any, is left for mercy? How can generosity exist in a world governed by justice? How can a judge know a person's guilt and with a wave of the hand dismiss the case *and then* give them a bonus, as if they were just named employee of the month? Or have we become so familiar with "justice and grace" that we don't even see the problem? Or, God forbid, we understand the problem "in the Old Testament" and are quick to explain, "that's why we needed a new covenant, the New Testament way of doing things" (my fingers almost refuse to type these words onto the screen). Unfortunately, these conscious or often unconscious attitudes infect or sway the results of our study before we can begin. In its extreme form, we say (or think) that since the answer is Jesus, the God in the Old Testament is not allowed to offer and give forgiveness of sin through sacrifice, which he does (see Lev. 5:10, 13, 16, 18; 6:7), or extend grace without sacrifice, which he also does (see Exod. 34:6–7; Isa. 1:15–20; Jonah 3:4–10), or include mercy alongside justice in the book of Proverbs.

So with full recognition of the place justice holds in the worldview of the sages and awareness of our tendency to find justice in the Old Testament and mercy in the New Testament, we now look for the presence of mercy in Proverbs. In what follows, we will discover that mercy is not only present in Proverbs, it flourishes.

Hebrew Terms for Mercy

Four Hebrew words and their derivatives used in the book of Proverbs include in their spectrum of meaning some concept of mercy, grace, favor, or honor:

- *hen:* 3:4, 34; 11:16; 13:15; 17:8 (lit. "stone of favor"); 22:1, 11; 28:23[8]
- *hanan:* 14:21, 31; 19:17; 21:10; 26:25; 28:8
- *raham*: 12:10; 28:13
- *hamal*: 6:34

8. *Hen* occurs in other texts and is variously translated as a "fair" garland (1:9; 4:9), "adornment" (3:22), "graceful" doe (5:19), and "charm" that can be deceitful or misleading (31:30).

In total these four terms occur well over a dozen times in Proverbs. Our search for mercy, therefore, begins with these terms, followed by special consideration of a fifth term (*kasah*, "to cover").

Hen

The Hebrew word *hen* as a noun or adjective means favor, mercy, gracious, or graceful. For example, we read texts in Proverbs in which *hen* is best understood as:

- A result of positive character traits: Good sense earns favor (*hen*, 13:15). Loyalty and faithfulness lead to favor (*hen*) with people and God (3:3–4). A good reputation brings favor (*hen*) that is better than silver or gold (22:1). And offering correction finds more favor (*hen*) than flattery (28:23).
- Favorable or gracious character traits lead to a blessing or reward: a gracious woman receives honor (*hen*, 11:16), and gracious (*hen*) speech may lead to friendship with a king (22:11).

One text clearly uses *hen* for mercy or grace:

- "At scoffers He scoffs, but to the lowly He shows grace" (3:34 NJPS). God gives grace, favor, or blessings to those who are humble, but as for the proud, God returns their taunts, sneers, and ridicule.

Hanan

The meaning of the Hebrew word *hanan* ranges from kindness to mercy:

- An enemy may speak graciously (26:25) to mislead and hurt another person.
- Neighbors of the wicked find no mercy (*hanan*) from them (21:10b).
- A person who gains wealth through high-interest loans to the poor will forfeit their wealth to those who are generous (*hanan*) to the poor (28:8).
- Those who are kind (*hanan*) to the poor honor God (14:31b). They will be blessed (14:21b) and are assured that the Lord will repay them in full (19:17); but those who despise and oppress the poor are sinners (14:21a) who insult God, their maker (14:31a).

Raham

The Hebrew word *raham* conveys the idea of mercy or merciful in two texts.

- Righteous owners are attentive to the needs of their animals and extend compassionate care to their herds. But even the mercy (*raham*) of the wicked is cruel (12:10).
- Mercy (*raham*) or forgiveness is available to the person who will admit their wrongs and leave them behind, but one who tries to hide their wrongdoing will not prosper (28:13).

Hamal

The Hebrew word *hamal* occurs only once in Proverbs with a clear, although negative, meaning of forgiveness or compassion. In this text, a man has had a sexual affair with a married woman, crossing an ethical line that is like going over a cliff—it is impossible to return or reset matters as if it hadn't happened. So when the woman's husband discovers the affair, his jealousy and rage will lead him to show no mercy or forgiveness (*hamal*, 6:34), no matter what bribe or plea bargain the offender may offer.

Kasah

The Hebrew word *kasah* means "to cover," as in concealing or hiding knowledge (12:23), keeping a confidence (11:13), hiding violence (10:6), concealing hatred (10:18; 26:26), covering the disgrace of an insult (12:16), or hiding sin (28:13). Twice, however, the word appears to indicate an act of mercy. In the first instance, a sage observes that hate stirs up or agitates a conflict, but love covers (*kasah*) all offenses (10:12). In other words, love motivates mercy and forgiveness that resolves the conflict. The second text bears strong resemblance to the first: a person who covers (*kasah*) an offense forgives the offense and fosters friendship (17:9).

To summarize our findings: from the original candidates based on vocabulary, we have identified eleven texts that speak explicitly about mercy:

- Three texts speak about people who refuse to extend mercy to individuals (6:34), neighbors (21:10), or animals (12:10).

- The Lord shows grace to the humble (3:34b), forgives those who confess and turn away from their sins (28:13b), and blesses those who are kind or compassionate to the needy (14:21b).
- The efforts of the wicked to gain wealth by taking advantage of the poor angers the Lord (14:31a) and results in their working for money that will be handed over to those who are merciful to the poor (28:8).
- The Lord favors the poor and those who help them, who imitate his compassion and honor him (14:31b). Their kindness to the poor is regarded as a loan to the Lord, and the Lord will pay them back in full (19:17).
- A person who loves will cover over or forgive an offense, but the person motivated by hate will stir up a conflict (10:12). Covering or forgiving an offense also fosters friendship (17:9).

No longer do we need to ask if mercy and forgiveness are present in the book of Proverbs, for of course the sages speak of mercy and forgiveness. However in comparison to explicit references to justice, mercy falls far behind (twenty-two references to justice, only eleven to mercy), leading us toward a new question: What accounts for the disparity between mercy and justice? Why such an apparent emphasis on justice over mercy? Before exploring this question, however, we must determine if the disparity continues in implicit references to mercy in Proverbs.

Implicit References to Mercy in Proverbs

As we saw in our study of justice, the communities who crafted individual proverbs were not limited by our vocabulary lists. So if we are to find all that the book of Proverbs says about mercy, we must continue our radical method of study: reading the book of Proverbs. Only when we read the text can we hear the sages express in their own unique way the ideas of mercy, compassion, forgiveness, and generosity. In addition as we read, it will be helpful to watch for secondary terms that are frequently found with expressions of mercy, for example terms for the poor and verbs that are antithetical to mercy, such as to crush, to oppress, or to rob.

As before, what follows is the result of my attempt to read and listen to the sages. I make no comprehensive claim about finding everything Proverbs has to say about mercy. No doubt if I keep listening, I will hear more. But for now, I offer three observations.

Observation #1: Helping the Poor

The proverbs bring to mind the Japanese pictorial maxim of the three wise monkeys who embody the principle "see no evil, hear no evil, speak no evil." Except for one small detail—each principle is reversed in Proverbs. The sages urge readers not to "*close their ears* to the cries of the poor" (21:13 CEB, emphasis mine) or they will not be heard in a time of trouble. In the same way, readers must not turn "a blind eye" to the poor, because those who do "will get many a curse" (28:27b). In contrast, those who see and give to the poor "will lack nothing" (28:27a).

Lemuel's mother taught him to speak on behalf of those who cannot speak for themselves and "for the rights of all who are vulnerable" (31:8 CEB). A wise person should "speak out in order to judge with righteousness and to defend the needy and the poor" (31:9 CEB). So instead of being like monkeys who sit quietly and cover their eyes, ears, and mouths—or instead of being quiet, compliant citizens who never rock the political or social boat over injustices done to the vulnerable—the sages claim that to live with wisdom requires knowing the rights of the poor (29:7), seeing the needs that exist, speaking out, and acting in mercy (24:10–12).

Observation #2: Not Oppressing the Poor

Another set of texts warns against taking advantage of the poor or needy just because these groups appear to lack the resources to defend themselves. Four scenarios unfold before the reader. First, it might look easy to oppress the poor and give to the wealthy in order to gain more influence and produce more wealth. But in fact, this strategy will backfire and lead to poverty (22:16).

Second, the laws in Deuteronomy require landowners to pay day laborers at the end of every day because these workers live by day: what they are paid today buys food for their family today. If they are not paid, their family goes hungry. Deuteronomy warns that if this happens, the poor will cry out to the Lord against the landowner's injustice, who will incur guilt (Deut. 24:15). In Proverbs, those who "withhold what is due" or do not pay workers at the end of the day will "suffer want" (Prov. 11:24). Why an employer would withhold pay is not clear. Maybe it was a strategy that further oppressed the workers, making sure they returned the next day, or maybe it was to dispute the value of their work, or maybe they did not have the money to hire workers in the first place and were taking advantage of the laborers' need and trust. Or perhaps it is for the same reasons given today in fields filled with migrant workers: workers labor at the mercy of an employer who holds the power to withhold or minimize their pay.

Third, others may employ a different strategy of taking advantage of the poor, moving a boundary stone or otherwise encroaching on or taking land, assuming the poor will be unable to defend themselves (23:10). These claim jumpers, as we called them during the gold rush days in Colorado, California, and Alaska, make a serious miscalculation because the redeemer, defender, and avenger of the poor is strong. God will take up the cause of the poor and defend their rights against all types of theft and predatory practices (23:11).

Fourth, the greedy are warned not to attempt to rob the poor or needy in court because the Lord will take up the case of the needy and "press the life out of those who oppress them" (22:22–23 CEB). Much like today, the wealthy had more resources and more influence over the courts with the best attorneys, connections to judges, etc., than the poor. Appearances, however, do not always reflect reality. The Lord will make his presence known when he defends the poor against oppression in court.

Observation #3: Generosity

Generosity is the way of life for those who are wise (21:26), a path that is counterintuitive from almost every perspective. After all, aren't we all taught to save and invest in companies that make money? Giving our wealth away hardly seems to be a wise strategy. Nonetheless, it is the best strategy for living a life that is good.

Instead of keeping everything for their own pleasure, those who share their food with those in need are happy and blessed (22:9). Those who withhold what is owed do not get further ahead, but suffer want, an ironic contrast to others who give freely and grow wealthier (11:24–25). The community blesses people who sell grain when it is needed. But people curse those who hoard grain or who increase prices when the need is great, price gouging the market (11:26).

Perhaps the counterintuitive nature of generosity will help us understand one of the enigmas of Proverbs:

> *If your enemies are hungry, give them bread to eat;*
> *and if they are thirsty, give them water to drink;*
> *for you will heap coals of fire on their heads,*
> *and the* LORD *will reward you.* (Prov. 25:21–22)

In the letter to the Romans, Paul cites these verses (12:20) and then adds:

Do not be overcome by evil,
but overcome evil with good. (Rom. 12:21)

This enigma in Proverbs 25 may be resolved by recognizing the counterintuitive nature of other proverbs in this chapter. The proverb says nothing about how the enemy will react. Speculation runs wild, from they will be shamed to they will become a friend. The text speaks only about the wise action of giving enemies what they need, when typical human behavior would withhold even basic necessities from enemies. I began a research project on this text some years back to discover how these actions "heap coals of fire on their heads" and what this phrase means. Finally after filling a three-ring binder with reading notes, I came to the conclusion that I had found no satisfying explanation. Theories appear to multiply like rabbits, but every explanation I have seen so far lacks credible evidence or support. My only caution in choosing an interpretation is to remember that the ethic of love for enemies is equally present in the New Testament (Matt. 5:43–44) as it is in the Old Testament (Exod. 22:21–24, 23:4–5, 9; Lev. 19:17–18, 34; Deut. 10:18–19; Prov. 24:17–18).[9]

Conclusion

Imagine every proverb to be the brush stroke of a master artist, every theme a color, every subtheme a different hue on the palette. To bring all the brush strokes about justice and mercy together into anything other than a bad painting requires the talent of a Rembrandt or Picasso: heavy, thick strokes here, delicate strokes soft as a cloud there, a radiant color here, shadows there. The "ghost painting"—painted on the canvas before the beginning of time—of the sharp patterns of justice still lay behind the masterwork of Proverbs. Misunderstood, justice may easily run amok and devolve into a socially conservative program that ensures the status quo for the wealthy and powerful at the expense of the weak. The sages, however, advocated justice that ensures the wealthy and powerful do not take advantage of the poor. Even more, they understood the Lord to stand behind and enforce such justice, because the Lord models the practice of merciful justice. The Lord

- Shows favor or mercy to the humble (3:34b)
- Forgives those who confess and turn away from their sins (28:13b)

9. See the discussion of 31:6–9 in ch. 9.

- Repays those who are gracious to the poor (19:17)
- Takes the case of the needy and poor, and presses "the life out of those who oppress them" (22:22–23 CEB)
- Brings charges against those who attempt to encroach on the land of an orphan (23:10–11)

In other words, according to Proverbs the Lord practices mercy within justice.

As a result, those who follow the Lord will resist the problems associated with "only justice" and follow the Lord's example.

- They refuse to take advantage of another person just because it's easy and they can get away with it (14:31a).
- They refuse to charge high interest on loans (cf. 28:8). Instead, they freely loan money or give whatever is needed to the poor, as if they were giving to God (19:17; 14:31b).

Based on texts reviewed in this chapter, we could add other practices to this list that derive from the Lord's practice of mercy. Nonetheless, these examples suffice to show that those who are merciful and kind to the poor not only follow the Lord's example; they will also be happy and blessed (14:21b).

Finally, we return to the imbalance between justice and mercy. Why does Proverbs place such a heavy stress on justice and a lighter emphasis on mercy? At least part of the answer lies in the nature of society. For example, in early Israel the tribes devolved into a collection of individuals doing what they wished, what was best for them without regard for community well-being (see Judg. 17:6; 18:1; 19:1; 21:25). To exist, communities must have a foundation of righteousness, justice, and equity, a backbone strong enough to order and regulate society, a role that mercy alone cannot perform. However to be human—and like God—this strong skeleton needs soft skin that can touch, feel, comfort, and embrace. Otherwise our just communities become tyrannical robots. We must recognize that it is always easy for those who have privilege, wealth, and status to appeal to what is right, even to the detriment of those who are just trying to survive. It is easy to cry for justice when we feel threatened and want to protect our own—and in the name of justice leave others on the street, starving as they look at us through the windows of our expensive restaurants. Or to call to justice individuals or groups who have acted in desperation, breaking our just laws for the sake of life—a life we are not willing to share. This, my friends, is not justice but selfishness.

The prophet Micah may not have been a sage, but he expressed the sentiments of the sages when he said,

> *He has shown you, O mortal, what is good.*
> *And what does the LORD require of you?*
> *To act justly and to love mercy*
> *and to walk humbly with your God.* (Mic. 6:8 NIV)

To act with justice *and* to love mercy at the same time—this is our challenge.

DISCUSSION QUESTIONS

1. This chapter is data heavy. It includes many proverbs and almost as many points or observations. What verses or observations surprised or caught your attention? Please explain why.
2. Which of the qualities—justice or mercy, would you say is your strong suit? Why? Which is your weakness? Why?
3. In light of Proverbs, provide analysis of your own culture: Where is a greater sense of justice needed? Where is the greatest need for mercy? Support your analysis with specific references to your culture. What do the sages say about your situation?
4. Do you agree with my claim that justice should be the skeleton of community existence? Give examples of where you see the skeleton of justice at work in your community. How does justice provide structure? In what ways is this framework of justice tempered with mercy? Where does mercy provide a softer touch?
5. Describe the ways in which justice and mercy are interwoven. In what situations do we most often see justice out of control? In what situations do we see mercy out of control? What wisdom or principles might guide our efforts to act with justice and to love mercy at the same time?

PROJECT CHALLENGE

Here is a case study in justice and mercy. Politicians and the media (to name only two) have had much to say in recent years about immigration policies and the crisis of illegal immigration. How does what we have seen in Proverbs intersect with this debate? In your wisdom, in what ways does justice need to guide any resolution of the problem? In what ways should mercy contribute to a resolution?

PART THREE

Applied Topics for a Life That Is Good

CHAPTER 7

Speech: A Kiss on the Lips or a Club to the Head?

Sticks and stones may break my bones,
but words will never hurt me.

—Anonymous

Rash words are like sword thrusts,
but the tongue of the wise brings healing.

—Proverbs 12:18

How great a forest is set ablaze by a small fire! And the tongue is a fire. The tongue is placed among our members as a world of iniquity; it stains the whole body, sets on fire the cycle of nature, and is itself set on fire by hell.

—James 3:5b–6

TO PREPARE FOR READING THIS CHAPTER

Read the proverbs in either #1 or #2:

1. Proverbs 2:10–12, 16; 4:23–24; 6:16–19, 23–24; 7:18–21; 10:6, 8, 11, 14, 18, 20–21, 31–32; 11:9, 11–13; 12:6, 13–14, 17–20, 22–23, 25; 13:1, 3; 14:5, 23, 25; 15:1–2, 4, 12, 23, 26, 28; 16:13, 21, 23–24, 27–30; 17:4–5, 20, 27–28; 18:2, 4, 6–8, 13, 17, 20–21; 19:9, 25, 27–29; 20:15, 19; 21:6, 11, 28; 22:10–11; 24:9, 24–26; 25:11–15, 18; 26:4–6, 9, 20–26, 28; 27:5; 28:23; 29:5, 8; 30:10; 31:8–9, 26
2. Proverbs 4:23–24; 6:16–19, 23–24; 10:6–8, 18–21, 31–32; 11:9–13; 12:13–14, 17–25; 14:23–25; 15:1–4, 26–28; 16:21–24, 27–30; 17:4–5, 27–28; 18:2–8, 20–21; 19:27–29; 22:10–11; 24:9–12, 24–26; 25:11–15; 26:4–6, 20–28; 31:8–9

It only takes a little time reading the book of Proverbs to see that words and speech are a major theme. Jutta Hausmann writes, "No other corpus in the Old Testament offers such an extensive reflection concerning the possibilities and functions of language, as Proverbs."[1] Still, if we read Proverbs slowly over a period of weeks or months, it is possible that the degree to which the sages stress words and speech might slip by us unnoticed, like a ship on a dark and cloudy night.

In a conservative estimate, Roland Murphy claims that twenty percent of Proverbs 10–29 has to do with speech.[2] My own survey includes the entire book of Proverbs and counts all mentions of speech, general and specific, for example wicked or evil speech and lying or boasting, as well as those who speak and those who listen (see Figure 7.1). I found in my survey that over thirty percent of the book of Proverbs relates in some way to the theme of speech.

Speech in the Book of Proverbs

Introduction to Wisdom Proverbs 1–9	77 of 256 verses	30.08%
Solomon I 10:1–22:16	136 of 375 verses	36.26%
Words of the Wise I 22:17–24:22	16 of 70 verses	22.86%
Words of the Wise II 24:23–34	5 of 12 verses	41.67%
Solomon II 25:1–29:27	57 of 138 verses	41.30%
Sayings of Agur 30:1–33	11 of 33 verses	33%
Sayings of Lemuel 31:1–9	4 of 9 verses	44.44%
Ode to the Capable Wife 31:10–31	1 of 22 verses	4.54%
Proverbs 1–9	77 of 256 verses	30.08%
Proverbs 10–31	230 of 659 verses	34.90%
All of Proverbs	307 of 915 verses	33.55%

1. Jutta Hausmann, *Studien zum Menschenbild der älteren Weisheit*, FAT 7 (Tübingen: Mohr Siebeck, 1995), 186. Translated by Roland Murphy, *Proverbs*, Word Bible Commentary 22 (Nashville: Thomas Nelson), 259.

2. Murphy, *Proverbs*, 258.

Beyond frequency, these words about words also describe the value and power of the spoken word. What we say has enormous potential to benefit others. Our words can cheer up another person (12:25b), supply nourishment (10:21), and even provide health and healing (16:24). In a word, what we say can bring life:

> *The mouth of the righteous is a fountain of life* (10:11a)

> *A gentle tongue is a tree of life* (15:4a)

Or instead of a fountain or tree of life, our words can be "like a scorching fire" (16:27). As anyone who survived middle school knows, it is simply not true that "Sticks and stones may break my bones, but words will never hurt me." What we say to or about other people has tremendous power to harm them: to destroy (11:9), break their spirit (15:4b), or even bring death (18:21).

Words also have enormous potential to harm the speaker. We can set a trap for others and catch ourselves with what we say (12:13), stir up trouble and invite others to beat us up (18:6), or ruin our own lives (18:7). Or to reverse directions, what we say can fill our lives with good things (12:14). To put the challenge in a single proverb:

> *Death and life are in the power of the tongue,*
> *and those who love it will eat its fruits.* (18:21)

The choice is ours not merely to get our words right but to get our hearts right, for from our hearts our words bubble over (4:23; see also Matt. 12:34).

So if we are looking for the most important themes in Proverbs, we just stumbled over a vein of pure gold. All that remains in this chapter is for us to take up our pickax, sledge hammer, dynamite, and shovel and find how deep and in what directions this vein will lead us. Or to leave the metaphor for a moment, I will ask two sets of questions: 1) What misuses of speech does the book of Proverbs identify, and what ideal traits? and 2) Why is speech such a major concern for the sages who wrote Proverbs? What motivated the sages to spend a third of what they wrote on what we say? What's so important about words—what's at stake?

Question #1: What Does Proverbs Say about Speech?

The questions raised, we are ready to start digging and follow this vein wherever it may lead us.

Negative Speech

Most often the sages write about speech in negative terms, identifying improper words or misuses of speech and the consequences. Four stand out: lying, gossip, flattery, and slander or malice.

Lying

By definition, a lie is the intent to deceive, a deliberate action whether large or small (the little white lie), spoken by word or by silence. The sages stress that whatever benefit the liar may gain will be short in duration, lasting only a moment (12:19b) or as fleeting as the vapor we exhale on a subfreezing morning (21:6). They also name the truth that motivates a lie: liars hate their victims, the ones to whom they lie (10:18; 26:28). Consequently, God hates lying lips; they are an "abomination" to him (6:16–19; 12:22).

Gossip

Gossip is more difficult to define. In general terms, gossip is speaking about a person or situation when I am not part of the problem or part of its solution and my motivation is salacious, scandalous, or against the well-being of those involved. The sages label someone who divulges secrets a "gossip" or a "whisperer" (11:13; 20:19). If only the gossip would stop, the fire of a scandal would go out (26:20). The problem, however, is that gossip tastes so good, it is difficult to restrain ourselves (18:8; 26:22).

Flattery

Related to lying, flattery is an insincere compliment (a little "white lie") given to advance our standing with the object of our flattery (26:28). On the one side, flattery lays a trap for its victim (29:5). On the other side, the sages try to convince us that speaking difficult truth or correction is far more effective for long-term friendship or favor (28:23).

Slander or Malice

Also related to lying, slander may be truthful or untruthful speech (10:18). What defines slander is whether or not our intent is to harm the person about whom we speak. Proverbs warns us against using slander to get ahead or take revenge (30:10). Chapter 26 also provides an extended description of a person who speaks with slander or malice:

> *Like the glaze covering an earthen vessel*
> *are smooth lips with an evil heart.*
> *An enemy dissembles in speaking*
> *while harboring deceit within;*
> *when an enemy speaks graciously, do not believe it,*
> *for there are seven abominations concealed within;*
> *though hatred is covered with guile,*
> *the enemy's wickedness will be exposed in the assembly.* (26:23–26)

Notice the terms used to describe this person's heart: it is evil (v. 23b), harbors deceit (24b), conceals "seven abominations" (v. 25b), and is full of hatred (v. 26a). Yet this person speaks graciously (v. 25a) with "smooth lips" (23b). In other words, watch out—don't trust people like this because they are not trying to help us or be our friend. In time, their true nature will be exposed (v. 26b). Meanwhile, the sages warn us to exercise great caution around these people.

Positive Speech

The common theme behind positive speech patterns is knowing what to say and when to say it (10:32). For those who are wise, the ability to speak "a word in season" is not only a joy (15:23), it is fine art: "like golden apples in a silver basket" (25:11 NLT). Thus, on the positive side, we may briefly highlight three characteristics of virtuous speech mentioned in the book of Proverbs: honesty, gentleness, and patience or restrained speech. (See further development of these themes below in "An Underlying Concern for Character Formation.")

Honesty

Earlier in the book, Woman Wisdom asserts that she is one who speaks truth, so she can be trusted (8:7). The "Words of the Wise" (22:17–24:22) begin with the same claim. The sages have written sayings to show what is "right and true" (22:21) so that "your trust may be in the LORD" (22:19a). And at the end of the book of Proverbs, Lemuel's mother testifies, "Every word of God proves true; he is a shield to those who take refuge in him" (30:5). Like previous texts, she connects truth or truthfulness to trust. Or simply put, honest speech fosters trust. In contrast, God hates lying lips but "favors those who do what is true" (12:22 CEB) or "those who act faithfully" (NRSV). The benefits from lying are brief in duration, but "truthful lips endure forever" (12:19). And certainly, the sages commend truthfulness in the court (12:17; 14:25), a place where an honest answer is indeed like "a kiss on the lips" (24:26).

Gentleness

Though described as "soft" or "patient," we should not confuse gentle speech with weakness. In fact, gentle speech has tremendous power, even to break a bone or its equivalent, to persuade rulers (25:15). Gentle speech can also deescalate a situation and turn away anger (15:1) or provide life itself: "a gentle tongue is a tree of life" (15:4a).

Patience or Restrained Speech

Among the "best practices" of speech is the ability to restrain and control it (17:27). Such restraint certainly stands beneath an ability to speak with gentleness, to use appropriate words at appropriate times, and to speak truth (e.g., 21:28). However, in Proverbs, the sages most often emphasize restraint in connection to listening. Wisdom comes when a person stops speaking long enough to listen to advice and correction (12:15; 13:10; 19:20). A word aptly spoken may be like golden apples (25:11), but a "wise rebuke to a listening ear" is a gold ring or golden ornament (25:12). A person who guards their lips preserves their life (13:3). But when a person is unable (or unwilling) to restrain their speech they will ruin their lives (10:8, 10), a hallmark trait of a fool (see the discussion of 17:28 in ch. 4).

Question #2: Why Such an Emphasis on Words and Speech?

Our second entry point into this vein of study raises a different set of questions. We begin with geology, or how this particular vein of gold about speech came into existence. From a historical perspective, proverbs tend to originate in oral form, then are written in small collections, and are ultimately brought into larger collections, such as the book of Proverbs. This history sharpens our question to a sharper, more incisive edge. Why did the people of the time generate so many proverbs about speech? Why did so many of these sayings engage Israel's collective memory so much that they were written down? And why did those who edited the book of Proverbs choose to include so many texts about speech? To reword our questions, why did so many proverbs about speech follow the long, winding road into the final edition of the book of Proverbs? Why do the sages who wrote and compiled the book place such an incredible emphasis on speech?[3]

All the talk in Proverbs about speech signifies that more than mere words are at stake. Certainly the sages were interested in words and proverbs for teaching proper, God-fearing ways of speaking to others. It is wise to speak cautiously and truthfully and not to gossip, slander, insult, or belittle others. Still, the emphasis on speech indicates that even more important principles are at stake for the sages. In fact, what we discover has been found by generation after generation: words matter. Often we may attempt to deflect this truth as nothing more than an example of the liberal police arresting us for not using politically correct language or listeners we claim are too sensitive or nitpicky. However, the sages argue that words matter and so does the thought behind the words. People who fear the Lord should speak in ways that befit their master, with words that are righteous, just, fair, and sensitive.

As with justice and mercy, godly language is not developed by following rules and guidelines. Such an approach to language is impossible for simple if not obvious reasons: we could never write enough rules to cover every situation, and if we could, we would not have enough time to read all the rules and even less time to learn them. Instead, what we find in the book is a diverse collection of sayings about speech that were ultimately developed from and driven by four core values. These values dictate the importance of speech and form the Israelite understanding of godly language.

3. For further introductions to this topic, see the short studies by Murphy, *Proverbs*, 258–60; and Lucas, *Proverbs*, 363–82.

An Underlying Concern for the Community

Others have noticed the first core principle behind the attention to speech in the book of Proverbs. For example, D. A. Hubbard writes, "Speech and community go hand in hand. Community depends on communication—upon information and attitudes shared in common."[4] Bruce Waltke also asserts, "The importance of *eloquentia* [effective speech] cannot be overemphasized. All social values depend on some form of communication."[5] Their claim is substantiated not only by Proverbs but elsewhere in the Old Testament. After the great flood of Genesis 6–9, the shared common language enabled humans to act in defiance of God. They organized to build a city with a tower that would reach into the heavens (Gen. 11:1–4), until their project caught the Lord's attention. He made an excursion down to see this "tall" tower and determined that it posed an unacceptable threat (Gen. 11:5). As long as the people shared a common language he said, "nothing that they propose to do will now be impossible for them" (Gen. 11:6). Their speech brought them together into a united front against God to elevate their community to rival God. So God confused their language and scattered them, unraveling and crushing their united community simply by confusing their communication (Gen. 11:7–8).

So too in the book of Proverbs, speech is important because it has the power to build or destroy community. For example:

> *When it goes well with the righteous, the city rejoices;*
> *and when the wicked perish, there is jubilation.*
> *By the blessing of the upright a city is exalted,*
> *but it is overthrown by the mouth of the wicked.* (11:10–11)

"The mouth of the wicked" is an explicit reference to speech (11:11b), in contrast with "the blessing of the upright." As the antithesis of "the mouth of the wicked," "the blessing of the upright" implies a general claim for speech that exalts a city or community. True to its nature, however, the book of Proverbs avoids generalities in favor of identifying particular forms of speech. Thus, the sages recognize four types of speaker that impact the community: the false witness, the mocker or scoffer, the gossip, and the wicked.

4. D. A. Hubbard, *Proverbs*, Communicator's Commentary 15a (Dallas: Word, 1989), 214.

5. Bruce Waltke, *The Book of Proverbs 1–15*, New International Commentary on the Old Testament (Grand Rapids: Eerdmans, 2004), 102.

The False Witness

Obviously related to the liar (see above) are the dangerous people in communities who will not tell the truth when called to witness (14:5). These false witnesses are not just worthless; they also mock justice (19:28a) and could cost others their lives (14:25). In fact, a person who gives false testimony about their neighbor might just as well hit them in the head with a club or shoot them with an arrow (25:18). After all, a liar hates his or her victims (see above) and/or appears to profit in some way from their downfall (21:6). The sages assure the community that a false witness will be punished, perhaps even losing their life (19:5; 21:28). "Lying lips are an abomination to the LORD" (12:22), and for that reason, readers are assured that a "lying tongue lasts only a moment" (12:19b; see also 21:6). Nevertheless, false witnesses may last long enough to irrevocably harm their community.

The Mocker or Scoffer

A mocker or scoffer is proud and acts with arrogance in ridiculing others (21:24). As opposed to being kind, they belittle people (14:21) and demonstrate their own lack of sense (11:12). A scoffer is dead weight to a society because they never learn or possess the desire to learn (1:22–25; 14:6), and they are unresponsive to correction (13:1; 15:12). Worse, mockers with their quarrelsome nature and scoundrels with their speech could be charged with arson because they set entire communities ablaze with their stupid arguments (16:27; 26:21; 29:8).

Witnesses who mock justice with their testimony will not fare well when they are on trial: they will be condemned (19:28–29). They even mock the guilt offering, turning their back against the Lord and rejecting his forgiveness (14:9). No wonder the Lord is scornful of those who have acted scornfully (3:34), and people regard scoffers as abominations in the community because they cause more trouble than those who devise mischief and folly (24:9). Only when society drives out mockers will quarreling and abuse finally come to an end (22:10).

The Gossip

We have defined gossip as speaking about a person or situation when we are not part of the problem or the solution or worse, we are opposed to the well-being of those involved. Now we consider the consequences of such behavior. The sages call "gossips" those who repeat secrets shared in confidence (11:13). Those who listen to and repeat rumors and separate close friends are also gossips (16:28). These people often refuse to forgive an offense, choosing instead to dwell on the wrong done to them and "alienate a friend" (17:9). And like a mocker or scoffer, a "whisperer" adds fuel to the fire of a quarrel, ensuring that it will continue to burn and destroy the community (26:20).

The Wicked

Proverbs brings up the danger posed to the community by the words of a broad category of people the sages label "the wicked" or "the godless." For example because they don't think through their answer, their mouths "pour out evil" (15:28). Even more dangerous than folly is the violence these people hide behind their words (10:6, 11). They use words to set deadly ambushes (12:6) and attempt to destroy their neighbors with their mouths (11:9).

An Underlying Concern for the Family

Though not as strongly stated as concern for the community, the sages also demonstrate concern for speech that affects the family, especially marriage. However, their rhetoric is limited by the absence of women within the target audience of the book (see ch. 1).[6] So we are left to imagine, regrettably, what a female sage might have to say to women about men and the words they use. As we have seen, the sages warn men against the seductive speech of women who can destroy their lives and their marriages (2:16–19; 6:23–24; 7:4–5; see ch. 2). Parental words and speech attempt to keep young men from listening to the words of these "other" women and falling into their hands. They are concerned about this seductive speech not merely because of the words themselves but because of what listening to them can do to the young man's marriage and family (5:3–14; 7:23–27).

Outside of the introductory chapters (Prov. 1–9) are only a few sayings regarding speech and the relationship of husband and wife. Regrettably, the

6. Female sages are mentioned in the Bible, for example Lemuel's mother (Prov. 31:1–9) and the "wise woman from Tekoa" (2 Sam. 14:1–20), but their perspective on men and marriage does not appear to be a part of the book of Proverbs.

most memorable proverbs identify the type of women who through their speech can make a young man's life miserable. For example:

> *A wife's quarreling is a continual dripping of rain.* (19:13b)

> *It is better to live in a corner of the housetop*
> *than in a house shared with a contentious wife.* (21:9, 25:24)

> *It is better to live in a desert land*
> *than with a contentious and fretful wife.* (21:19)

The sages lament the husband's future because he can do little to change his fate.

> *A continual dripping on a rainy day*
> *and a contentious wife are alike;*
> *to restrain her is to restrain the wind*
> *or to grasp oil in the right hand.* (27:15–16)

The sages of Proverbs might have been able to get away with such a one-sided critique, but to do the same today in our culture would most certainly be a foolish use of these texts—like the drunk swinging a branch from a thorn bush, he will hurt others and himself (26:9). It's true enough that living with women who share these speech patterns creates a difficult life; and it's just as true that living with men who share these and other types of derogatory and even abusive speech patterns can be beyond merely difficult. (See discussion question #2 at the end of this chapter.)

An Underlying Concern for Integrity

Integrity exists when our actions match our inner commitments, our true selves—what Proverbs often calls "the heart" (10:8; 23:15). In fact, the sages' frequent use of the Hebrew word *leb* (lit. "heart) warrants a brief excursus into the ways in which this term is deployed and translated in the book of Proverbs before we speak about integrity. Simply stated, the sages use *leb* to denote one of two related ideas.

- *The Heart Is the Seat of Thought*: In Proverbs, to possess heart means to have "an intelligent mind (*leb*)" (18:15), but to lack or be "without heart (*leb*)" means to have no sense (7:7; 9:4; 11:12; 15:21), or to be "senseless" (17:18), lack understanding (28:16), and have no desire to learn (17:16). In addition, because the sages understand thinking or mental activity to occur in the heart, it may make plans ("The human mind [*leb*] plans the way" [16:9; see also 16:1; 19:21]) or concoct evil ("a heart that devises wicked plans" [6:18; 12:20]).

- *The Heart Is the Seat of Emotion*: Positive emotions in the heart include gladness (23:15; 24:17; 27:11), cheerfulness (15:13a, 15b; 17:22a; 27:9), delight (29:17), and serenity ("a tranquil mind (*leb*)," 14:30a). Negative emotions include sorrow (15:13b; 17:22b; 25:20), illicit desire (6:25; 7:25), despising or hatred (5:12), envy (23:17), anxiety (12:25), hopelessness (13:12), bitterness (14:10), sadness (14:13), and rage (19:3).

Those who have a disconnect between their heart/mind and their mouth alarm the sages; in other words—the sages are troubled by a lack of integrity. Such people may have "smooth lips" that flatter or say kind things but an evil heart (26:23), or they may tell a lie, disregarding the Lord's ability to see inside the human heart (24:12). Those who lack integrity are dangerous to the community because of the difference between what they truly feel or think and what they say.

A person with integrity, however, speaks from the heart/mind, truthfully reflecting what they think, believe, or feel. In fact, when a person with wisdom couples their heart with gracious speech, they can have great influence (16:21), just as those "who love a pure heart" and speak graciously "will have the king as a friend" (22:11). That is to say, everyone will want to be their friend. These texts preview what Jesus says: the heart is the source of our words and actions (Matt. 15:18–19). For this reason, the sage warns us to "Keep your heart with all vigilance, for from it flow the springs of life" (Prov. 4:23). Integrity is a matter of wholeness and consistency of thought and action; our speech will either reflect and promote our integrity or it will erode us from the inside out.

An Underlying Concern for Good Character Formation

One of the strongest metaphors in Proverbs is the path or trail that leads a person on a continual trek of learning the content of wisdom and applying what they learn to their lives. In other words, wisdom is not a destination at which we finally arrive but a way of life (3:21–24; 4:10–12; 8:20–21). It is the path chosen by the wise not because it is the easiest path, but because it offers a way to live with the Lord; the path of least resistance is a trap into which the gullible fall to their death (7:21–23). The metaphor of the path also requires a conscious decision each day to follow it by practicing certain disciplines that lead to the formation of good character. For example, Dave Bland explains that good character formation comes as the result of conscious repetition of actions or attitudes until they become a habit.[7] As they walk this road, young sages accept, remember, and put into practice the advice and teaching of others walking in the same direction (10:8; 12:15; 13:10).

Speech factors into this process of character formation in three distinct ways: listening to the wise, promoting heart transformation, and demonstrating good character in speech.

Listening to the Wise

The young person must decide to whom they will listen and what words they will internalize and make a part of their identity. As we have already seen (see chs. 1 and 2), Proverbs 1 provides one example of this battle of words over a young man's way of life. The mother and father identify the rhetoric of the "gang" to expose the lifestyle they offer to the youth: a lifestyle filled with excitement, fast money, and acceptance as an equal but which leads to death (1:8–19). If the son accepts the gang's rhetoric, he will become violent, greedy, and selfish.

But if the son will listen to those who are wise, he will begin to understand the good and right way. If he follows this way, wisdom will come into his heart (2:1–10) and save him from the way of evil. As he walks on the path of wisdom, he will come to understand what is right, just, and equitable (2:9; 8:20). He will walk with integrity (28:8) as he grows in insight (9:6) and becomes upright (15:19). And as he walks, he will listen to instruction (10:17) and give thought to his ways (21:29). So good character formation, walking on the right path, begins and depends on identifying and listening to words that will lead toward wisdom.

7. Dave Bland, *Proverbs and the Formation of Character* (Eugene, OR: Cascade, 2015), 1–3.

Promoting Heart Transformation

Once youths decide to follow wisdom, the sages urge them to listen intently with their heart (2:2; 22:17–18; 23:12) and retain instruction in their heart (3:1; 6:21). In time, this continual process will transform their character and cause them to no longer trust in themselves but to trust in the Lord. The sages give this advice to develop this trust:

> *Trust in the* LORD *with all your heart,*
> *and do not rely on your own insight.* (3:5)

> *Do not let your heart envy sinners,*
> *but always continue in the fear of the* LORD. (23:17)

Sages also encourage youths to remember:

> *Those who trust in their own wits are fools;*
> *but those who walk in wisdom come through safely.* (28:26)

Walking on this path day after day, listening, learning, and applying wisdom will instill attitudes and habits of the heart that will develop the good character of wisdom: doing what is right, just, and equitable (1:2–3).

Showing Good Character in Speech

Our character, the truth of our heart or our truest self, is revealed by our speech. As Roland Murphy points out, "Speech is perhaps the truest indication whether one is wise or foolish. It betrays who one is."[8] Here, we expand on the three characteristics of positive speech introduced above, especially as these speech patterns show the quality of our heart or character.

Honesty

A person who speaks honestly does so as a result of a heart devoted to truth, a character trait highly prized in Proverbs: "one who gives an honest answer gives a

8. Murphy, *Proverbs*, 259.

kiss on the lips" (24:26) and "truthful lips endure forever" (12:19a). For example, a trustworthy messenger refreshes the spirit of his master like a snow during harvest (25:13), and "a truthful witness saves lives" (14:25; cf. 25:18; 21:28; see above).

Gentleness

A gentle or kind heart is evident in the gracious words that a person speaks (15:26b). These texts illustrate the ways in which a kind heart will speak: softly, gently, and pleasantly.

> *Pleasant words are a honeycomb,*
> *sweetness to the soul and health to the body.* (16:24)

> *Anxiety weighs down the human heart,*
> *but a good word cheers it up.* (12:25)

Patience or Restrained Speech

The wicked and fools blurt out folly without restraint (10:8; 12:23; 15:28). However, the wise show a patient heart or attitude by not rushing to speak. They are "cool in spirit" (17:27) and exercise patience and self-control by sometimes holding back their thoughts instead of speaking (10:14; 13:3a; 20:3). When they do speak, it is after carefully considering their words (15:28a) so that they are judicious and persuasive (16:23). The connection between patience or self-control and speech is so strong that even fools would be considered wise if they held their tongue (17:28). The problem, of course, is that a fool can no more control their tongue than we can control an avalanche once it has begun (12:23b, 15:28b).

Conclusion

Because of the close connection between our hearts, character, and speech, it comes as no surprise that Proverbs includes sweeping claims about speech and the heart.

> *The tongue of the righteous is choice silver;*
> *the mind of the wicked is of little worth.* (10:20)

> *There is gold, and abundance of costly stones;*
> *but the lips informed by knowledge are a precious jewel.* (20:15; see also 25:11)

The Lord sees our heart (15:11), weighs our heart (21:2; 24:12), and tests the quality of our heart (17:3). Consequently, we must do all we can to—

> *Keep your heart with all vigilance,*
> *for from it flow the springs of life.* (4:23)

For the sages, speech functions as both a thermometer and a thermostat. As a thermometer, speech detects the wellness of a person's heart: truthful, kind, and gentle words denote a wise heart becoming like God. But lies, gossip, flattery, and slander are symptomatic of a confused, if not self-centered heart. As a thermostat, our heart determines how we will live and is ultimately responsible for our speech that affects our communities, our families, and our own character development.

There is a unique and ironic danger that comes with writing a chapter about speech in Proverbs, or preaching or teaching about our words; namely, we must open our mouths or our pens and speak. And the sages make it clear that the more we open our mouths, the less likely it will be that we engage our minds and hearts at the same time. The wise person remembers to hold back, not say so much, and be restrained (12:23; 17:27) because those "who open wide their lips" come to ruin (13:3b). The book of James describes the same danger with a different set of images and warns us of the responsibility that comes with standing up to teach, or sitting down to write (Jas. 3:1–2). We might control a horse or a ship with small tools, and we might tame every species of animal. But no one can control or tame the tongue: it will burn us every time (Jas. 3:3–8).

The sages have this heart and mouth idea in mind throughout Proverbs, but Jesus sharpens the point: "The good person out of the good treasure of the heart produces good, and the evil person out of evil treasure produces evil; for it is out of the abundance of the heart that the mouth speaks" (Luke 6:45; see also Matt. 15:18–20). This is the challenge: until our hearts are pure, our language will be impure. Trying to control our speech without heart transformation is as useless as expecting gold to come out of a coal mine. Wisdom leads us to guard and protect our heart because our heart is the source of life and the source of speech (Prov. 4:23).

DISCUSSION QUESTIONS

1. Does the emphasis on speech in Proverbs surprise you? If so, what surprises you and why? If not, why does it not surprise you? How important would you say speech is to the sages? Why?
2. Once again because Proverbs addresses men, at several points it includes sayings about the speech of wives (Prov. 21:9, 19; 25:24; 27:15). Turn these proverbs around. In your wisdom, what features of a husband's speech or behavior will make a wife's life miserable? Compose new proverbs to express your observations.
3. We sometimes hear people speak or act as if words really don't matter. After all, "they are just words." How would the sages respond to this claim? According to the sages in Proverbs, why do words matter? What can you add to the sages' observations about why words matter?
4. Review the list of negative speech in this chapter. Which of these speech patterns is the greatest problem in your culture or community? Is another misuse of speech that is not listed more significant? Please explain. What is your greatest weakness in speech?
5. Ideally, a person's heart and speech should be united, as well as their heart and other actions. What images would you use to describe a person who is divided–their heart believes or thinks one thing, but they speak and act another way? What special danger, if any, does this person risk?
6. If the sages of Proverbs were relocated to our time and place, what else might they say about speech? What special concerns might they have today? What would they commend as a wise practice?

PROJECT CHALLENGE

I mention the shared language at the tower of Babel and its importance for that community. Reflect on the idea of a "common language" and respond to one or more of the following questions.

- Today much of the world shares a common language through computers. What prospects or positives does this hold? What dangers?
- In addition to speech, what qualifies as a shared or common "language"? How do these common languages unite communities?

- What unique phrases and words, or practices, unites your faith community? What "words" in your language might an outsider not understand? How frequent is "insider language" used in your assemblies? What are the positives and negatives in using this kind of language?

CHAPTER 8

If I Were a Poor Man: Wealth and Poverty

Sometimes, I want to ask God why He allows poverty, famine, and injustice in the world when he could be doing something about it, but I'm afraid he might ask me the same question.

—Abdul Baha

If you want to know what God thinks of money,
just look at the people he gave it to.

—Dorothy Parker

TO PREPARE FOR READING THIS CHAPTER

Read the proverbs in either #1 or #2:

1. Proverbs 1:13–14, 18–19; 3:1–2, 5–6, 9–10, 13–16, 27–28, 33, 35; 4:7–9; 6:6–8, 9–11; 8:10–11, 18–21; 10:2–4, 11, 16, 20–22; 11:1, 4, 17–18, 23–26, 28–29; 12: 9–12, 14, 24, 27; 13:2, 4, 7, 11, 18, 21, 23, 25; 14:4, 20–21, 23, 31; 15:15–16, 25, 27; 16:8–9, 11, 16, 19, 20, 26; 17:1, 8, 23; 18:9, 11–12, 16, 20, 23; 19:1, 4,6–7, 15, 17, 22–24; 20:4, 10, 13–15, 17, 21, 23; 21:5–7, 13–14, 17, 20–21, 25–26; 22:1–2, 7–9, 13, 16, 22–23, 28; 23:4–5, 10–11, 20–21; 24:3–4, 30–34; 25:16, 27; 26:13–16; 27:7, 20, 23–27; 28:3, 6–8, 11, 15–16, 19–20, 22, 25–27; 29:3, 4, 7, 13–14; 30:7–9, 14–15; 31:4–9, 13–16, 18–20
2. Proverbs 1:18–19; 3:1–2, 9–10, 13–16, 27–28; 4:7–9; 6:6–11; 8:10–11, 18–21; 10:2–4, 20–22; 11:17–18, 23–29; 12:9–12; 13:2–4, 7, 11, 21–23; 14:20–21; 15:15–16; 16:8–9; 18:11–12, 20; 19:6–7, 22–24; 20:13–15; 21:5–7, 13–14, 20–21, 25–26; 22:1–2, 7–9, 22–23; 23:4–5, 10–11, 20–21; 24:3–4, 30–34; 26:13–16; 27:23–27; 28:3, 6–8, 15–16, 19–27; 29:13–14; 30:7–9, 14–15; 31:4–9

A favorite, low-energy, irrational, cheap, and delusional way that my wife, Dana, and I have found to pass the time on long trips is to play "the Lotto fantasy game." If the jackpot is above fifty or sixty million dollars, we buy a single ticket, confident that we will not match a single winning number (guaranteed if I buy the ticket). But since the promotional signs tell us the money goes to fund education, why not help? To play the game, we take the advertised payoff, deduct fifty percent for taxes, and begin to decide what charitable efforts or organizations will be the beneficiaries of our skilled choice of numbers. Standard options include student scholarships and endowed faculty positions at the university and an expansion of the education building, the Housing First initiative in Abilene, and an assortment of relatives and friends (let the competition begin!). We would only keep money for retirement and a smallish cabin in Colorado to escape summer heat in Texas and write in the cool mountain breeze. Of course we would let family and friends enjoy the space and allow other professors to use the cabin for a writing retreat. Frankly, our plan is so good, I don't understand why God who controls "the lots" (16:33) hasn't already given us the money. All I can reckon is that God still loves us too much to ruin our lives with so much money at once (see 13:11).

We appear to share the Lotto fantasy game with a few million friends who also purchase their tickets, driving up the jackpot, and who share a common outlook on life. In fact, we appear to share the same "cultural bubble" that existed in ancient Israel prior to and after the Babylonian conquest of 587 BCE. During the era of Israel's decline prior to exile and in the era of rebuilding after the exile, the people just wanted to return to the good ole days of their ancestors when they could live the good life of affluence and privilege in a socio-economic state fueled by the inflow of money and inexpensive goods produced with cheap labor. Transposed onto our culture, they wanted more small pieces of paper printed with one dollar, five dollars, ten dollars, and twenty dollars that would bring them happiness and enable them to buy a brand new chariot. However as in ancient Israel, in our society today the divide between the few at the top and the majority at the bottom is growing larger by the day, an alarming and dangerous trend for our future.[1]

It should come as no surprise that the mirror topics of wealth and poverty receive extensive attention in the book of Proverbs. In their own way, the sages recognized the gravitational pull of wealth and fought against the delusion

1. See the critical analysis and prophetic summons by Walter Brueggemann, *Reality, Grief, Hope: Three Urgent Prophetic Tasks* (Grand Rapids: Eerdmans, 2014).

that wealth is capable of providing a life that is good. Some examples of their proverbs on the delusions of wealth include the following:

- The wealthy may have many friends (14:20), but when their wealth disappears, so will their friends (19:4, 6–7).
- The wealthy have the power of affluence and connections to get them what they want when they want it. Sometimes, however, their method is nothing less than bribery (15:27; 17:8, 23; 18:16; 21:14).
- The wealthy tend to believe their prosperity creates protection, but in truth, their bank statement gives a false sense of security (10:15a; 18:11–12).

Despite having the sages, priests, and prophets, the Israelites still bought into the lies of "the good life." And tragically, doing so cost them their lives. Yet three millennia later, not only have we not learned from their mistakes, we seem hell bent on imitating them. We chase wealth at all costs and have such high esteem for wealth that we even pretend to be wealthy when we have nothing (see 13:7). Even more, because the art of deal making is such a crucial mark of "the good life," we love to brag about our ability to negotiate for bargains, despite the loss for others (see 20:14).

Don't misunderstand; the sages do not deny the benefits of wealth or the hardships caused by poverty. They know that in contrast to the wealthy, the poor have fewer friends (14:20; 19:7). Because they lack power or influence, they must ask, even beg, for help (18:23), and they live without the guardrails and safety nets the rich take for granted. Without wealth, the poor are vulnerable to oppression. For instance, those with wealth and power may decide to

- Withhold payment for work completed (Prov. 3:27–28)
- Use false weights and measures to cheat buyers (11:1; 20:10, 23)
- Move boundary markers on property to steal land (22:28; 23:10–11)
- Scheme to rob the poor, specifically taking advantage of their poverty (22:22)
- "Crush the afflicted at the gate" where the courts were often held (22:22b), or in our culture, "lawyer up" to complicate and extend a legal case so that the poor never stand a chance of a just settlement
- Refuse to sell their excess food when others are in need (11:26a), so the poor go hungry
- Rule over the poor as lenders rule over borrowers (22:7)
- Unjustly take away a poor person's crops or means of income (13:23; 28:3, 15)

Lacking power, the poor can do nothing to defend themselves from these practices—nothing but look as if they are lazy or trying to live off society. However, the sages in Proverbs tell the truth about the poor without watering down their words.

> *All the days of the poor are hard* (15:15a)

> *The wealth of the rich is their fortress;*
> *the poverty of the poor is their ruin.* (10:15)

Or as you may have heard,

> *Life is but a game for the rich*
> *and a battle for the poor.* (Jeremy Limn)

In response to the inequities and harsh realities of life for those on the margins of society, the sages bypass temporary fixes and get at the heart of the issues related to wealth and poverty—the human heart. In other words, the book of Proverbs paints a vision for life like a master artist using six brush strokes. Some strokes paint over the existing image by identifying the fatal flaws within any life, personal or corporate, that regards money as the most important objective in life. Other strokes reimagine a view of wealth and poverty rooted in wisdom and the fear of the Lord.

Stroke #1: We Never Have Enough

The first flaw in attempting to build a life that is good on a foundation of wealth is simple: we never have enough money. The only way to maintain a lifestyle built on wealth is to acquire more and more money, because what provides the good life today will not satisfy us or be enough next year. The sages describe this "never enough" syndrome using the following images:

- Death, the grave, and human eyes (27:20)
- A leech and her two daughters who constantly cry for more (30:15a–b)
- The grave, a barren womb, a land without water, and fire (30:15c–16)

This brush stroke also reveals the tendency to glut ourselves with the goods bought by our wealth to the point that we no longer enjoy them (25:16,

27; 27:7a). Much like an addict, "the good life" requires us to find stronger and greater pleasures that demand more and more money. Also like an addict, we may be unaware that our life is growing out of control when we depend on wealth more and more to give us one more "trip" or "high."

Stroke #2: More Valuable Than Money

The second brush stroke reveals a flaw that grows like an insidious cancer the moment we begin to regard money as the most important tool for acquiring the good life. In response, the sages turn the equation around to identify what is more important than money: wisdom, righteousness, family, humility, and integrity.

Wisdom

Wisdom, coupled with "the fear of the LORD," is a rather obvious first choice for what the sages consider to be more important than money. The "fear of the LORD," or an appropriate relationship with the Lord, is more important than riches and all the trouble that comes with immense wealth (15:16). Wisdom brings prosperity and material wealth through the diligent work of the wise (8:18; 10:14b; 12:27b). But wisdom also provides an income better than wealth and more precious than jewels (3:13–16; 8:10–11; 8:19). For example, wisdom and understanding are better than gold or silver (16:16), and "lips informed by knowledge" are more valuable than precious stones (20:15). Wisdom provides what money cannot buy: long life and honor (3:16) or, in other words, genuine life that is good.

Righteousness

The Lord's blessing is on the house of the righteous (3:33) and children who are righteous make their parents happy (23:24). More specifically, righteousness, doing right, is more valuable than wealth. The sages stress this comparison in two different ways. First, they assert righteousness to be more valuable than any amount of wealth generated by wicked means.

> *Treasure gained by wickedness does not profit,*
> *but righteousness delivers from death.* (10:2)

Better is little with righteousness
than a large income with injustice. (16:8)

This theme is consistently reiterated in Proverbs: no matter how wealthy or happy the wicked may appear to be, it is better to be righteous than wicked (10:30; 11:19, 21, 28; 12:3, 7, 13, 21; 21:21).

Second, the sages claim that righteousness produces a profit more valuable than whatever the wicked may gain.

The hope of the righteous ends in gladness,
but the expectation of the wicked comes to nothing. (10:28)

The wicked earn no real gain,
but those who sow righteousness get a true reward. (11:18)

What the righteous hope for will end in good or happiness, but not so for the wicked (10:24; 11:23a). The wicked want to grow wealthy, but only the righteous grow fruit (11:23b; 12:12; 13:25). In fact, while prosperity rewards those who are righteous, misfortune and trouble follow whatever the wicked may gain (13:21; 15:6; see also 10:16, 11:4).

Family

A simple meal shared with a loving family who care for each other is much better than a feast every day with constant bickering and hatred (15:17; 17:1). The food may be great, but the cost of admission paid by their families is too high. In comparison to wealth, the sages also point out the greater value of a good wife or spouse. Wealth and houses may be inherited from parents, but "a prudent wife is from the LORD" (19:14) and a "capable wife" is "far more precious than jewels" (31:10, cf. ch. 2). And though children are not compared to wealth in Proverbs, the sages consistently identify wise children as a source of joy to their parents (10:1; 15:20; 23:15; 27:11; 29:3), as opposed to foolish children who cause grief (10:1b; 17:25) or stupid children who bring ruin to the family (19:13).

Humility

"It is better to be of lowly spirit [humble] among the poor than to divide the spoil with the proud" (16:19). Why? Because "Pride goes before destruction, and a haughty spirit before a fall" (16:18). The sages also write,

> *Better to be despised and have a servant,*
> *than to be self-important and lack food.* (12:9)

The proud or "self-important" people are determined to look wealthy no matter the cost—which could lead to a lack of food. In contrast, it's better to be "despised" or humble, without concern for what others think, and have a servant. The irony is thick: a conceited person might spend everything to look wealthy and as a result have nothing, while a humble person is not caught up in a race to the top and as a result has more to spend.

Growing out of humility is the willingness to listen and learn from others as opposed to self-reliant pride that disregards wisdom. Two proverbs warn of "poverty and disgrace" for the person who ignores instruction (13:18), and the news is even worse for those who despise instruction. They bring "destruction on themselves" (13:13).

Integrity

Integrity is also far more important than wealth. People of integrity have determined principles to guide their lives, and they live by their principles. They are not perfect, but it's better to be poor with integrity than "crooked" and rich (28:6) or to be a fool with dishonest speech (19:1). A person's reputation is inseparable from their integrity; a good reputation is built on the foundation of integrity. So it comes as no surprise that the sages claim our reputation is more important than our bank statement. A "good name" should be chosen over riches because the "favor" or esteem that comes from a good reputation has more value on the street and in life than money (22:1).

Integrity leads us to be loyal to friends. And according to the sages, having loyal friends is better than wealth (19:22a). People value loyal friends more highly than wealthy friends, as well as friends who do not take advantage of us just because we have money (see ch. 10).

Together, these five elements of life that are better than wealth are the sages' second brush stroke in their effort to paint a composition that exposes "the good life" built on wealth. Wealth is not better or more important than wisdom, righteousness, love and peace, humility, listening and learning, integrity, loyalty, or our reputation, and certainly not more important than our relationship to God. Perhaps it's just my curiosity, but this list raises two "wonder questions." First, I wonder why the sages identify these particular things as more important than wealth as opposed to other items? They could have named other things as more important than wealth, but they don't. So, why these eight? Second, I wonder what the sages would identify as less important than wealth? Is anything less important than wealth?

Stroke #3: Getting Wealth by the Wrong Means

The third brush stroke identifies what might work to acquire money, but is unethical and will ultimately backfire. Gaining wealth through these tactics is somewhat like wearing a suicide vest—it may work, but it will kill us in the process and hurt others.

Cutting Corners

Those in a hurry to get rich are apt to cut a few corners and put at least a toe or two over the line of the law. As a result they "will not go unpunished" (28:20b). These people are motivated by greed and will not only hurt others in their mad pursuit of wealth (28:25a), they will also harm their own families (15:27a), and kill themselves (1:17–19). In the end, they will be left with nothing (21:5b; 28:22).

Robbery

One of the quickest ways to get rich is robbery: taking what we did not work for at the expense of those who did (10:2). It's easy to give an example of what we would never do: I'd never rob a library of all its books on the Old Testament. Better examples challenge our wisdom and our practices: illegally copying a CD or DVD, downloading free music (is this theft?), being slack at work (see 18:9), or overpricing goods and services (by inaccurate weights or scales in Israel, see 20:10, 23). The major issue here is whether we live in such a way that we must constantly watch for lines we should not cross or we might get caught, or if we live in pursuit of wisdom and a life that is good so that our effort leans toward the heart of God and far away from the clear or faded lines we shouldn't cross.

Aggressive Oppression

Aggressive tactics that oppress the poor may be effective to "gain riches" (11:16b), but the money will not last (11:18a), and worse, the harsh tactics will ultimately "lead to loss" (22:16, see also 11:17b). Perhaps the clearest example of aggressive tactics that take advantage of the poor in our culture is the personal loan industry. Companies charge exorbitant interest on loans to those desperate to get by until payday so they can get a car repaired, purchase required work tools, or buy food. According to the sages, such aggressive business plans will amass wealth, but it will be given to those who are kind to the poor (28:8).

Deceit

Deceit is a broad term for multiple forms of dishonesty, such as lying, false advertising, trickery, and cheating. But acquiring wealth by deception is a "fleeting vapor" and "a snare of death" (21:6) and will even turn into gravel as we eat (20:17). Examples of deceit today include a con artist, a roofing company that takes money up front and skips out of town, or the person who plays loosely with the truth on their tax forms.

Getting Rich Quickly

Finally, the sages warn that getting rich quickly, by legal or illegal means, is not necessarily a good thing. Often, such wealth goes as quickly as it came (13:11a). Or as we have seen from follow-up reports about lottery winners, all that money ends up ruining the lives of those who win it (20:21).

The first three brush strokes by people who spent their lives observing the world and how life works are negative and suggest just how strongly their culture defined "the good life" in terms of wealth. Then as now, to gain this good life people will do everything from the blatantly immoral to the secretive and shady. But greed for wealth is a tumor growing within that will eventually kill the individual and the society. So with each brush stroke, the sages unleash a barrage of truth and reality to kill this tumor. In other words, the sages have a lot to undo and deconstruct before they can begin to build a sustainable model of *a life that is good* in relationship to wealth.

Stroke #4: Acquiring Wealth by the Right Means

The fourth stroke and first constructive movement of the brush describes ways in which wealth may be acquired in harmony with a life that is good.

By Wisdom

Those who walk in the way of wisdom acquire riches, including "enduring wealth" (8:18–21). They gain wealth because they are diligent and gather it "little by little" (12:27a; 13:11b, see below). Also, wise people do not devour or spend everything they earn, like fools do (21:20). Wisdom is the cornerstone in building an enduring family, wisdom that fills every room with "precious and pleasant riches" (24:3–4). Wisdom will keep a person from losing wealth through disaster (19:23) or through pursuing wealth by the ways described above. As we have seen, to walk with wisdom requires fearing the Lord, which includes trusting the Lord, through which a person will "be enriched" (28:25b). Proverbs 22:4 sums up the results of fearing the Lord:

> *The reward for humility and fear of the* Lord
> *is riches and honor and life.* (22:4)

Beneficial wealth in a life that is good only comes by wisdom.

By Righteousness

Righteousness is another requirement for acquiring true riches and flourishing "like green leaves" (11:28; see also 14:11). The Lord's blessing is on the home of the righteous (3:33b), filling it with treasure (15:6), and making them rich without the sorrows wealth sometimes brings (10:22). Whatever the righteous person pursues ends in good (11:23a), and "The Lord does not let the righteous go hungry" (10:3; 13:25a). It's as if the righteous are trees that produce good things, bearing fruit (12:12b) and a "true reward" (11:17–18) and prosperity

(13:21b; see Ps. 1:1–3). The righteous also bless others with their words (Prov. 10:20–21), words that give life like a fountain (10:11). One proverb states the issue with precision:

> *Whoever pursues righteousness and kindness*
> *will find life and honor.* (21:21)

The true riches of a life that is good come only to those who pursue righteousness.

By Diligence

The sages also stress disciplined, diligent work for gaining wealth (12:14b; 12:27; 14:23). Those who work their land (12:11; 20:13; 24:27), tend their plants or trees (27:18a), and carefully watch their flocks and herds (27:23–24) will have a harvest to sustain their family (13:4b; 28:19a) along with milk and clothing (27:25–27). Twice the sages present an ant colony as a model of diligence and wisdom, for they work all summer for harvest in the fall (6:6–8; 30:24–25). These and other proverbs suggest the context on the family farm (also 31:13, 19, 22).

Another set of "diligence" sayings appears to originate in urban settings where work differs from typical rural tasks. In these texts, the "plans of the diligent will surely lead to abundance" (Prov. 21:5), and "those who are attentive to a matter will prosper" (16:20). And the "fruit of the mouth," or spoken word, brings a satisfying return (12:14b, 13:2, 18:20–21). The "hands of the diligent" also rule, in contrast to being put into "forced labor" (12:24, also consider 27:23–24).

By Giving

Counterintuitive to most financial plans, the sages state that giving charitable donations—giving to those other than family or even friends—is an act the Lord not only repays but also causes to enrich (11:24–25). Such generosity may be directed in three directions: 1) giving to the poor and needy (22:9; 28:27a; 31:20; cf. 3:28; 25:14); 2) giving in helpful ways to one's enemies (25:21–22; see ch. 6); and 3) giving the Lord a gift of our firstfruits (which also results in rich rewards, with a rare reference to the teachings of the priests [3:9–10; Lev. 23:9–14]).

The sages acknowledge the presence of one other type of gift: a bribe. They also admit (with descriptive proverbs) that bribes may be effective. A bribe is like a "magic stone" to the person giving the bribe—"wherever they turn they prosper" (17:8). A bribe or "paying someone off" may enable a person to escape trouble or the anger caused by prior actions (21:14; see also 18:16). And yet, while bribes may work, it is the wicked who accept bribes "to pervert the ways of justice" (17:23). Proverbs 15:27 connects bribes to those who are greedy and concludes that it is only "those who hate bribes" who will live. Ultimately, this type of gift belongs with the ways to obtain wealth in the wrong way—and in the process, destroy ourselves.

All of these good means of acquiring wealth, obvious and not so obvious, contribute to communal welfare, as well as the health of the family and individual worker.

Stroke #5: Best Use for Wealth Is to Help the Poor

The fifth brush stroke dares to paint across the grain to depict how those in positions of wealth and power can best help those who are poor. As already stated, Proverbs encourages kindness and charitable giving (11:24–25; 14:21b; 21:26b; 22:9; 31:20), a reflection of the God we serve. But the sages suggest that even the best short-term answers to poverty do not offer long-term solutions, for the problem has roots that are deeply interwoven with cultural values. In fact, they look to more viable long-term plans to bring about true change.

Recognize Equality

The sages appeal to those with resources and power to recognize their common origin and shared humanity with the poor (22:2; 29:13). The sages recognize that separation and distinction between me and my group and others (them) is the first step toward exercising brutality or justifying the inhumane treatment of others. Once we have this attitude, it is easier to label the "others" as less intelligent, less hard working, and ultimately less human. Then it is much easier to send *them* to different schools, force *them* to use different bathrooms, or ban *them* from entering *our* country. So long as we speak about *them*, the other group exists without a human face.

Use Honest Business Practices

The Lord requires fair business practices such as honest "balances and scales" (16:11; 11:1; 20:10) and hates those who use power and status to pay some less than others for their work and overcharging those in need for goods and services. Examples include the company store that charged high prices and kept miners in constant debt, forcing them to continue dangerous work at an unfair wage. Similar today are "food deserts," the absence of grocery stores in poorer neighborhoods where residents cannot afford personal transportation, forcing them to buy their food at much more expensive convenience stores.

Protect the Vulnerable

The sages urge those who fear the Lord to act like the Lord, who protects the widow's property from being taken over by those who are more powerful (15:25). In ancient Israel, land was "leased" to families in perpetuity by the Lord, who owned the land (Lev. 25:23). Nonetheless, widows were vulnerable throughout ancient Near Eastern cultures because they did not have husbands to argue their case or sons to defend them from those eager to take advantage of them.

Defend Human Rights

"The righteous know the rights of the poor" (Prov. 29:7a) and understand these rights in the context of social practices, in contrast to those who lack this understanding (29:7b) and are "cruel" oppressors who use their power like roaring lions or charging bears to oppress the poor (28:15–16). Here knowing or understanding denotes more than just knowing information about the poor. True understanding of their situation should lead to defending the poor against oppression. For example today, going beyond prayer to stand up against unjust city ordinances that evict the poor from their homes, or confronting those who manipulate the law to take advantage of the poor. Just as "the LORD pleads their cause" (22:23), we too should use our wealth and influence to stop those who otherwise "crush the afflicted" (22:22).

Listen

The wealthy and powerful often refuse to listen to the poor. But those who fear the Lord and are wise should not close our ears to the cries of the poor—or we will risk one day crying out ourselves and having no one hear (21:13). To open one's ear to the poor means more than hearing a sound. It means acting on what we hear: genuinely listening to the poor so that we help provide what they really need.

Act

The wealthy and powerful often act against the poor. But the sages in Proverbs encourage us to use wealth and power to become activists:

> *Speak out for those who cannot speak,*
> *for the rights of all the destitute.*
> *Speak out, judge righteously,*
> *defend the rights of the poor and needy.* (Prov. 31:8–9)

My treatment of this topic here is brief in anticipation of fuller discussion in chapter 9. Former professor and minister James Forbes summarizes the matter in his adage, "Nobody gets into heaven without a letter of reference from the poor." Those with money and influence must learn to see the daily struggles of the poor and understand how societal systems make it enormously difficult for those without wealth and power to pull their way up. Yes, exceptions exist, but only a few. It is time for the wise to take up their cause persistently until the status quo can no longer stand.

Stroke #6: The Problem of Self-Inflicted Poverty

The sages' final brush stroke on the topic of wealth brings us to difficult images and words that describe how poverty can be self-inflicted. In other words, sometimes personal poverty is a direct result of a person's foolish actions. I have deliberately left these descriptions until the end so that we have a better context in which to place them, after we have recognized how social systems and the greed of many not only cause poverty but keep those who are poor in a state of perpetual poverty. Only with this recognition is it fair to identify the ways in which some who are poor have brought poverty on themselves.

Laziness

The most frequent self-induced cause of poverty in Proverbs is laziness. Some translations describe a lazy person as a "sluggard"—like a snail without a shell. The sages' depiction of the lazy is a caricature that uses the most common and extreme forms of laziness. Obviously, a lazy person doesn't like to work—they would rather sleep in late (6:9; 10:5; 19:15; 20:13). Yet they don't seem to understand that their laziness is the root cause of their hunger (10:4; 13:4; 21:25; see also 20:4) or the reason their farm is falling apart (24:30–31). To their surprise, poverty comes on them like a thief or armed warrior while they are sleeping (24:32–34). Nor can they comprehend that their laziness is what keeps them in trouble with their employer (10:26; 18:9) and keeps them stuck in positions of "forced labor" (12:24). And if a friend tries to point out the link between cause and effect, a full-blown sluggard will blow them off, believing they are far smarter than seven sages (26:16).

I am old enough to remember watching *The Tonight Show* before Jimmy Fallon or even Jay Leno. Back in the good ole days, Johnny Carson would engage the audience in his monologue by stating some terrible condition, "The traffic on I-405 was so bad today." And Johnny's sidekick, Ed McMahon, would lead the audience in asking, "How bad was it?" Johnny then hit the punch line: "It was so bad a man on a Vespa walking his Chihuahua passed me in traffic." So in the spirit of this tradition, I now say with the sages: "A sluggard is so lazy!" And you ask: "How lazy is he?"

- *A sluggard is so lazy* that as he lies in bed, he turns from side to side like a door on its hinges (26:14).
- *A sluggard is so lazy* he makes ridiculous excuses for not going to work: "There is a lion outside!" If I try to come to work "I shall be killed in the streets!" (22:13).
- *A sluggard is so lazy* he puts his hand in a dish to pick up his food, but is too lazy and "tired" to lift his hand to his mouth to eat (19:24; 26:15).

Wickedness

A second self-induced cause of personal poverty is wickedness. Those who are wicked often find it difficult to make financial ends meet, and they seem to always be hungry (13:25b). While they may not have the moral sense to grasp why this is so (10:20b–21), the sages understand: the Lord's curse is on their house (3:33a). Because of their disobedience and rebellion, the Lord thwarts their craving or desire (10:3b) and misfortune pursues them (13:21a). Ultimately "the house of the wicked is destroyed" (14:11), and they are "cut off from the land" (2:22; 10:29–30). Even if they should earn some money, their effort is futile because trouble will take it away (15:6b), so that they never really get ahead (11:18; see also 10:2). Because of their wickedness, their hopes and expectations will only end in disappointment and anger (11:23).

Greed

A third self-inflicted cause of poverty is greed and being in a hurry to get rich. The parents warn their son that those who are greedy to get rich only trap and destroy themselves (1:17–19). The greedy stir up trouble for themselves and others (28:25), but they seem unaware that "loss is sure to come" (28:22). Like the wicked, the one chasing fast money "will not go unpunished" (28:20b).

The irony for those who are in a hurry to get rich is that their rush will not only cause them to fail, but it will put them into an even worse situation (13:11a; 21:5b). This could be because people often use illicit means for gaining wealth quickly (see above), or maybe because they are thrown into the foreign situation of inheriting a large sum of money or winning the lottery, and do not have the sense to manage it wisely. Either way, "An estate quickly acquired in the beginning will not be blessed in the end" (20:21).

Love of Pleasure

The sages provide several distinct examples of a fourth cause of poverty, the love of pleasure. A person who "loves wine and oil will not be rich" (21:17). A glutton or drunkard will land in poverty (23:20–21). And love of sexual pleasure will likely lead to squandering money on prostitutes (29:3). The problem may be described in different ways and affect people differently. But fundamentally, a love of pleasure leads people to overindulge—in wine, in food, in sex, or today in drugs, alcohol, or other practices (see below). And the result is personal poverty.

Pursuit of Fantasies

I suppose every society has ways for people to chase fantasies of fame and wealth or other worthless pursuits (12:11b; 28:19b). I don't know what these might have been in ancient Israel: perhaps daydreaming of a way to sell food from a chariot or starting a business of converting used chariots into a tiny houses. However, I do know a few fantasies and worthless pursuits today. My first image, from my days of teaching, is the young person who does not know how to play a musical instrument (not even the triangle) and can't carry a tune in a bucket, but their dream is to be in a rock band. A second image is the dream of becoming a wealthy and famous player in the NFL—when we are slow, small, and without skill. This is not to say that all dreams are worthless pursuits. What makes the difference, at least in part, is whether or not people have talent for the dream and are doing all they can to achieve their goal, or if they are simply dreaming about the day they will be famous and not working at worthwhile pursuits.

Beyond these self-destructive behaviors that lead to personal poverty we may also add spending everything and not saving (21:20b), a failure to listen to others and respond appropriately (13:18a), trusting in our wealth, not God (11:28a), or pride that leads to our downfall (15:25a). All of these practices may cause financial failure.

Life Then and Now

The spirit of wisdom, continually learning from our world and experience, demands that we pause here to raise questions and even objections based on how we view the world today compared with Israel's sages three millennia ago. For example, the sages viewed loving pleasure too much as a road to poverty. However if we watched the same people, we might conclude that they have an addiction. It is also true that some people are lazy and love to sleep too much. But we have learned that some struggle to stay awake or may appear lazy because of narcolepsy, clinical depression, bipolar disorders, or other physical conditions. We treat these conditions through medications and programs such as Alcoholics Anonymous—not words that describe these people as fools.

Neither Proverbs nor wisdom will let us sneak past before we grapple with how to deal with new human insights, at least not if we live with wisdom. The epistemology of wisdom or how the wise know what they know is thoroughly based on human experience and learning how life works, not special revelation (see ch. 1). This pillar of wisdom stands with a second: careful observation and study continues to reveal new insights into human behavior. So the question we must answer is what to do with these insights? Do we reject them because all wisdom is limited to what the sages knew and recorded in the book of Proverbs? Or do we receive these new insights with open arms, even if it means rethinking, emending, or rejecting what we previously thought and what the sages of Israel recorded in the book of Proverbs? These questions are easy to express, but certainly not easy to answer. Make no mistake; our answer has the potential to change how we think about such contemporary subjects as same-sex attraction, addictive behaviors, and family structures and roles. What role, if any, will we allow contemporary wisdom to play in these and other discussions?

Conclusion

Given the matter-of-fact way in which the sages acknowledge the benefits of wealth and the hardships that come with poverty, we might expect the sages to advocate for the acquisition of wealth as a primary goal of life. But they and we know better, in part because wealth often comes with a new set of problems: the temptation to trust our money (11:28), to become stingy (28:22, 27), to become proud (28:11), or to love money (see also Luke 12:15; 1 Tim. 6:9–10; cf. Prov. 21:17). So the sages include two texts in Proverbs that in many ways bring to a fine point all that they have to say about wealth and poverty. The first is on the ethereal quality of wealth and why we should not work too hard to get it:

> *Do not wear yourself out to get rich;*
> *be wise enough to desist.*
> *When your eyes light upon it, it is gone;*
> *for suddenly it takes wings to itself,*
> *flying like an eagle toward heaven.* (23:4–5)

With this counsel is a prayer of the wise:

> *Two things I ask of you [God];*
> *do not deny them to me before I die:*
> *Remove far from me falsehood and lying;*
> *give me neither poverty nor riches;*
> *feed me with the food that I need,*
> *or I shall be full, and deny you,*
> *and say, "Who is the Lord?"*
> *or I shall be poor, and steal,*
> *and profane the name of my God.* (30:7–9)

Sages pray for the middle path—a place lacking the pitfalls of wealth and the dangers associated with poverty. It's an easy prayer and at the same time incredibly difficult. In other words, it's easy to ask for just what we need, at least until we think about it. To be honest, I like the prayer, but I can't recall a time when I didn't prefer to be a little more comfortable and to have a little more than I really needed (or a lot more). In fact, it is difficult for many, perhaps most of us, to imagine what we really need versus what we really want. Our rampant consumer-driven economy infects us from birth, creating needs we don't have in order to sell us products we don't need. And this economy continues to drive a deep wedge between the wealthy and the poor. No wonder what Israel's sages have to say about riches and poverty rings so true in our ears.

Consequently, we need a sage's vision for a different path—a society built on the ideals of a life that is good.

- Stroke #1: We need to recognize the allure of wealth and its trap: requiring us to constantly stretch for more and more to just stay even.
- Stroke #2: We need to chop the appeal of wealth down to size by recognizing the things that are much more important than wealth.
- Stroke #3: We need to deconstruct unethical means of acquiring wealth that hurt others and destroy us.
- Stroke #4: We need to replace unethical ways of getting money with approaches that are in harmony with a life that is good.
- Stroke #5: We need to use our power and privilege to help the poor and vulnerable and break the insidious cycle of poverty.
- Stroke #6: We need to identify and avoid self-induced causes of poverty and help others to understand and avoid these pitfalls.

I find it far too easy to exercise "drive-by wisdom" as I travel through a neighborhood and think to myself, "If they would only . . ." or "If they weren't so lazy . . ." or to quote an anonymous awful proverb:

If you are born poor it's not your mistake,
but if you die poor it's your mistake.

The hubris in this saying fails to recognize that most Americans achieve status and wealth by being born into the middle or upper class, not by making their own wealth. It also fails to recognize the odds against those born into poverty, odds maintained by those who live at their expense and who are often unaware of what they are doing. I am not suggesting that the problem and its solution are simple. Quite the opposite; the problem of poverty and its solutions are complicated. But rather than throwing up our hands in resignation to the status quo, we can and we must begin a conversation that employs the best of our tools: economics, business management, psychology, and theology—in other words, *all of our wisdom*. And as our wisdom reveals the direction, we desperately need to follow step by step on its path.

DISCUSSION QUESTIONS

1. The sages claim that wisdom is of greater value than gold, silver, and jewels and state that wisdom will give us wealth and enduring prosperity. How can they express both ideas at the same time? How can something that is more valuable than wealth bring or provide wealth? How do you resolve this paradox?
2. In the lists of ways by which the rich may oppress the poor or a person might unethically acquire wealth, I sometimes give examples and sometimes do not. Review these lists and the examples. In your opinion, are my examples weak or questionable? Why? Provide contemporary examples for points in which they are lacking.
3. I identify eight things that the sages in Proverbs claim are better than wealth. Review this list and consider why the sages make these comparisons. Why do they point out these aspects of life as more important than wealth and not others? What might the sages have included, but didn't? Why?
4. The sages point out lazy people do not realize their laziness, cause trouble for their employer, and "will be put to forced labor" (Prov. 12:24). What types of trouble does laziness cause employers? What does "forced labor" denote in our culture? What types of jobs would be equivalent to "forced labor"? Do people realize their laziness? Why or why not?
5. If the ancient Israelite sages lived among us, what would they do with new insights into human life and the world? Would they reject them because all wisdom is limited to what they can read in the book of Proverbs? Or would they receive new insights with open arms, even if it means rethinking, emending, or rejecting what they previously thought? What will we do?
6. What is the difference between chasing a fantasy and pursuing your dreams? What makes one foolish and the other heroic?

PROJECT CHALLENGE

What unique challenges do the poor face in your community? What factors create a cycle of poverty? What intervention strategies are most effective to help the poor break out of this cycle? What do those who are poor most need to do? What do those with wealth or moderate wealth most need to do to help bring about change?

CHAPTER 9

Which Way Did They Go? The Wisdom to Lead

Power tends to corrupt, and absolute power corrupts absolutely.
Great men are almost always bad men.

—Lord Acton in a letter to
Bishop Creighton (1887)

If you want to make God laugh,
tell him about your plans.

—Woody Allen

TO PREPARE FOR READING THIS CHAPTER

Read the proverbs in either #1 or #2:

1. Proverbs 11:2, 11; 12:10, 15; 14:8; 15:22–23, 28; 16:1, 3, 9, 12–14, 32; 18:12; 19:21; 20:18, 28; 21:1, 22, 29–31; 22:8; 23:3–6; 25:4–7, 12, 27; 27:3–4, 21, 23–27; 28:2–3, 10, 12, 14–16, 23, 26, 28; 29:2, 4, 7, 11, 12, 14, 16, 23, 25; 31:1–9
2. Proverbs 15:22–23; 16:9–14; 21:29–31; 23:3–6; 25:4–7; 27:3–4,23–27; 28:2–3, 10–16, 26–28; 29:2–4, 11–16, 23–25; 31:1–9

Regardless of your political party—Republican, Democrat, Independent, or none of the above—I believe we can all agree on one thing: our country suffers from lack of effective, principled leadership. It seems that we elect fresh faces to Washington who promise to "change the system," but they step into their new offices and pivot 180 degrees. They begin to print their reelection fund-raising brochures, fill their calendar with special interest lunches, and make decisions based on what will keep them in office. Yes, there are remarkable exceptions. But truthfully, the only thing strange about any of this is that we are still so surprised when it happens, again.

Another sage from the Bible, masked behind the title "Qoheleth," the preacher (NIV) or teacher (NRSV) of Ecclesiastes, told those willing to listen that this cycle of corruption occurs over and over. A popular, wise youth rises up to the throne, replacing the failed leadership of an old, foolish king who no longer listens to advice, only to become foolish himself (Eccl. 4:13–16). Only a few verses later, Qoheleth also warns us not to be so surprised when we find government corruption that oppresses the poor and violates justice. Political systems seem built to break good leaders as one official watches over another, who watches another, who watches someone else (Eccl. 5:8). Mix a little greed and self-promotion into the equation, and Lord Acton is once again proven correct: power corrupts. Power is an intoxicating narcotic and highly addictive. Without strong resolve, the character to resist, and God's help, the drug will lead us to seek more and more power, fame, and control until we push too high, grab too much, and die from an overdose, killing ourselves spiritually, relationally, and legally—if not actually losing our lives.

Proverbs as Preparation for Leadership

We have already discovered in the introduction to Proverbs that the book primarily addresses young men (1:4; see ch. 1). Here we push further toward the identity of these young men and the purpose of Proverbs. Some have suggested that these young men were in training for leadership positions in the royal court as counselors, scribes, or other roles and the book of Proverbs was part of their curriculum. However, most are suspicious of these claims due to the lack of strong, consistent evidence. It does appear that these young men were on the verge of taking on more responsibility for life decisions. They were becoming or were already young adults in their culture. They were old enough to become involved with gang-like activities (1:11–14), to be sexually active (see 2:16–19; 5:3–20; 6:24–35; 7:6–23), or in some cases were already married (5:15–19).[1]

The book of Proverbs attempts to help these young men by teaching them: 1) the content of wisdom and how to understand these words, and 2) what it means to live wisely by doing what is right, just, and fair (1:2–6). It is also safe to say that the sages understood the importance of wise leadership because they frequently speak about leaders or rulers from several different perspectives. In

1. Women in ancient Israel married in their early teens, men somewhat later. See Edwin Yamauchi, "Marriage," *Dictionary of Daily Life in Biblical and Post-Biblical Antiquity*, edited by Edwin Yamauchi and Marvin Wilson (Peabody, MA: Hendrickson, 2016), 3:221.

general terms, they recognize the value of wise leaders who do not bypass counsel because of pride but who listen to and accept sound advice (12:15; 15:22). That said, every year my students objected to the wisdom of Proverbs 21:22:

One wise person went up against a city of warriors
and brought down the stronghold in which they trusted.

My students challenged the idea of one wise person going up against a city of warriors: "This isn't wise," they said. "It's reckless." I see their point. Nonetheless, I think they miss the basic contrast and message of the proverb: when compared to the strength of warriors, wisdom comes out ahead. Wise warriors are stronger than those who only have brute force (24:5; see also 16:32). One young man with wisdom, such as David, can outsmart a giant in battle armor, such as Goliath, by reshaping the rules of single combat to a slingshot in the hands of an expert marksman (see 1 Sam. 17). In reality, the giant never stood a chance, which unfortunately wrecks all of our sermons and metaphors about David against Goliath.[2]

We can find further evidence to support the claim that the sages were concerned with developing wise leaders. The sages advise those who work in the royal court (16:13–14; 25:6–7). The king would also do well to listen to some of these proverbs (15:22; 21:30; 28:2, 12, 15). Sometimes the sages speak of the wise leadership of those who take responsibility for the lives of their animals and affirm those who look after their home (12:10a; 27:23–24). In all these proverbs, the sages address the subject of effective leadership. Our wisdom, however, should keep us from confusing a concern for wise leadership in Proverbs with the claim that Proverbs was designed to train future leaders—at least until we take a closer look at three subunits that especially speak of leadership.

Proverbs for Kings

The high volume of direct and indirect speech to kings leads Bruce Malchow to identify Proverbs 27:23–29:27 as a "manual for future monarchs."[3] Here we read, for example—

2. See Bruce Halpern, *David's Secret Demons: Messiah, Murderer, Traitor, King* (Grand Rapids: Eerdmans, 2001), 6–13.

3. Bruce Malchow, "A Manual for Future Monarchs," *Catholic Biblical Quarterly* 47 (1985): 238–45.

When a land rebels
it has many rulers;
but with an intelligent ruler
there is lasting order. (28:2)

Like a roaring lion or a charging bear
is a wicked ruler over a poor people. (28:15)

When the righteous are in authority, the people rejoice;
but when the wicked rule, the people groan. (29:2)

I encourage you to read and identify other proverbs to or about a ruler in these chapters.[4] Assuming for the moment that we accept Malchow's argument enables us to imagine a context of leadership behind these chapters and consequently read and interpret almost every verse in chapters 28–29 with some idea of leadership, though we might not initially make the connection (e.g., 28:14; 29:25).

Instruction of Amenemope *and Proverbs*

There is near universal agreement that Proverbs 22:17–24:22, "The Words of the Wise," relies to some extent on the *Instruction of Amenemope*, an Egyptian collection of wisdom. Of significance here is the beginning of the Egyptian text: "The beginning of the instruction about life, the guide for well-being, all *the principles of official procedure, the duties of the courtiers*" (emphasis mine).[5] In other words, the primary objective of the *Instruction of Amenemope* was to train young men who were preparing for leadership positions in the Egyptian royal court. It stands to reason then that to the extent Proverbs 22:17–24:22 relies on the *Instruction of Amenemope*, it too addresses young men training for leadership positions in Israel's royal court. However this issue is the sticking point for the claim: To what degree does "The Words of the Wise" reflect the

4. My results from the NRSV: First, thirteen verses clearly refer to leadership: 28:2, 3, 10, 12, 15, 16, 28; 29:2, 4, 12, 14, 16, 26. Second, if we assume that the text addresses leaders especially, nineteen additional verses may also be read as statements to or about leadership: 28:1, 5, 6, 8, 14, 21, 23, 26, 27; 29:7, 8, 9, 11, 18, 19, 20, 22, 23, 25. Thus, thirty-two of fifty-five verses may be about or apply to leadership.

5. William Kelly Simpson, trans., "The Instruction of Amenemope," *A Reader of Ancient Near Eastern Texts*, ed. Michael Coogan (New York: Oxford University Press, 2013), 191.

Instruction of Amenemope? And are the similarities close enough to support the claim that this text in Proverbs is also designed for leadership training?

The Words of King Lemuel's Mother

We find a short text explicitly addressed to monarchs in Proverbs 31:1–9, the teaching of a non-Israelite mother to her son, Lemuel, the king. One of the last units in Proverbs, the words of King Lemuel's mother present a fascinating case study in leadership, to which we return later in this chapter.

Training Young Men for the Royal Court

So we have three units, Proverbs 27:23–29:27, 22:17–24:22, and 31:1–9, that present at least some material for training young men for the royal court; a significant but not large amount of text (134 total verses), with similar material scattered throughout Proverbs 10–31. Does this evidence, however, convince us that Proverbs was tailor-made for leadership preparation? Michael Fox, a leading expert in Proverbs and ancient Egyptian wisdom, and most other scholars are unconvinced. Fox points out that the content of Proverbs,

> with the exception of a few passages treats everyday life, not the grand affairs of state, history, cult [temple/worship], or law. It gives guidance in challenges we all face: how to get along with people, how to be a good and devout person, how to make the best choices in personal and business affairs, how to win God's favor and avoid disaster.[6]

I believe Fox is correct in his assesssment. As a whole, most proverbs feature subjects other than the king or explicit royal concerns. For example, consider the chapters in this book about subject matter other than the royal court (e.g., becoming a fool, justice and mercy, friendship, and family values). Consequently, while Proverbs does have much to say about leadership, it is unlikely that the book as a whole was primarily compiled to prepare leaders for the royal court.

This conclusion leaves us with another good question: if the book of Proverbs was not primarily compiled for leadership development, why does

6. Michael Fox, *Proverbs 1–9*, Anchor Bible 18A (New York: Doubleday, 2000), 7.

it have so much to say about leaders and leadership? The answer is quite simple: those who most often rise to leadership positions of any type are those who are recognized for their wisdom. People develop into leaders because they have developed wisdom; others recognize those with wisdom and place them in positions of leadership. Wisdom has a natural relationship to leadership. So it is little wonder that the most important quality of highly effective leaders, according to Proverbs, is wisdom. To this end, three aspects of wisdom, each with multiple subcategories, stand out as primary for those who lead or will lead. These ideas are not organized like individual points in an outline, but build one upon the other like a pyramid.

Leadership and Character

Contemporary studies of leadership carry on the process of wisdom including close observation of life to formulate principles for effective leaders. Over the years, especially during my short time in academic leadership, I read my share of the most popular books in leadership and management. While I found overlap in the principles identified by Proverbs and contemporary books, I also discovered one glaring difference. Consider, for example, the four keys of leadership described by Markus Buckingham and Curt Coffman:[7]

1. Select for talent
2. Define the right outcomes
3. Focus on strengths
4. Find the right fit

Or consider the seven habits of effective leaders identified by Stephen Covey:[8]

1. Be proactive
2. Begin with the end in mind
3. Put first things first
4. Think win/win

7. Markus Buckingham and Curt Coffman, *First Break All the Rules: What the World's Greatest Managers Do Differently* (New York: Simon & Schuster, 1999).

8. Stephen Covey, *The Seven Habits of Highly Effective People: Powerful Lessons in Personal Change* (New York: Free Press, 1989).

5. Seek first to understand, then to be understood
6. Synergize
7. Sharpen the saw

I find Buckingham, Coffman, and Covey to be fair representatives of the field today. Books about leadership typically emphasize the wisdom of identifying goals, managing time, recruiting and supporting the right personnel, and taking time for personal renewal. The book of Proverbs, however, begins with the leader's *character* including disposition, temperament, and truest self. This idea has minimal presence in contemporary discussions of leadership. In fact after the 2016 presidential election, it was not unusual to hear someone on either side explain their vote by saying, "I set character issues to the side and voted only on the policy positions taken by the candidate." Not unusual perhaps for non-believers, but alarming for those of faith who want their leaders to be wise, especially when Proverbs makes it clear that no leader can be effective or wise unless they pursue character development in relationship to God and other people.

A wise leader with "upright" character brings strength to a home (24:3–4); the upright exalt a city (11:11); and righteousness establishes a king's reign (16:12; 20:28; 25:4–5). When people of good character triumph, "there is great glory" (28:12a) and "the people rejoice" (29:2). When a ruler is committed to what is right, just, and fair, as opposed to what is convenient or self-serving, the land retains stability (29:4). In the same way, those who give special attention to the poor and vulnerable also establish stability in the land and enjoy a long reign (29:14). These character qualities take us back to the definition of wisdom at the beginning of Proverbs as acting with "righteousness, justice, and equity" (1:3), built on the foundation of "the fear of the LORD," the right type of relationship to God.

Proverbs also attests to what happens when leaders lack wisdom and good character. "When the wicked rule, the people groan" (29:2b) and "go into hiding" (28:12b, 28:28a) because a wicked ruler is "like a roaring lion or charging bear" (28:15), or simply put, "a cruel oppressor" (28:16a). The sages assert with force what we often ignore: character matters. When the wicked rule, we should expect trouble:

> *When the wicked are in authority, transgression increases.* (29:16a)

> *If a ruler listens to falsehood,*
> *all his officials will be wicked.* (29:12)

People who lack good character created by wisdom cannot promote values higher than their own. Instead, their wickedness will spread through lower ranks of government and to following generations, a principle for which we find a case study in the story of the Northern Kingdom of Israel (1 Kgs. 12–2 Kgs. 17). In fact, not only did the Northern Kingdom of Israel fall because of the iniquity of the leaders, the Southern Kingdom, Judah, also suffered the same fate. Manasseh "misled them to do more evil than the nations had done that the LORD destroyed before the people of Israel" (2 Kgs. 21:9). Not even later reforms could stop what Manasseh put into motion among the people (2 Kgs. 23:26–27; see also 22:14–17).

As for Jeroboam, first king of the Northern Kingdom, he was afraid that he would lose the kingdom the Lord had promised to him, so he established two shrines to rival the temple in Jerusalem, competing holy days, and an open priesthood, and had two golden bulls fashioned to equal the ark of the covenant (1 Kgs. 12:25–33). Originally, the bulls were no more "gods" than was the ark of the covenant in Jerusalem. Jeroboam's intent appears to have been to adapt local Baal culture by using the bulls as the Lord's portable throne, just as the ark of the covenant was a portable throne. Soon, however, the bulls became the objects of worship, and the king led the nation into a long era of revolt against the Lord, with the people following the king into sin (1 Kgs. 12:30). In fact, every king to follow Jeroboam is compared to him. A few are better, some worse, and most about the same. Together they set a low standard of leadership above which the people were unable to rise. (See the explanation of the Northern Kingdom's downfall in 2 Kgs. 17.)

We learn from Jeroboam the danger of leading from a position of fear. Instead of trusting the Lord, he was afraid of losing the nation and his life. Jeroboam's fear overrode his ability to fear the Lord and trust in him. So Jeroboam, and most other Northern Kingdom kings, took matters into their own hands, a move with only one possible outcome: failure and collapse from their pride (Prov. 29:23a). The wicked may rule for a time, but eventually "the righteous will look upon their downfall" (29:16).

Humility

Proverbs describes humility as a critical character trait of a wise leader. In general terms, humility means recognizing the truth about who we are and what we can do, as opposed to pride built on the myths of self-sufficiency and self-determination, an illusion that will ultimately collapse and cause disgrace

(11:2), humiliation (29:23), and destruction (18:12). However, wise leaders recognize that they do not control the outcome of events. God and God alone is in control. So while leaders are responsible for making decisions and preparing for the future, wise leaders recognize that their plans are always subject to the Lord's sovereignty.

> *The king's heart is a stream of water in the hand of the* L*ORD*;
> *he turns it wherever he will.* (21:1)
>
> *The human mind plans the way,*
> *but the* L*ORD directs the steps.* (16:9)
>
> *The human mind may devise many plans,*
> *but it is the purpose of the* L*ORD that will be established.* (19:21)

Without abandoning their responsibilities, the humility of wise leaders will enable them to recognize their limitations and inability to see everything. They will understand that a course of action might *seem* to be right but could actually lead to disaster (16:25). By humbly acknowledging their limitations, wise leaders will commit their work to the Lord and defer leadership to him. If God approves, ultimately their plans will become the Lord's plans, and the work will flourish (16:3). To act otherwise, trusting in our wisdom and relying on our limited vision and ability to know what is best is to act like a fool (28:26a).

Sometimes leaders give the appearance of listening to other points of view, but only *after* they have made their decision. They really listen to pacify or please those who feel compelled to provide insight or information that would contribute to a wise decision. I dare say that we have all found ourselves in this situation: we shared our concerns, provided information the leader did not know, and cautioned against foolish actions while providing vision for another way forward. While we were speaking, the leader appeared to be hanging on every word and may even have gushed with gratitude for all we said. Only later we discovered that the decision had already been made and plans already set in motion. Maybe this is the idea behind the first line of Proverbs 21:29, "The wicked put on a bold face," while the second line offers the contrast, "but the upright give thought to their ways." People who put on a *bold face* act as if they are listening, truly contemplating the direction to go. But humble leaders don't have to act. They are genuinely interested in wise counsel because they recognize their own limitations.

Humble leaders possesses the strength of character to listen to all views, especially those that oppose their initial idea. As a result, their plans are established by wisdom. In particular, Proverbs emphasizes listening to counsel for success on the battlefield.

Plans are established by taking advice;
wage war by following wise guidance. (20:18)

Wise warriors are mightier than strong ones,
and those who have knowledge than those who have strength;
for by wise guidance you can wage your war,
and in abundance of counselors there is victory. (24:5–6)

However when a person leads an army to success on the battlefield—or at the office, temple, or church—the praise and honor that comes from the accomplishment will further test the strength of their character and humility (27:21). Some will believe their own press release about how excellent their plans and work had been and seek praise or become proud (25:27). According to Proverbs, praise is a dangerous trap for leaders that threatens to damage our character and cause us to replace reliance on the Lord with trust in ourselves and to forget the true reason for our success (21:31).

Compassion

A second critical character trait of wise leaders is compassion. Instead of pride that focuses us on ourselves—our needs, our entitlements, and our rights—wise leaders have genuine concern for others, especially those for whom we are responsible. In Proverbs, the sages first state this principle in agrarian terms:

Know well the condition of your flocks,
and give attention to your herds;
for riches do not last forever,
nor a crown for all generations. (27:23–24)

The righteous know the needs of their animals,
but the mercy of the wicked is cruel. (12:10)

Both proverbs work at a literal and metaphorical level:

- *Literal*: good shepherds pay close attention to the health, safety, and needs of the four-legged sheep for which they are responsible.
- *Metaphorical*: good leaders pay close attention to the health, safety, and needs their two-legged sheep, the people who follow them.

In Psalm 23, the Lord is an excellent example of a shepherd leader who provides (23:1), guides (23:2–3), protects (23:4–5), and loves those he leads (23:6). The Lord does all these things because of his constant concern for and presence with those he leads.

A shepherd's time with the flock observing and recognizing personalities pays dividends in the present and the future. One of the first lessons I learned from my predecessor, Dr. David Wray, early in my tenure of academic leadership was the simple practice of walking the halls, looking for office doors that were ajar or wide open, knocking, stepping in and asking simple questions such as "How are you doing? How are your classes going? How are your research projects progressing?" This practice enabled me to enter the lives of people in my department, support their work, and deal with problems while they were still small. Sometimes we would talk about their needs and the possible solutions or help my office might provide. Most often, however, all they really needed from me was my presence, a leader who knew them and cared about them. I only wished it had been this easy to connect to people while I was in pastoral ministry.

Of course, the point of knowing the flock is to know those we serve and their most urgent needs. A leadership character that includes humility and compassion will help us see and care about those in need. Also for those of us who are privileged (most of us), it is easy to be blind to those who lack the blessings we have enjoyed all our lives. As long as the needy are out of our sight because we live in affluent neighborhoods, drive around the "rough part of town," and have laws to keep "them" off street corners, we can ignore that they exist. We have successfully erased them from our lives.

In earlier chapters, we mentioned the counsel of King Lemuel's mother and her initial concern for two things that could sink her son's reign: affairs with women other than his wife and getting drunk and perverting the rights of those who are suffering (Prov. 31:1–5). Now we will listen to the remainder of this remarkable mother/son conversation:

Give strong drink to one who is perishing,
and wine to those in bitter distress;

let them drink and forget their poverty,
and remember their misery no more.
Speak out for those who cannot speak,
for the rights of all the destitute.
Speak out, judge righteously,
defend the rights of the poor and needy. (31:6–9)

Her advice to Lemuel is not only from another time and country; it is totally foreign to our way of thinking: give "strong drink" to those in bitter distress, help them forget "their poverty" and "their misery." Her advice is unimaginable to any benevolence committee or church I have ever known. When I was in ministry, I was taught never to give cash because the recipient might go to the liquor store and waste it. Somewhere along the way I missed Proverbs 31. The last thing we want to do is support or enable someone's addiction, possibly the very cause of their poverty and suffering. After all, Lemuel's mother also tells him to avoid drunkenness (31:4–5). So what are we to do?

Markus grew up in a home that privileged him with physical beatings and sexual abuse.[9] He was a throwaway kid who no one knew about or cared enough about to rescue. So as a young teenager, he rescued himself by going to the streets of San Antonio, eventually landing in an old vacant hotel with a family of others living out the same story. Soon enough he was escaping his living nightmare through drugs and alcohol, a path to freedom that was temporary at best. What gave him relief also chained him to the demands of addiction, defined by Proverbs as folly.

I don't know the details or even the basic story of how Markus found recovery, but he did. As of today, Markus has been in recovery for years, sober and drug free. In fact, he gave his life to God, volunteered at church, worked his way through a GED, and even enrolled in college where my wife, Dana, met him. Dana has a talent for engaging others in conversation and learning their stories. So over the course of the semester, Markus talked to Dana about what it was like to be unloved and homeless. Part of what Markus told her still haunts me.

> A lot of people seem to think they know all about homeless people and what our lives are like. They don't. These same people usually have simplistic solutions and are quick to judge. For me, nighttime was the worst part of the day: I was cold, alone, and afraid [we could also add that he was

9. I have changed the name and location of "Markus" to conceal his identity.

> just a kid]. There in the dark, what I needed most was a bottle, something strong enough so that I would not be so alone and scared, and I could make it through the night.

I immediately notice the correlation between what Markus said and the words from King Lemuel's mother. At the same time, I recognize the pattern of his addiction. So again, what are we to do? Ideally, the best thing would be to help people get off the street and into good housing, with beds, blankets, and doors that lock: projects such as Housing First, which builds apartments for those who live on the street as a first step in permanently leaving homelessness behind.

At the same time, I can't deny what the text says for relieving the misery of the poor (31:7). I'd prefer the text limit this short-term solution to those who are dying and suffering (31:6); and maybe this image is supposed to guide our understand of the "poor"—those suffering from illness. Or maybe the key here is to remember that proverbs are not absolute statements of truth, but conditional, based on time and circumstance. Perhaps all I can really say is what Dana and I try to do in view of these words—not so much Markus's statement about the bottle but his indictment of those who think they know all about the homeless and their needs. First, we support projects such as Housing First, long-term solutions. Second, we've changed our personal policy. If someone asks us for money, we do not grill them about what they really need, but with discernment we give them money. We have decided that we will no longer judge people that we don't know or provide only what *we* think a person like *them* should need or should have. As for those making these decisions in the temple or church, I understand the problem: I've been there. But until we are ready or able to rescue people from the streets, to provide for their needs, including long-term solutions to their poverty and addictions, it seems that our primary responsibility is to give and to give freely—with wisdom, but not with judgment.

I hope we have all experienced the presence of compassionate shepherds in our lives, women and men who have led and mentored us. I regret that in all likelihood we have also dealt with the opposite: a leader who does not know or exhibit any genuine concern for us. The sages know what it is like when those we look to for guidance let us down:

> *A ruler who lacks understanding is a cruel oppressor;*
> *but one who hates unjust gain will enjoy a long life.* (28:16)

I doubt this leader intends to be a cruel oppressor, but his lack of empathy and possibly his desire for money under the table leads him to neglect those who need his care. Unfortunately, he may even reach the point where the mercy he offers is itself an act of cruelty (12:10).

Other proverbs on the characteristics of a compassionate leader emphasize the need for them to understand what constitutes a fair response (29:7), as opposed to a ruler who doesn't care and oppresses those already marginalized by their financial situation.

> *A ruler who oppresses the poor*
> *is a beating rain that leaves no food.* (28:3)

A compassionate leader "ponders how to answer" (15:28) instead of responding with little thought for people or their needs, and only fools give full vent to their anger (29:11).

We need to add only one more specific tile to complete the mosaic of leaders who are connected to the lives and needs of the people they lead. Compassion sometimes requires having difficult conversations, and of course, knowing what to say and the right time to say it (15:23). But leaders are human: it's easier to support and encourage than it is to speak difficult words of truth. So the sages remind us:

> *Better is open rebuke*
> *than hidden love.* (27:5)

> *Whoever rebukes a person will afterward find more favor*
> *than one who flatters with the tongue.* (28:23)

> *but those who rebuke the wicked will have delight,*
> *and a good blessing will come upon them.* (24:25)

Conducted with wisdom, humility, and compassion, difficult conversations will lead to more favor than just "letting it go" and not saying anything. In fact, in time such a rebuke will lead to delight and a blessing. Speaking honestly, even when it is not easy, will be like a "kiss on the lips" (24:26). An open rebuke expresses love far more than love that doesn't want to hurt a friend. It is an act of compassion and precious gift to correct a person who looks to us for guidance (25:12). Proverbs states and my experience affirms that speaking the truth works best in existing relationships; strangers have no reason to believe or accept my hard words.

Solomon and Proverbs

The sages responsible for the final shape of Proverbs associated their work with Solomon (1:1), an act that leads some to claim Solomon as an ultimate example of wise leadership. Solomon did appeal to the Lord for wisdom to lead the people (1 Kgs. 3:4–9), a request the Lord granted (1 Kgs. 3:10–14) so well that Solomon became famous for his wisdom (1 Kgs. 4:29–34). Unfortunately, read against the text of Proverbs, Solomon's life doesn't measure up to the standards of godly wisdom built on the irreplaceable foundation of "the fear of the LORD" (see ch. 1).

At the beginning of his reign in Jerusalem, Solomon secures his position on the throne by following his father's advice to settle scores for him: cases in which David had promised not to kill a person, but that Solomon should deal with "according to [his] wisdom" (1 Kgs. 2:5). In other words, David advises Solomon to kill Joab (1 Kgs. 2:5–6) and Shimei (2:8–9), which he does later in the chapter. Additionally, when Adonijah (the oldest son of David who initially claimed the throne for himself, 1:5–53) comes to Solomon with a request for Abishag (the young woman who kept David warm, 1:1–4), Solomon seizes the opportunity to have Adonijah killed (2:13–25). Solomon also banishes Abiathar (who initially supported Adonijah as king, 1:7) and his family from serving as priests (2:26–27, 35). At the end of these bloody events the text reports, "So the kingdom was established in the hand of Solomon" (2:46). Perhaps these were all wise political moves to make, but I have to wonder if the brutality stemmed from a lack of trust in the Lord who promised to secure his throne (1 Kgs. 2:1–4). In other words, Solomon did not yet "fear the Lord" enough to trust the Lord (cf. Prov. 16:12).

After a brief time of trusting God, Solomon engaged in other questionable activities: amassing enormous wealth and opulence (1 Kgs. 10:14–25, 27), conducting a massive buildup of the military (1Kgs. 10:26, 28–29), and marrying seven hundred royal wives as the result of signing treaties and building power through political alliances (1 Kgs. 11:1–3)—all in direct violation of the monarch code in Deuteronomy 17:14–20. One final example from Solomon's life was the manner in which he established taxation districts with a heavy tax burden on districts outside of Judah (1 Kgs. 4:7–23) and conscripted labor from Israel for his building projects (1 Kgs. 5:13–18). Later, the nation regarded Solomon to be a cruel oppressor (1 Kgs. 12:3–4, compare to Prov. 28:16a). He had become a king who overtaxes and ruins his country (Prov. 28:3; 29:4), a significant factor in the division of the nation (1 Kgs. 12:1–24, also consider Prov. 11:2; 18:12; 29:23).

As an example of a great leader with wisdom built on the fear of the Lord, Solomon comes up short. The book that bears his name testifies against him. Solomon may have been an incredibly wise administrator and expert in national affairs (cf. Solomon's request in 1 Kgs. 3:6–9 and recall the first definition of wisdom in ch. 1). But before we hold him up as an example of the wisdom taught by Proverbs, we need to look carefully and study his life against the text. The Lord gave Solomon the wisdom to rule the people (1 Kgs. 3:10–14) but from all indications, Solomon failed to develop and maintain the character he needed to be truly wise. Consequently, instead of being a great example of wisdom, the book that bears his name suggests that Solomon was a larger-than-life illustration of a fool.

Conclusion

From simple firsthand observation, I argue that the most common values and principles for leadership in North America, whether explicitly recognized or assumed to be true, feature one or more of the following ideas:

- *Methods and Strategies*: These include select the best talent, cast a vision, get people to buy into your vision, empower your people to do their work, and attend seminars so you can learn more strategies.
- *The Leader's Personality*, not to be confused with character: A person who employs engaging rhetoric in their own "hip" or "down home" style, when in reality the leader is disconnected from genuine relationships. The leader's personality can fuel explosive growth or productivity as long as the leader maintains the culturally attractive persona.
- *Top-Down Power*: Nothing of substance can be done outside of the leader's awareness and approval, and everything must fit within the leader's vision. Failure to gain prior authorization is apt to cause serious repercussions. A leader who is unable to control the actions of others is deemed weak and replaced.
- *Situational Power*: These leaders prey upon people's fears and insecurities and promise to deliver security, which is a highly effective method for obtaining power. The history of our world witnesses to how these leaders managed to grab power at just the right time to influence world events.

However, Proverbs has a different vision of effective leadership than what surrounds and influences us today:

- *Wisdom*. Wise women and men recognize the Lord as the true ruler and live in relationship with him. They trust in the Lord, not in their ability, their plans, or their power.
- *Character*. Leadership in Proverbs is first and foremost about character, who we are as a person rather than what we can do. Good leaders have integrity that brings strength and stability. Good leaders maintain justice and ensure that the needs of the most vulnerable are met.
- *Humility*. This character attribute of wise leaders is a strength rather than weakness. Humble leaders recognize the one who can control an outcome, and it is not them. Humble leaders still carry out their duty to make plans and lead, but always in conversation with other people and with God. Any success that comes is recognized for what it is, a blessing of God, not a human achievement.
- *Compassion*. Wise leaders who fear the Lord lead with genuine compassion for people. They care enough about their flock to spend time with them, get to know them, and learn how to best serve them—not how the flock may best serve the their purposes—even if it means causing short-term pain for long-term benefits.

These two visions for leadership—the North American model and the Proverbs model—are incompatible with one another. The character-based leadership of Proverbs cannot be one more add-on to the list of habits or practices for successful leadership. In the American model, the aim is for rewards, moving up, grasping more power and more money: "the good life" for the leader. In the other model from Proverbs and the sages, the goal is the well-being of the people and leading them to lives that are good. Here we confront the basic theological challenge that the wisdom of Proverbs asserts against the commonplace ways of our world. Are we seeking "the "good life" and the ways to achieve our dreams? Or do we want what Proverbs has to offer: disciplined, character-based leadership that reaches out to those hungry for a life that is good? The choice is between two different paths, two ways of being and leading—with the wisdom of God or with the wisdom of the world. May we choose wisely.

DISCUSSION QUESTIONS

1. What is the common definition of leadership? How do you define leadership (not explicitly stated)? Are all people leaders, as is sometimes

claimed? Or does Proverbs assume a more limited definition? How does Proverbs appear to define leadership?

2. Read Proverbs 27:23–29:27 and note every statement about leadership, explicit or implicit. If time permits, repeat this exercise with a different translation. Malchow asserts that this text was originally a manual for rulers. Would you agree with his hypothesis? Be prepared to defend your answer.
3. Describe one of the best leaders you have ever known personally. What special traits did your leader demonstrate? Compare these to what we have seen about a wise leader. What do you notice?
4. Describe one of the worst leaders you have ever had the misfortune of being under. What traits or practices made them so bad or ill suited for leadership? Compare these to what we have seen about a wise leader. What do you notice?
5. Consider Solomon as a wise leader. In what ways was Solomon wise? In what ways was he foolish? What can we learn from Solomon?
6. Reconsider Proverbs 31:1–9. Have you ever noticed this text before? If so, how has it influenced you? How might "forgetting what has been decreed" deprive the poor of their rights? What does Lemuel's mother advocate? Recognizing the general nature of Proverbs, what situations does this advice best fit?

PROJECT CHALLENGE

Based on what we have learned from Proverbs, assess David as a leader. This project will require careful reading of the David narrative (1 Sam. 16–1 Kgs. 2). How does the book of Proverbs engage with David's life? In what ways was David wise or foolish?

PART FOUR

Relationships in a Life That Is Good

CHAPTER 10

Destroying and Creating Friends: Wisdom for Relationships

Friendship, like phosphorus,
shines brightest when all around is dark.

—Anonymous

Hold a true friend with both your hands.

—Nigerian Proverb

Some friends play at friendship
but a true friend sticks closer than one's nearest kin.

—Proverbs 18:24

TO PREPARE FOR READING THIS CHAPTER

Read the proverbs in either #1 or #2:

1. Proverbs 3:3–4, 27–30; 6:1–6; 10:12; 11:9, 12–13, 15, 26; 12:5–6, 18, 26; 13:17, 20; 14:7, 29; 15:1, 18, 23; 16:18–19, 28–32; 17:9, 17–18; 18:1, 24; 19:4–7, 22; 20:6, 19; 21:10; 22:11, 24–27; 24:1–2, 28–29; 25:7–10, 14, 17–20; 26:18–19; 27:6, 10, 13–14, 17; 28:7, 23; 29:3, 5, 22, 24; 30:33
2. Proverbs 3:3–4, 27–30; 6:1–6; 11:9–15; 12:5–6; 13:17, 20; 16:28–32; 17:9, 17–18; 19:4–7; 20:6, 19; 22:24–27; 24:1–2, 28–29; 25:7–10, 17–20; 26:18–19; 27:13–14; 29:3–5, 22–24

Any quick internet search for surveys or studies of friendship in America will find the same conclusion: fewer and fewer people have strong, close friends, people with whom we discuss our lives, important issues, and decisions and whom we would call without hesitation if a crisis came at three o'clock in the morning. If the stock market counted best friends instead of money, we would be in a fifty-year depression, every year a little worse than the one before.

Yet at the same time, or perhaps for this reason, many of our favorite songs celebrate the comforts and joys of strong friendships. Just select your decade and sing along:

- "With a Little Help from My Friends" (The Beatles, 1967)
- "You Got a Friend" (James Taylor, 1971)
- "Thank You for Being a Friend" (theme from *The Golden Girls*, Andrew Gold, 1978)
- "That's What Friends Are For" (Dionne Warwick, Elton John, Stevie Wonder, and Gladys Knight, 1986)
- "Where Everybody Knows Your Name" (theme from *Cheers*, Judy Angelo, Gary Portnoy, Julian Williams, recorded by Gary Portnoy, 1989)
- "I'll Be There for You" (theme from *Friends*, David Crane, et al., recorded by The Rembrandts, 1995)
- "You Got a Friend in Me" (theme from *Toy Story*, Randy Newman, 1995)
- "We're Going to Be Friends" (Jack White, recorded by The White Stripes, 2002)
- "My Best Friend" (Rivers Cuomo, recorded by Weezer, 2005)
- "Count on Me" (Bruno Mars, Philip Lawrence, and Ari Levine, recorded by Bruno Mars, 2010)

Now, either you will read this chapter with the tune of your favorite song stuck in your mind, or given the number of top hits on the subject of friendship, you will wonder why I didn't include the most obvious choice—your favorite song.

There is more than enough blame to spread around for the decline of friendship and have leftovers for tomorrow's lunch. One easy target is the mobility of our time. Far behind us are the days of growing up in one community, leaving home for college or the military or another temporary purpose, and moving back to live out our days in the same community. A few will stay in their hometown, and a few will make one move for the sake of a job and settle in for the duration, but the percentage is not high. Most adults will make multiple moves from one job to another and one town to another. Fueling our lives as sojourners moving from place to place was the mass production of the automobile. It opened up the world to us but brought problems in the trunk we did not foresee. We also have less commitment to "the company" we work for because the company has less commitment to us and can no longer be trusted to provide work for a lifetime; pink slips could be handed out without notice at any time. And motivating these developments is the rugged individualism fostered by our culture. I can't decide which comes first: loss of community or the primary commitment to self? All I know is that today we are a nation of individuals with individual rights searching for "the good life for me," not us, not you, and certainly not others.

The impact our mobility has on our relationships doesn't take a "rocket surgeon to figure out," as one of my close friends, who now lives in another town, liked to say. We never stay around long enough to develop friendships that are more than casual or are outside of work. At best, our relationships will just be beginning when our friends move, we move, or one of us takes another job or retires. We may do our best to keep our friendship alive, but we both know what will happen—hard-earned friendships will eventually dry up and blow away like tumbleweeds. In fact, many of us may even avoid pouring ourselves into friendships that we know will never last.

Yet despite our fifty-year depression, these days it is possible to deceive ourselves and hide our lack of close personal friends behind the smokescreen of social media. For example, as of today I have 1,959 "friends" on Facebook™, many of whom I have never met in person, but by personal invitation and deliberate decision, we have decided to be friends. Our situation is further aggravated by the unique ability in our time to be with many people but not be fully present with anyone. Several years ago I watched two young couples dressed in tuxedos and evening gowns for the prom later that night walking toward a restaurant. The two guys walked together a few steps behind their dates who were both fully engaged in multiple nonstop conversations with other friends through text messaging. They were present with their dates on a beautiful spring evening along the River Walk in Bricktown, Oklahoma City, but they were absent at the same time, no closer to their dates than they were with those on the other end of their messages. Sadder still, not only have you and I seen the same behavior elsewhere, odds are high that a little honest reflection will remind us that we have done the same thing. Without critical self-assessment, we can fool ourselves into thinking that we have many good, close friends, when in fact we have none.

To some degree I blame whoever began the myth of multitasking, the idea that our brains are able to process two, three, or even four things at the same time. So we believe it is possible to be fully present with our date and also chat with two friends across town who are with their dates. Experience has shown us our folly. In other words, wisdom has taught us better. We know how it feels when someone at the table or in conversation has left us to engage someone else on their phone. Accident statistics and growing public concern for DUI-P, driving under the influence of phones, also testify to the problem. But the star witnesses are neuroscientists who have learned that the human brain is incapable of conscience thought about more than one thing at a time. We truly are simpleminded. It is not possible to think about two or more things at the same time. This is the reason why meditation is such an effective tool for pain management: if I can focus my mind on one thing, visualizing a favorite vacation place or studying a rose across the room, I can forget about or lessen the degree to which I notice the pain signals going off like fireworks on the fourth of July in my legs. And to the objection, "But I can multitask," all we can say is that you have just become very good at rapidly switching back and forth from one thought to another. But know that whether we do this while driving or while we are with a close friend, we are rapidly turning our thoughts on and off and our presence on and off. And just as certainly as we know when this is happening to us and how it feels, our friends know when we are at best half present.

Ancient Israel's sages recognized the value of good friends. "Two are better than one," the teacher in Ecclesiastes writes, because together they will have will have greater productivity in work (Eccl. 4:9), greater help when one falls and can't get up (4:10), and greater protection against attacks (4:12). The teacher concludes that a rope made from three cords will not easily break (4:12b), which is a simple way of saying we are better and stronger when we live in close relationship with other people. The sages who wrote Proverbs make the same point by praising the value of good friends:

There are persons for companionship,
but then there are friends who are more loyal than family. (18:24 CEB)

A friend loves at all times,
and kinfolk are born to share adversity. (17:17)

The first of these proverbs recognizes the difference between companions and good friends who may in fact be closer than siblings. The second may be best understood as a parallel statement, each line reinforcing the other. A friend, like family, loves at all times, especially when trouble comes and they are needed. Taken together, these proverbs remind us that a friend may be closer than family, an insight that is especially apt in our mobile society in which parents and siblings may live hundreds of miles away from each other. This situation is envisioned in the second half of Proverbs 27:10:

Better is a neighbor who is nearby
than kindred who are far away.

A crisis has come, but one's family lives some distance away. In this case, it is far better to have close friends near to us than family who live across the country.

Like other topics in this book, Proverbs has much to say about friendship. The sages teach us how to make close friends. First, they identify character types that the reader must avoid. We begin with a sketch of these character types. Second, the sages identify the traits of an ideal friend, not only so we know what to look for (although not easy to find, 20:6), but also so we know what to become to be a good friend. Third, the sages point out the attitudes and behaviors that will sabotage a friendship more quickly than we can repair the damage.

As I have said before, the further we progress in our study, the more prior chapters overlap with the topic at hand. For example, our friendships are influenced for good or bad by our wisdom or folly (chs. 3 and 4), our practice of mercy and justice (ch. 6), our habits of speech (ch. 7), and our use or misuse of wealth (ch. 8). Wisdom is a holistic enterprise in relationship with God and others and in the process of character formation. Consequently, character traits or practices are not isolated silos but interwoven and interdependent. Anything less would produce a split personality, for example being one person when we go to worship, a different person at work, still a different person at home, and who knows what on the road.

Character Types to Avoid

We may identify two levels of concern within Proverbs regarding potential character traits to recognize and avoid. On the first level the sages identify traits of those we should not befriend or not make a close companion. On the second the sages escalate their concern for behaviors and characteristics in others to be on guard against at all times. As for level one, only a handful of proverbs explicitly identify persons with whom we should not become friends.

Those Who Make Bad Friends

The Sinner

Opening the first lecture in Proverbs the parents warn and plead with the son not to believe and join up with a gang of "sinners" (1:10) who promise excitement, fast money, and equal standing as a member of the gang. In reality, however, they are setting a trap that will eventually catch them and lead to their death (1:17–19, see ch. 4). The sages also warn that sinners are pursued by misfortune (13:21) and are repaid for their wicked actions on earth (11:31). It makes little sense to envy sinners (23:17) or, in view of these realities, to want to be their close friend.

The Wicked

Closely related to sinners, the wicked pose a similar threat. Their "minds devise violence," and their mouths speak of plans to harm others. So the sages warn the reader "not to envy the wicked," to want what the wicked have, or to desire to be with them (24:1–2). An earlier proverb drives home the point; all the wicked want to do is evil and their neighbors or friends "find no mercy in their eyes" (21:10). The sages warn those eager to join the wicked that what the wicked do to other people, they will certainly do to you in time. Don't fool yourself into believing they won't.

The Thief

The sages also caution against becoming a "partner of a thief" (29:24a), associated with or friends with a thief, even if you are not involved in the crime. The danger of such a relationship comes when we are called as a witness in our friend's trial: we may hear the curse and pain of the victim but disclose nothing of what we know (29:24b), in the process compromising our integrity for our friend.

The Hotheaded or Easily Angered

The next three categories are related. The sages state, "Make no friends with those given to anger" or "hotheads" (22:24) because as you spend time with them, you "may learn their ways and entangle yourself in a snare" (22:25). Other texts add to the warning: "the one given to anger" stirs up trouble and causes much sin (29:22; see also 15:1b, 18; 30:33), and a quick temper is the mark of a fool (12:16; 14:29).

The Prostitute

One proverb contrasts the happiness that children who love wisdom will bring to their parents against children who "keep company with prostitutes" and squander their wealth (29:3). Other texts also mention prostitutes. In 7:10, the seductive married woman is dressed "like a prostitute," suggesting what she is after. Proverbs 23:27 warns that when men go to prostitutes, they fall into "a deep pit." Therefore it is easy to see why prostitutes do not make good friends—with them we squander our money and fall into a hole that is difficult to climb out of.

The Glutton and the Drunkard

The "companions of gluttons shame their parents" (Prov. 28:7). A second text also warns the reader not to be among the gluttons or the drunks because these groups eventually "come to poverty," and their drowsiness brought on by too much food and wine "will clothe them with rags" (23:20–21; cf. 26:10, drunkenness creates poor employees). Those who drink too much have a tendency to forget promises they make and infringe on the rights of others, especially the poor. For these reasons it is especially dangerous for a king or leader to have drinking problem (31:4–5), though both consequences should also alert potential friends to problems that will come in a close relationship with someone who drinks too much—forgetting and not following through on promises and mistreating us. And with these dangers is the stark reality that "strong drink" is a "brawler" or "leads to fights" (20:1 CEV), either way—along with or against our drunken friend—we should expect to be fighting. (See also 23:29–35 on the effects of alcoholism.)

The One Who Lacks of Self-Control

A common thread holds these groups together. Each group lacks self-control, an inability to control their response to an insult, their appetite for sex, and their intake of food and drink. Those who are wise exercise self-control, but this is especially hard to do if we are friends with those who lack self-control.

Obviously, these three groups still exist today, but life has also changed or developed to give us new expressions of the same problem. Along with food, drink, and sex we also recognize drug, gambling, smoking or nicotine, and shopping addictions (among others). And just as addictive behavioral problems spelled trouble for friendships in ancient Israel, these more recently recognized addictions are apt to cause problems today. Today, through wisdom we understand better these behaviors, their causes, best treatments, and even the ways in which they affect addicts and those living close to them (e.g., secondhand smoke). In fact, we've learned a great deal about the addictive nature of human behavior, including genetic predispositions towards certain addictions. For example, because of genetic factors it takes little for some people to become alcoholics, while others may drink socially without ever facing addiction. Some may take one opioid pill and be hooked; with all the physical pain I deal with I thank God that I did not inherit that gene. Each of these addictive behaviors will affect friends in different ways, a task that I leave for your discussion of this chapter.

The Gossip

Our excursion into types of speech in chapter 7 included a short analysis of gossip in Proverbs. There we observed that gossip wouldn't be such a problem if the words didn't taste so good (18:8; 26:22). In other words, not associating with a gossip also requires exercising self-control. But the sages motivate the reader to "not associate with a babbler" by warning that gossips will reveal secrets, including our secrets (20:19). A gossip will also separate us from our closest friends (16:28). We must resist the folly of thinking our new friend will tell us secrets about other people but will not divulge our own. Unless we want our secrets revealed to the world and we want to lose our best friends, we must avoid becoming friends with a gossip.

The Fool

Finally, we come to the most obvious character type we must not befriend: the fool. Since we already explored this character in detail (see ch. 4), I mention only two texts here. In the first, the sages warn that "the companion of fools suffers harm," compared to those who walk with the wise and become wise (13:20). The second text advises us to, "Leave the presence of a fool, for there you do not find words of knowledge" (14:7). Assuming that the reader of Proverbs wants wisdom, this advice makes sense: if we seek wisdom, we will not find it among fools.

People to Avoid Entirely

While the sages discourage readers from being friends with these eight types of people, they save their strongest rhetoric for extreme behaviors and characteristics. Here friendship is not even on the table or considered to be an option. Instead, the reader must avoid these people *entirely* at risk of losing their own lives.

Troublemakers

This group includes "the perverse" who naturally create problems by their actions (16:28), who plan "perverse things" (16:30), and who are bad messengers who bring trouble (13:17), perhaps because they arrive late or confuse the message. In either case they are unreliable. The common feature of these people is the trouble they cause for those who grow close to them or rely on them.

Deceivers

The second group is best known for the different ways they "entice" or lead their companions into a trap. They include the violent who "entice their neighbors" and lead them in directions that are not good for them (16:29). The wicked also give advice that is "deceptive" (12:5b CEB, "deceitful" NASB, NIV), setting a deadly "ambush" (12:6a or "deathtrap" CEB). In addition, the sages also describe insincere compliments or flattery as being like the profuse "kisses of an enemy" (27:6). Deceptive people use flattery to distract us from the net they are spreading to catch us (29:5). All of these types of deceivers are dangerous to be around.

Guarantors of Surety

The last group consists of those who have been convinced in some way or have decided to provide "surety" for someone else, whether for neighbors or companions, or even worse, strangers or foreigners. To provide surety is roughly equivalent to our practice of cosigning a loan for someone who does not qualify for a loan because of their credit history. For example it is not unusual for parents to help their children in this way. But Proverbs warns that to do this for a neighbor is senseless (17:18), and if we have already caught ourselves in this trap, we should do everything we can to get out of the contract (6:1–5). Worse, the sages go ballistic at the foolishness of cosigning a loan for people we don't even know, the "strangers." Doing so brings trouble (11:15), and whoever does this should have the collateral they pledged taken away—perhaps to teach them what they stand to lose (27:13). The sages even ask the question: why do you guarantee loans when you have no money to pay the loan? Should the borrower default, you stand to lose your bed (22:26–27). The answer may be "to gain a friend." The sages, however, give no indication that this will ever work and advise us to stay away from those who ask us to stake our reputation and well-being on their reliability. Few if any stable friendships will emerge as the result of guaranteeing a loan for someone else.

Allow me to clarify one potential misunderstanding: to guarantee a loan and to help the poor are two different matters. The wise are to give to the poor with a generous heart. They may also extend a loan to the poor, but when they make such a loan, they should regard the money as a potential gift and not charge much interest, if any. In ancient Israel if the poor had not been able to pay off the loan before the Sabbatical Year, the debt was to be erased (Deut. 15:7–11; cf. Exod. 21:1–6). By contrast, the person who asks another to cosign or guarantee a loan may be taking advantage of the cosigner's good nature and skip out of town with the goods or drop the debt burden on the cosigner.

To avoid friendship and even causal companionship with the all of these character types is not the easiest thing to do—not in ancient Israel nor in our time. Nor is it simple to know a person's character until we have been with them a while, even long enough that ending the relationship will be awkward. Even so, in our hearts we know the sages are telling us the best ways to be happy and live well. It's just hard to be patient as we search for friends we can rely on (see Prov. 20:6).

The Traits of an Ideal Friend

What are the traits of an ideal friend? Most of us can recall what our parents or grandparents taught us: 1) the only person you can control or change is you, and 2) to have a good friend you must first learn to be a good friend. So now we turn the question around: what must we do or who must we become to be a good friend? As we might expect, many character qualities of a good friend are the mirror opposites of the negative traits the sages warn us about.

Loyalty

What people want in a friend is loyalty (19:22; 20:6), someone who will not cut and run at the first sign of trouble (27:10a). As the sages state, if you will bind "loyalty and faithfulness" around your neck and "write them on the tablet of your heart," you will find favor with God and people (3:3–4). Loyalty is also expressed through keeping a confidence (11:13), being a faithful envoy (13:17a), and by not taking advantage of others, or only staying around until the gifts and the money run out (19:4). We need our friends to be reliable people we can turn to in the dead of night, especially if our family is far away (18:24; 27:10c–d).

Love

It is difficult to distinguish love from loyalty because the two have similar outcomes. A friend "loves at all times" (17:17a). Friendship requires us to be slow to anger and slow to become offended (14:29; cf. 15:18; 16:32) and to ignore an insult rather than reacting in anger (12:16).

We want friends who love so much that they are willing to forgive, for this kind of love "covers all offenses" (10:12). In fact, "One who forgives an affront fosters friendship" (17:9a). If we take offense at every intentional or unintentional slight and hold onto the pain and our "right" to get even, we disable any chance of a long-term friendship. It is not humanly possible for a friend to never make a mistake. Nor is it possible for us to forget what has happened or the pain it caused us. However, we can surrender our "right" to take revenge and choose to forgive. Otherwise, we will never establish and keep good friends.

Wise in Speech

Those who attract friends and make good friends exercise wise speech. They know when to speak and when to remain silent, what to say and how to say the appropriate words for the situation (15:23). The wise speak words that encourage (12:25), heal (12:18), provide good advice (12:26a), or calm a tense situation with a soft, sensitive reply (15:1a). However, pure speech like this cannot be externally manufactured for long. Wise speech comes from a pure heart (22:11), an idea taken up and expanded in the New Testament (Matt. 13:34;

cf. Jas. 3:1–12). Wise speech that encourages and genuinely helps a friend is not always pleasant or easy to speak, or receive. Sometimes the most loving thing to do is correct a friend or to accept their words of correction. Such "wounds" from a friend are well intended (27:6a), and in the long run these words strengthen friendships (28:23).

Humble

Finally, one other quality of heart that we need to develop and we want to find in those who become our friends is humility (see 16:19). The sages teach that humility precedes and brings wisdom (11:2). When coupled with the fear of the Lord, humility also results in riches and life (22:4a). And most of all, humility brings honor (15:33; 18:12; 22:4b; 29:23). Humility is the quality of character that enables us to recognize our limitations so that instead of trusting in ourselves, we trust in God. We also recognize our need for other people in our lives to help us, and not just so we help them (this is a proud savior complex, not friendship). If we become like our friends and participate in their lives, we need to befriend those who are humble, those who can lead us to wisdom, honor, and the life that is good.

No doubt we could arrange and rearrange these texts to describe other desirable characteristics such as wisdom, righteousness, and respect for equity. The characteristics above, however, will suffice for us to realize that Jesus alone is not all we need. From the beginning of our story, we were created as social beings designed to live in relationship with one another (see Gen. 2). Consequently, how and with whom we live in relationship is the concern of the sages and of all who want to live a life that is good.

How to Sabotage Our Relationships

We have examined what the sages in Proverbs advise on who to avoid as a friend and what characteristics we need to develop and to seek in others to start and maintain good friendships. What remains are what Proverbs says are sure-fire ways to sabotage and end a friendship. A few of these behaviors have already been mentioned. Most present new ideas, and many strike deeply into our experience. We know all too well what the sages are talking about in these warnings.

Seek Revenge

We begin with the familiar. The only way any good friendship stands a chance is if we operate within a framework of mercy and forgiveness. If, however, we decide to pursue vendettas to settle scores with everyone who hurts us, including friends, we will never have longterm friendships (24:29). Forgiveness "fosters friendship" but grudges "will alienate a friend" (17:9).

Break a Confidence

The day we decide to tell others what a friend told us in confidence is the day we begin killing our closest friendships (11:13; 16:28). If those to whom we speak are wise, they will know not to entrust us with their secrets or their friendship. They may enjoy hearing us reveal secrets about others, but they also learn that we are not to be trusted. If we sold out other close friends today, what's to stop us from telling the secrets of our new friends tomorrow?

Withhold Good

The sages of Proverbs warn against withholding "good from those to whom it is due" when it is within our ability to give it (3:27). The reference may be to a debt we owe and could repay, but delay paying. More likely, however, it speaks of a friend who has come to us in need, but we refuse to give them anything. We might even send them away with empty promises that we will help them tomorrow even though we could help them today (3:28). Another proverb speaks to a similar situation: people bless those who open their granary and sell when it is needed, but "people curse those who hold back grain" (11:26). The time to help a friend or community is when they need our help, not when it is convenient for us. To delay is selfish and damages the friendship: like a windy overcast day without rain is a person "who boasts of a gift never given" (25:14).

Pursue Frivolous Lawsuits

The father warns us not to "plan harm against your neighbor" by starting a quarrel for no reason, especially when our neighbor trusts us (3:29–30). Proverbs 25:7c–10 describes a similar situation, hastily bringing suit against our neighbor or friend instead of first going to them to work out the problem. The sages warn that taking a friend to trial may force our friend to turn the tables against us, bring shame on our reputation, and destroy our friendship. In the same way, the sages also warn against becoming a false witness against a neighbor or friend because we are angry with them (24:28–29). Proverbs 25:18 states the warning in vivid terms:

Like a war club, a sword, or a sharp arrow
is one who bears false witness against a neighbor.

We will not only hurt a friend who has done nothing to harm us, the gun will also backfire, destroying us.

Belittle People

In our younger days, we might remember the practice of "dissing" or belittling a friend to get a laugh. When our friend got upset we would say, "I was just kidding." Does this bring to mind any memories, even painful memories? The sages respond with a simple statement, "Whoever belittles another lacks sense" (11:12a). As if they were writing today, they also assert:

Like a crazy person shooting deadly flaming arrows
are those who deceive their neighbor and say, "Hey, I was only joking!"
(26:18–19 CEB)

Belittling words followed by "Don't take it so seriously" and "I was just kidding" are still deadly, fire-tipped arrows that pierce and burn up our friendships, causing irreparable damage. "I was only joking" is no joke for relationships.

Monopolize Time

A traditional American proverb attributed to Benjamin Franklin says, "Guests, like fish, begin to stink after three days." Ancient Israel's sages were well ahead of ole Ben:

Let your foot be seldom in your neighbor's house,
otherwise the neighbor will become weary of you and hate you. (25:17)

At issue in this proverb is monopolizing our friends' time, smothering them with our presence whether in their house, apartment, or dorm room. As a result, our friend and our friendship cannot breathe, and we will destroy the very thing we treasure.

At first glance, Proverbs 27:14 often made little sense to my students:

If anyone loudly blesses their neighbor early in the morning,
it will be taken as a curse. (NIV)

I helped my students understand the text by offering to call their room on Saturday to tell them how much I loved them. I promised to call as soon as I woke up, between 5:00 and 6:00 am. Suddenly, no one wanted me to call and bless them with a loud voice. Like monopolizing a friend's time, at issue here is consideration of another person's needs and wishes as opposed to focusing only on my selfish desires.

Be Insensitive to Feelings

We conclude with a mysterious proverb (in part because of an uncertain Hebrew text) translated by Michael Fox:

Like taking a cloak away on a cold day,
like vinegar on soda,
the one who sings songs to a sad heart. (25:20)[1]

Or from the New International Version:

Like one who takes away a garment on a cold day,
or like vinegar poured on a wound,
is one who sings songs to a heavy heart.

The first line makes sense: taking away a cloak on a cold day makes a person colder. The second line presents another picture of an unhelpful action, but it is difficult to translate and understand. Fox's pouring "vinegar on soda" will cause the soda to sizzle and is not helpful. In contrast, the NIV's "vinegar

1. Michael Fox, *Proverbs 10–31*, Anchor Bible 18B (New Haven: Yale University Press, 2009), 785–86.

poured on a wound" may promote healing but will also be painful. Thus, the third line assumes an action with a negative result: singing songs to a heavy heart is not helpful but hurtful to a person who is sad. This opposes the idea that music calms or soothes someone in pain, as in the story of David and Saul (1 Sam. 16:23). So we are left with the question, how is singing to someone with a heavy heart good or bad? The answer, I think, has to do with the type of song we sing. Soothing music may help a tortured soul, but upbeat, happy music is out of place and only makes the pain worse. Once again, the issue is appropriateness. We need to shape our response to our friend's needs. When it is time to weep, we cry with our friend, and when the time comes to laugh, we laugh with them (see Eccl. 3:4). Instead of focusing on our discomfort with pain and sadness and attempting to force our friend to get past their grief, we prioritize our friend's need to grieve.

Conclusion

How we relate to other people, friends, acquaintances, strangers, or family (see ch. 11) is often a clear indication of whether we are still trying to live "the good life" or if we are trying to live a life that is good. Those who chase the good life want their wishes and desires met. So they select us to be their "friend" based on their perceived needs and goals. Then they manipulate and control us to accomplish their own purposes, sometimes with such skill that we don't even realize we are being used until we are no longer of value and they toss us aside. But those who want to live a life that is good recognize that they are not the center of the universe. We described the depression of friendship at the beginning of this chapter. We can add to its causes the epidemic of narcissistic self-love in our society in which many people are self-centered, self-admiring, and self-absorbed. Instead, the sages call us to put others first, to honor their dignity as persons created by God, and to help them as much or more than they help us.

The sages caution that opening our lives to others makes us vulnerable to internal damage. When we need and rely on our friends, they may let us down—like a bad tooth or a lame foot (Prov. 25:19). A psalmist conveys the risk we take and the depth to which we could be hurt when he describes the brutal, unrelenting attack of an enemy (Ps. 55:1–11). He recognizes the assailant as his close friend—a blow that is as indescribably painful as it is surprising (55:12–14).

Nonetheless, opening our lives to close friendships provides the unique benefits of the presence of another: strength, resiliency, protection, and help to pick us up when we fail or fall. Even more important for living a life that is good, close friendships give us the opportunity to bless another person's life. We can provide security, a safe ear to listen, advice when called for, and dependable help in a crisis. Just as "iron sharpens iron," we help our friends and they help us become wiser and stronger (27:17). Maybe this is the idea behind the mysterious statement in Proverbs 18:1, given here in common translations for comparison:

> *The one who lives alone is self-indulgent,*
> *showing contempt for all who have sound judgment.* (NRSV)

> *An unfriendly person pursues selfish ends*
> *and against all sound judgment starts quarrels.* (NIV)

> *Unfriendly people care only about themselves;*
> *they lash out at common sense.* (NLT)

The first line somewhat literally says, "A person who wants to be alone." The idea is not that they live alone in a house, but that they see no need for other people, especially friendships. Based on the three translations above, it is obvious that the Hebrew in the second line is difficult to translate and understand. My best literal translation is, "he rails against all prudence," perhaps meaning that this person thinks he is above the need for others. His desire to be left alone without other people in his life, especially friends, ignores what the sages have said about good sense or wisdom. Perhaps he also "rails against" or speaks openly against the importance of friends in living a life that is good. We are created for relationships with other people, friends we can count on to be honest with us and who we can count on to still be around when everyone else has given up on us. Not even God, present as the Trinity or as the Son on earth, existed outside of relationships. Neither can we.

DISCUSSION QUESTIONS

1. Identify a person who is not a family member whom you would call in an emergency at three in the morning. If you are unable to think of someone now, has there been a time when you had such a friend? What has changed for you?
2. Do you agree with my claim that we are in a fifty-year friendship depression? If so, what contributes to or is causing this drought of close friend-

ships? What can we do to reverse this trend? If you disagree with my position, explain what you have seen or what leads you to differ.

3. What unites these types of behaviors: those easily angered, those who go to prostitutes, those who eat too much (gluttons), and those who drink too much (drunkards)? Who in our society belongs to these same groups or categories? Based on new insights, what have we learned about these types of behaviors that the sages of Israel did not know? How might we need to change our attitudes or approach to these groups?
4. Consider the traits of an ideal friend. Do you have a friend who exemplifies one or more of these attributes? If so, describe that person. In addition to the traits I identified, what other characteristics of a good friend do you find in Proverbs or in your experience of life? Describe these characteristics.
5. Consider the different ways in which the sages say we can sabotage our relationships. Have you experienced any of these behaviors? If so, what effect did it have on your relationship? In what other ways not mentioned in this chapter might a person sabotage or destroy a friendship?
6. Summarize the message of Proverbs regarding friendship. Beyond all the specific points, what major themes capture the message of the text?

PROJECT CHALLENGE

Investigate the ways in which text messaging, Twitter, and other social media platforms are changing the way we communicate with one another and the nature of friendship. What potential benefits are in these communication tools? What drawbacks or negative effects do they bring? What future do you see for these tools, and what changes will these tools bring to relationships? What wisdom do you have for how to live life well in this new world?

CHAPTER 11

Mom, Dad, and the Kids: Family Values in Proverbs

Families are like fudge—
mostly sweet with a few nuts.

—Author unknown

Grandchildren are the crown of the aged,
and the glory of children is their parents.

—Proverbs 17:6

It takes a village to raise a child.

—African proverb

TO PREPARE FOR READING THIS CHAPTER

Read the proverbs in either group #1 or group #2:

1. Proverbs 1:8; 2:16–19; 3:11–12, 13–18, 21; 4:3–9; 5:1–23; 6:20, 23–35; 7:1–27; 10:1, 5; 11:16, 22, 29; 12:4, 7; 13:1, 22, 24; 14:1, 11, 26; 15:5–6, 17, 20, 25, 27; 17:1–2, 6, 13, 21, 25; 18:22; 19:13–14, 18, 26, 27; 20:7, 11, 20–21, 30; 21:9, 12, 19–20; 22:6, 15; 23:13–26; 24:3–4, 13–14, 21–22, 27; 25:24; 27:8, 10–11, 15–16; 28:7, 24; 29:3, 15, 17; 30:11, 17; 31:1–3, 10–31
2. Proverbs 2:16–19; 3:11–12, 13–18; 4:3–9; 5:1–23; 6:20, 23–35; 7:1–27; 15:5–6; 17:1–2; 19:13–14; 20:20–21; 21:19–20; 22:6; 23:13–26; 24:3–4; 27:10–11, 15–16; 31:1–3, 10–31

The culture wars of the second half of the twentieth century in the United States featured what was frequently termed "the battle for the family" or the battle for "biblical family values." On one side stood the challenge of "liberal" (or postmodern) thought that questioned traditional family structures and values. On the other side, organizations such as Focus on the Family and the

Family Research Council dug in along the lines of "Christian family values" such as antiabortion, male leadership of the home, and rejection of homosexuality. For this side, Proverbs became a major resource for carpet bombing the opposition with one verse after another. From the other side, the longer the war went on, the more they pointed out that "biblical family values" are in fact nothing more than traditional American family values from the mid-twentieth century superimposed on favorite Bible verses, and they warned against confusing nostalgia for a bygone era with biblical principles.

Our examination of family values in Proverbs will push us to recognize and identify cultural practices at work behind the text. For example, the sages assumed that everyone in their world would marry. Most often, parents arranged the marriage, occasionally giving their sons and daughters some degree of choice, depending on the culture and historical era. For example, Rebekah was asked if she was willing to marry Isaac (Gen. 24:55–61), and Jacob arranged his own marriages (Gen. 29:16–30). Regardless, the book of Proverbs assumes that everyone will marry. Today of course not everyone chooses marriage or remarries after divorce or the death of their spouse. It is possible for a woman to work and support herself and her family, unlike most eras and places in the ancient Near East. And I don't hear of many who practice or advocate for the biblical practice of arranged marriages in the United States.

Second, the sages assumed that every marriage would produce children. Based on the rural setting of some proverbs (see 13:23; 24:27, 30–34; 27:23–27), social-science research suggests that reproductive patterns in ancient Israel may have been somewhat like those of early American families who farmed and raised livestock. Couples needed all the help they could get, especially sons who would not leave the estate as daughters did through marriage. Sons would also care for their mother if their father died first. In ancient Israel, however, the formation of a large family with four to six children was not easily accomplished. One problem then and now was infertility. Consequently when the first wife did not have children within the first few years of marriage, some Mesopotamian cultures allowed a husband to take a second wife of lesser status, or a concubine, or his wife could give him a slave as a surrogate mother.[1] We see this practice in the stories of Sarah and Abraham as well as Jacob and his wives (Gen. 16; 30:1–22). Also an issue in ancient Israel, though not as much in modern cultures, was high infant and adolescent mortality rates. Carol Meyers documents that only fifty percent of children lived to the age of

1. Elisabeth Meier Tetlow, *The Ancient Near East*, vol. 1 of *Women, Crime, and Punishment in Ancient Law and Society* (New York: Continuum, 2004), 56, 121.

eighteen. Women would have had to produce twice the number of children desired in order to achieve an optimal family size.[2] Meyers also reports that women faced significant risk of death in childbearing, a risk that made the average life expectancy for females thirty years, compared to forty years for males.[3]

Third, the size of the family and the enormous work load to survive led ancient Israelites to define "family" as the father, his wife (or wives), their sons and their families, and any slaves and servants all living together in a cluster of tents or buildings. Such a household or family might grow to the size of a small community of fifty to a hundred people. Obviously, we recognize that our definition of a "nuclear family" is incredibly different by composition, nature, and function.

Finally, it is also critical that we notice the gender bias of Proverbs, expressed in the prologue (1:1–7; see ch. 1) and systematically followed throughout the book. Proverbs aims primarily at men, especially young men who are taking more responsibility for their lives and their decisions. Consequently, the sages consistently spoke to men about their lives and about women only as they relate to men's lives and interests. Proverbs does not speak directly to women about their lives, about the men who threaten their well-being, or about the danger of marriage to a bad man. Four exceptions to this gender bias may exist, depending on how we interpret four texts or types of texts.

The longest text that may speak to women, "The Ode to the Worthy Woman" (31:10–31), might stand as an awkward exception at the end of a book that has not spoken to women in the prior thirty chapters. Or as discussed in chapter 2, the Ode may not be an exception or a surprise at all, but a depiction of life with Woman Wisdom and a fitting finale for a book about men and their interests.

Women are specifically mentioned in several statements that include both the father and mother (Prov. 1:8; 6:20; 10:1; 15:20; 17:25; 20:20; 23:22, 24–25; 28:24; 30:11, 17). These texts certainly recognize the son's mother as part of the parental unit, but to what extent she functions independently in these verses is unclear.

In a similar fashion, other texts use the Hebrew term *ab*: literally translated, "father" or "fathers," but sometimes meaning "parent" or "parents." The Hebrew language does not have a distinct word for "parent" other than *ab*.

2. Carol Meyers, *Discovering Eve: Ancient Israelite Women in Context* (New York: Oxford University Press, 1988), 112.

3. Meyers, *Discovering Eve*, 112–13.

Thus, we are faced with the difficulty of how to understand this term each time it appears in Proverbs. Consequently, English translations vary. To take one example, compare the translation of 15:5a.

> *A fool rejects his father's* (ab) *discipline* (NASB, see also the CEB, KJV)

> *A fool despises a parent's* (ab) *instruction* (NRSV, see also NIV, CEV, NLT)

Also see and compare the translations of 17:6, 21; 19:14; 27:10; 28:7; 29:3. In addition, the sages often use masculine pronouns to refer to the father (e.g., he, him, his), which may also be translated to include both parents. Again, to take one example, compare the translations of the masculine singular pronouns in 13:24, translated literally by the NASB.

> *He who withholds his rod hates his son,*
> *but he who loves him disciplines him diligently.* (NASB; see also KJV)

> *Those who spare the rod hate their children,*
> *but those who love them are diligent to discipline them.* (NRSV; see also NLT, NIV, CEB)

> *If you love your children, you will correct them;*
> *if you don't love them, you won't correct them.* (CEV)

Consider the same translation issue in 14:26; 20:7; 29:17. Without doubt, at least some of these texts are inclusive of both father and mother, but each case requires its own careful study and translation—beyond the space available here.

Finally, in a few texts, the sages recognize women for their potential in the formation of the home or family. On the positive side, a "wise woman builds her house" (14:1a), and a gracious woman will gain honor for herself (11:16), just as a good wife "is the crown of her husband" (12:4a; see also 18:22; 19:14). But from my perspective, it is unfortunate that when the sages do recognize women, most often their statements are negative. The sages compare a beautiful woman without sense to "a gold ring in a pig's snout" (11:22) and it is the mother, not the father, who is disgraced by a child who has not been properly trained or corrected (29:15). In addition to these, we also find several proverbs that speak about the problem of a quarrelsome or contentious wife (19:13; 21:9, 19; 27:15–16; cf. 12:4b; see below).

Though the book's wisdom includes discussion of women, it is not difficult to reach a verdict: gender bias is woven into the fabric of Proverbs. As in chapter one, I have no answers or solutions. It is easy for me, as a man, to say, "I don't like it, but to work constructively we need to accept the witness as it is." I see the problem, and as much as possible, I recognize the difficulty this presents to women, not only left out of the man's world again, but also blamed again for what men do wrong (e.g., 7:21–23). All I know to do is to be sensitive to the very real problem, listen well, and acknowledge the pain caused by these texts. Then together we can read these texts in context, discern the principles they present, do our best to transpose these values for our culture, and work to bring about change in the way we speak about families and family values, leaving no one out of the conversation.

In addition, as we move forward it's important to remember that though much or even most of the book of Proverbs originally addressed young men (see 1:4–5 and ch. 1 of this book), the values and principles of wisdom are true for everyone: young and old, male and female. The principles we have learned in prior chapters apply to family values and practices. For example, our families are affected for good or bad by our wisdom or folly (chs. 2 and 4), our practice of justice and mercy within the family and toward others (ch. 6), how we speak to one another (ch. 7), the family's handling of money (ch. 8), the way in which parents lead the family (ch. 9), and even the friends of the family (ch. 10). Wisdom is all-inclusive.

Family Values

Family values do not live on the surface of the text of Proverbs in specifics but behind the instructions and sayings, informing and prompting their existence. So to get at these principles, we need to learn how to do the Texas Two Step. And should this dance with the text not work, just remember you learned it from a guy who grew up in a tradition that viewed dancing to be a sin *and* a guy who now can't exactly do the Two Step in his wheelchair.

For each song or theme, the first step is to identify the descriptions or instructions that pertain to a common aspect of family life, while the second step envisions the desired outcomes of these proverbs. Outcomes or actions are not equivalent to family values, but indicators of one or more values. So in what might be called a final step, we will get a drink, sit down, and reflect on the family values that emerge from these texts. The band has begun to play our first song, so I ask in our final pages together, *will you dance with me?*

Song #1: Listen to Your Parents

Step One: Instructions

Even if we toss aside most of the father/son language of chapters 1–9 because it describes a teacher/pupil relationship (see ch. 1, nn. 5 and 6), we still find two speeches from the mother and father to the son (1:8; 6:20). Outside these chapters we also find other appeals for children to listen to the teaching and correction of parents, both mother and father. For example,

> *Listen to your father who begot you,*
> *and do not despise your mother when she is old.* (23:22)

And a little later:

> *The father of the righteous will greatly rejoice;*
> *he who begot a wise son will be glad in him.*
> *Let your father and mother be glad;*
> *let her who bore you rejoice.* (23:24–25; see also 10:1; 15:20; 30:17)

Worse than disobedience—and the ultimate end of children who do not respond to their parents' teaching and correction—are children who curse their parents and "do not bless their mothers" (30:11; cf. 20:20), those who rob their parents and don't consider it to be a crime (28:24), and those who "do violence to their father and chase away their mother" (19:26).

Step Two: Expected Actions

These proverbs anticipate children at home who listen to and obey their parents' instruction.[4] In ancient Israel, there were few if any alternative systems for instructing the next generation other than the family (see song #5 below). Consequently, a child's future depended on her or his willingness to learn from their parents. The same is true today, despite the presence of public and private schools, Sunday schools, and even vacation Bible school. It is through the practice of listening to and obeying our parents that we develop the virtue

4. For those living in family groups or compounds in ancient Israel, the instruction of parents extended well beyond the childhood or even adolescent years.

of being teachable: people who listen well, who learn how to learn, and who respond appropriately to those in authority. Becoming obedient children sets a pattern for the rest of our lives.

Song #2: The Good Wife and Husband

Step One: Instructions

Some proverbs speak positively about the impact of each spouse on the marriage and family. Regarding the woman, the sages write, "a gracious woman gets honor" (Prov. 11:16a), and "a good wife is the crown of her husband" (12:4a). "The wise woman builds her house" (14:1a). And the man who has such a wife "finds a good thing, and obtains favor from the LORD" (18:22). Parents may provide an inheritance, "but a prudent wife is from the LORD" (19:14).[5]

Other proverbs do not specifically mention a wife or husband, but establish basic principles that apply to both.[6] A house is built by wisdom and established by "understanding" (24:3). Through knowledge the rooms are filled "with all precious and pleasant riches" (24:4). The Lord blesses the home of the righteous (3:33b). Their house will not only "stand" (12:7b), but their "tent" will flourish (14:11b) and their work will bring "much treasure" (15:6a; 21:20a). The "good" will leave an inheritance to their children and grandchildren (13:22). It's no surprise that the children of the righteous who live with integrity will be happy or blessed (20:7). Finally, the fear of the Lord provides security for one's children (14:26).

Step Two: Expected Actions

Because the parents arranged the marriage of their children, a young man or young woman in ancient Israel did not "date" to select a husband or wife. Consequently, these statements about wives and husbands were not intended to guide a young person's selection of a spouse. Such an interpretation reads

5. Some may wish to include the virtues of the worthy woman (31:10–31) in this section (see ch. 2).

6. Because the book of Proverbs is primarily addressed to men, it may be assumed that these texts speak directly to them. Nonetheless, the principles are equally valid for fathers and mothers, husbands and wives, women and men.

too much of our society into the text. Instead, these proverbs identify and emphasize the character qualities vital to the well-being of a marriage, home, and children, virtues for both partners to seek and develop: graciousness, prudence, understanding, knowledge, and righteousness. In essence, the sages say that together, those who fear the Lord and are wise will build and establish a stable home.

Song #3: The Bad Husband and Wife

Step One: Instructions

We now reverse our movement to the negative descriptions, beginning with statements that apply equally to the husband and wife, and how they may negatively impact their marriages and families. Just as fools devour whatever they might earn or gain (21:20b), leaving nothing for their children to inherit, "those who trouble their households will inherit wind" (11:29). "The LORD's curse is on the house of the wicked" (3:33a). The Lord will cause trouble to come with their income (15:6b), just as a person who returns evil for good and a greedy person bring trouble on their homes (17:13; 15:27). The "Righteous One observes the house of the wicked" and "casts the wicked down to ruin" (21:12; see also 12:7a; 14:11a). In the same way, "the LORD tears down the house of the proud" (15:25a).

The next set of proverbs makes me wince in pain at the situations and the words the sages use to describe certain women. Here, the qualities of a bad wife and mother are on display with harsh metaphors not used for men. A quarrelsome wife is like a leaky roof or "a continual dripping of rain" (19:13b; 27:15). Such a wife is impossible for her husband to control; he would succeed just as well with trying to control the wind or holding oil in his hands (27:16). She will bring him shame (12:4b) and make his life so miserable that he will prefer living "in a corner of the housetop" (21:9) or in "a desert land" (21:19).

Perhaps it's not surprising that a book written by men to men would speak negatively about their wives, but not about men or husbands. Other than general statements mentioned above, husbands dodge harsh negative judgments. This makes the words about wives all the more hurtful and disappointing to us. Despite the silence, however, we know that wives in ancient Israel faced the same difficulties with their husbands as they do today (and perhaps more): critical attitudes, abusive words and actions, and destructive habits (e.g., drunkenness).

Step Two: Expected Actions

These proverbs commiserate with the husband or wife whose spouse is ruining their marriage and family. Even more, these proverbs acknowledge the power for good or ill within the actions of both the wife and the husband. As a result, each of us should hear an encouragement and warning to take our role seriously, recognizing the consequences our actions have on those we love. No one can control another person, despite self-assurances that "we will change him or her" or futile efforts to recreate our spouse into our ideal image. Instead, wisdom teaches us to focus on our own character, especially avoiding traits that will harm our spouses or families: greedily gaining wealth through dubious means, spending every dime that we earn rather than saving, growing in conceit or pride, and living wicked rather than righteous lives. In particular, the sages warn us against negative attitudes that lead us to complain (about everything) and to argue (about everything). Whether wife or husband, such attitudes and practices make our spouses miserable and eager to be away from us, not to mention our children.

Song #4: Stay True to Your Spouse

Step One: Instructions

Four speeches in chapters 1–9 warn the young man regarding involvement with an "other woman," any woman who is not his wife (2:16–19; 5:3–14; 6:23–35; 7:1–23). Our prior examination of these texts allows for brevity here (see ch. 2). The father warns his son that there is no quicker way to destroy himself and his family than by becoming involved with other women (married or unmarried). Those who engage in affairs typically convince themselves that they will never be caught, and even if they are, nothing terrible will happen to them. In response, the sages consistently and forcefully tell the youths that they are wrong about both claims. Three texts in Proverbs 10–31 reinforce these themes.

- A person who leaves home is like a bird that strays from the nest, unprotected from the elements and without a place to call home (27:8).
- A son who chases prostitutes wastes family resources (29:3).
- King Lemuel's mother warns him not to "give his strength to women" who will rob her son of his strength (31:1–3) and draw his attention away from what is most important (as in 31:4–5).

Instead, the sages encourage loyalty to one's own spouse (5:15–17) along with the general virtues of loyalty and faithfulness (e.g., 3:3; 16:6; 19:22; 20:6).

Step Two: Expected Actions

In principle, the sages encourage married couples to be loyal to each other with such singular commitment that they would never consider being with another man or woman. Fidelity in relationships is a virtue of wisdom. Sometimes, those who are married may be tempted to find fulfillment of some need that should be part of their marriage in someone, something, or somewhere other than their spouse. Psychologists recognize this need/fulfillment as the essence of infidelity, whether it is emotional, financial, or sexual. Consequently, not only does wisdom encourage us to be faithful to our spouses, it teaches us to be the kind of spouse who fulfills the needs of our partner. And though the sages' words appear to address solely those in covenant relationships (the norm in ancient Israel), wisdom also calls for the unmarried to recognize and respect the commitments made by marriage vows by not having any type of affair with a person who is married.

Song #5: Teach and Correct Your Children

Step One: Instructions

We began with the wisdom of children listening to and obeying their parents, a practice only possible if parents are, in fact, teaching their children. This final song may be heard amid many general proverbs that do not specifically address parents or spell out practices for the home. For example, we hear that a wise child harvests in summer, but those who love to sleep bring shame (10:5). It stands to reason that it is a parent's task to teach and correct their child so that they learn the value of work. Or since wise children bless or make their parents happy (10:1; 15:20), parents should teach and lead their children toward wisdom. In Proverbs 24, we find an example of a parent explicitly appealing to their child to "fear the LORD and the king" and not disobey them because of the awesome power they both wield (24:21–22).[7]

7. Depending on the identity of the father and son or child in Proverbs 1–9, we may have many examples of a father or father and mother teaching their children (see ch. 1).

In their teaching of children, the sages also advise parents to correct or redirect their children. For example:

> *Discipline your children while there is hope;*
> *do not set your heart on their destruction.* (19:18)

Despite the popular translation "discipline" (Hebrew *musar*), because of the associated baggage and misunderstanding surrounding this term, when *musar* has this meaning I choose to translate it "correction" or sometimes "redirection" (see discussion below). Perhaps because correction is not easy, the sages include several sayings that seek to motivate parents. They point out that while correction helps children, it is also good for the parents' future because instruction and correction produces adult children who give their parents rest and delight (29:17). There is no fate worse for a parent than to have a child who is foolish. Such a parent will experience grief and bitterness (10:1b; 17:25), trouble and a lack of joy (17:21), ruin (19:13a), shame, and reproach (19:26; 28:7b). In addition, their children may despise them (15:20b) or even curse them (20:20). But children who act in wise ways will make their parents happy (10:1a; 29:3) and bring them joy (23:15–16, 25). Avoiding the bad and enjoying the good motivate parents not only to teach, but to correct and redirect their children as necessary. How to achieve this correction raises the topic of corporal or physical discipline or correction, a topic that we temporarily defer for later discussion.

Step Two: Expected Actions

In ancient Israel, there were few if any systems for instructing the next generation other than the family. In recent years, researchers have debated the existence of schools in Israel, with the conclusion that if any schools existed, they were exclusively for young men from the royal family and other court personnel. Thus, responsibility for teaching children fell to the parents. Both parents would be involved, each teaching specific skills as well as common values. If children learned anything about their world or fearing God, it came from their parents with the support of others in the family community. To a large degree, despite our cultural differences the same is true today. We as parents often teach our children far more than we recognize because our children are watching and learning from us whether we realize it or not. They learn from watching how we interact with others, how we work, how we pray, how we talk, and so much more than just what we say to them as "instruction" or "correction." So the real question for us as parents is not whether or not we teach, but what do we teach our children?

The Third Step: Family Values

We have now listened to five tunes about the family from Proverbs (even if we refused to dance).

- Song #1: Listen to your parents.
- Song #2: The good wife and husband.
- Song #3: The bad husband and wife.
- Song #4: Stay true to your spouse.
- Song #5: Teach and correct your children.

Now it's time to get a drink, step back, and carefully consider the specific notes and words on family values in these songs. Before we sit down, however, the history of interpretation, or better stated the history of *misapplication*, leads me to add two reminders:

- We must remember that proverbs are general statements of truth that fit some but not necessarily all situations. If it required wisdom over two thousand years ago to know when and how to use a proverb, how much more wisdom is required of us as we try to make sense of these texts and use them.
- We must also remember that what we find in Proverbs is culturally conditioned. The wisdom of Proverbs is not expressed ahistorical, apart from history, but in the cultural clothing of ancient Israel. Sometimes people advocate for a specific practice because they read about it in Proverbs. But specific practices are only the clothing worn by the Israelites, their cultural expression of the values or principles.

I fear the potential damage we may inflict if we forget these or other aspects of how proverbs work (please see ch. 3). So with these brief reminders, let's sit down with a refreshing beverage of your choice and talk about family values.

Family Value 1: Passing on Wisdom

By nature, a child's heart is bound up with folly that only instruction and correction can take away (22:15). Left alone, a child will not become wise (29:15), a tragedy for both the child and the larger family unit, which needs children to develop wisdom and find their place within the family. Thus, the first family value that stands out in the book of Proverbs is the commitment to pass on wisdom to the next generation.

The sages assume that parents will teach their children about God and lead them to fear the Lord, the beginning point of wisdom (9:10). The sages also explicitly direct parents to teach their children:

> *Train children in the right way,*
> *and when old, they will not stray.* (22:6)

The book of Proverbs also frequently records the address of parents to their children, urging them to pay attention, listen, remember, and not forget their teaching. Thus, children will learn to fear the Lord and gain wisdom.

> *Hear, my child, and be wise,*
> *and direct your mind in the way.* (23:19)

> *Listen to your father who begot you,*
> *and do not despise your mother when she is old.*
> *Buy truth, and do not sell it;*
> *buy wisdom, instruction, and understanding.* (23:22–23)

> *My child, fear the LORD and the king,*
> *and do not disobey either of them;*
> *for disaster comes from them suddenly,*
> *and who knows the ruin that both can bring?* (24:21–22)

Parents also call upon children to follow their example (23:26).

If we take the frequency of the sages' words to be indicative, then it is crucial for parents to pass wisdom to the next generation by all forms of teaching, correction, and redirection. Success may often depend on the parents' commitment to raising wise children. However, the sages also recognize an individual's responsibility for their own decisions. As mentioned earlier in our discussion of how to read a proverb (see ch. 3), a parent's instruction does not guarantee that their children will be wise or walk on the right path (22:6). By nature, proverbs do not offer promises or guarantees, but express general truths for many situations. So yes, it is generally true that children who are trained well will follow the right path as adults, but this is certainly not always true. It is not the parent's fault every time a child leaves the path of wisdom. Rather, in Proverbs, the successful passage of wisdom from one generation to the next is a cooperative effort between parents and children.

Family Value 2: Harmony or Family Unity

Almost every category or group of proverbs includes wisdom for creating family unity: those on youths who listen to and obey their parents as opposed to rebelling against parental authority; those on parents who provide appropriate correction as opposed to neglect or heavy-handed approaches; those on marriage to a righteous and wise spouse as opposed to the discord caused by a wicked spouse who does not follow the path of wisdom; and those on strong, united marriages as opposed to those torn apart by affairs.

Like Proverbs, Psalm 133:1 states, "How very good and pleasant it is when kindred live together in unity!" In Proverbs, two texts express the value of family unity or harmony over the acquisition or presence of wealth:

> *Better a meal of greens with love*
> *than a plump calf with hate.* (15:17 CEB)

> *Better a dry crust with quiet*
> *than a house full of feasting with quarrels.* (17:1 CEB)

Ideally, family unity is the result of a common commitment to wisdom, beginning with the fear of the Lord or a proper relationship with the Lord. Notice, for example:

> *In the fear of the* LORD *one has strong confidence,*
> *and one's children will have a refuge.* (14:26)

> *Better is a little with the fear of the* LORD
> *than great treasure and trouble with it.* (15:16)

The fear of the LORD *is life indeed;*
filled with it one rests secure
and suffers no harm. (19:23)

Other proverbs, however, vividly warn against actions that threaten family harmony or unity:

- Children who mock or scorn their parents (30:17).
- Children who curse their mothers or fathers (20:20).
- Foolish women (or men) who to tear down or destroy their own homes (14:1).
- Family members, especially parents, who bring the threat of destruction and ruin because of their wickedness (14:11a; 21:12) and pride (15:25).

Instead, it is "tent of the upright" that flourishes (14:11b).

Family Value 3: Commitment to Marriage

A third family value is commitment to marriage. In Proverbs 1–7, the sages present strong arguments against sexual, emotional, or any other involvement with a person who is not our spouse (see ch. 2). The first comes early in the book. The father advocates the vigilant pursuit of wisdom and the Lord's gift of wisdom (2:1–8) as the most effective vaccine against a married woman who ignores her vows:

You will be saved from the loose woman,
from the adulteress with her smooth words,
who forsakes the partner of her youth
and forgets her sacred covenant (2:16–17, emphasis mine)

Positive encouragement to remain faithful to one's spouse is contained primarily in Proverbs 5:

Drink water from your own cistern,
flowing water from your own well.
Should your springs be scattered abroad,
streams of water in the streets?
Let them be for yourself alone,

and not for sharing with strangers.
Let your fountain be blessed,
and rejoice in the wife of your youth,
a lovely deer, a graceful doe.
May her breasts satisfy you at all times;
may you be intoxicated always by her love.
Why should you be intoxicated, my son, by another woman
and embrace the bosom of an adulteress? (5:15–20)

Instead of falling into the arms of another woman (5:3–10, 23), the sage exhorts the young man to be faithful to his wife and committed to her alone. It's not difficult to transfer their instruction to wives:

Drink water from your own cistern,
flowing water from your own well. . . .

Let your fountain be blessed,
and rejoice in the husband of your youth,
a stately deer, a strong buck.
May his love-making satisfy you at all times;
may you be intoxicated always by his love.
Why should you be intoxicated, my daughter, by another man
and embrace a man who only wants one thing?

Fidelity to our marriage vows, all of our vows, sexual and nonsexual, is a key family value for the sages in the book of Proverbs, a value that in its fullest expression calls upon women and men, married or single, to respect and support the marriage vows made by others.

Family Value 4: Commitment to Our Children and Corporal Punishment

It is obvious from what we have already seen that corporal or physical punishment was a common practice in ancient Israel, as it was throughout the ancient Near East. For example, *The Words of Ahiqar*, a wisdom text from Assyria, includes this proverb:

Spare not your son from the rod;
otherwise can you save him from wickedness?

If I beat you, my son, you will not die;
but if I leave you alone, [you will not live].[8]

The book of Proverbs includes a similar saying and other like-minded texts:

Do not withhold discipline from your children;
if you beat them with a rod, they will not die.
If you beat them with the rod,
you will save their lives from Sheol. (23:13–14)

Those who spare the rod hate their children,
but those who love them are diligent to discipline them. (13:24)[9]

Unfortunately, it's not uncommon to hear these proverbs quoted as proof that God supports harsh physical punishment of children: "Spare the rod and spoil the child" (a poor paraphrase of 13:24), or "It's not going to kill you" (a terrible paraphrase of 23:13). But worse, far worse is that it is not uncommon that a parent who abuses these texts also abuses their children.

For this reason, our work here calls for our best wisdom and listening to others with great care, including Ellen Davis and Dave Bland, among others.[10] We begin with important definitions of the key words that shape how we think and consequently how we act. First, the Hebrew word *musar* has a range of meaning that includes instruction, education, reminder, warning, correction, discipline. Sometimes *musar* is roughly equivalent to rebuke (12:1; 15:11) or reproof (3:11; 5:12; 6:23). Essentially, in Proverbs *musar* appears to denote anything done to help someone develop wisdom and good character. For example in the introduction, Proverbs claims the purpose "for learning about wisdom and instruction (*musar*)" (1:2) and explains that "fools despise wisdom and instruction (*musar*)" (1:7; see 15:32). Elsewhere in Proverbs, *musar* means correction, an action to stop or redirect negative behavior, specifically by means of "the rod" (13:24; 22:15; 23:13).

Second, the "rod" is synonymous with physical redirection, a negative response to stop a negative behavior. I avoid the English term "punishment" (for

8. James M. Lindenberger, trans., "Ahikar," in *A Reader of Ancient Near Eastern Texts*, ed. Michael Coogan (New York: Oxford University Press, 2013), 208.

9. See additional references to the "rod" in 10:13; 14:3; 26:3; 29:15.

10. See Ellen Davis, *Proverbs, Ecclesiastes, and the Song of Songs*, Westminster Bible Companion (Louisville: Westminster John Knox, 2000), 25–27, 87–89, 125–27; and Dave Bland, *Proverbs and the Formation of Character* (Eugene, OR: Cascade Books, 2015), 24–29.

musar) in these contexts because of its association with simple retribution or making someone pay for their mistakes, without the primary purpose of character formation or re-formation. In its original formulation, "the rod" meant striking with a rod. Ideally, the purpose for such an action was to "scrub away evil" and "purge the inmost being" (20:30 NIV), or to bring about a change of heart. In what follows, I propose that these definitions and the wisdom we have gained over the centuries about human development and behavior lead us to interpret "the rod" as the best method for stopping and redirecting foolish behavior—whatever that method may be for a given situation, not simply spanking, hitting, or physically striking.

Most responses to the issue of "the rod" fall into one of two extreme positions. At one extreme, some use these texts as a God-given advocacy to physically whip, spank, or hurt children in order to "discipline" them. At the other extreme, some dismiss these texts as old wisdom replaced today by better insights and understanding, or new wisdom. For example Ellen Davis points out that, "Contemporary psychology alerts us to the fact that the harsh discipline of young children frequently has violent repercussions when they become adults."[11] She also explains why the nature of wisdom requires growth and change: "[the wisdom] tradition is neither immutable nor closed. On the contrary, it *must* grow and change in order to be 'tradition,' literally '(a process of) passing on' from mind to mind, and not merely an artifact preserved in a history book. Tradition is *the shared learning of the community over time*."[12]

In other words, Davis brings us back to a critical question in our study of Proverbs that I introduced in chapter 1: To what degree or extent is our wisdom, observation, or experience of life relevant? Is our wisdom a valid source for theological reflection and decision making? Does it matter if we know or understand things now that the biblical sages didn't know then? In other words, does wisdom grow with human exploration—gaining new insights into human behavior, life, and relationships—and understanding God's world? Or is wisdom static: only what is said in Proverbs or another biblical text is wise?

Quickly, I must add that Davis *does not mean* that these particular proverbs have no relevance. While Davis values today's wisdom on the subject of redirection over the ancient traditions in Proverbs, she still wrestles with the principles that inform these specific practices and the bigger picture in the book of Proverbs. In this task, she is joined by Dave Bland, who takes a position toward the middle of the two extremes. He does not dismiss the ancient wis-

11. Davis, *Proverbs*, 87.

12. Davis, *Proverbs*, 88 (emphasis original).

dom, nor does he advocate harsh physical punishment. Instead, Bland argues for careful exploration of the "meaning of these proverbs in their theological context."[13] From different starting points, both Davis and Bland search for principles behind the specific practices that should guide our reading and application of these texts. Following their advice, I see three primary principles that gave shape to the Israelites' practices of instruction and redirection that should equally shape our actions.

Principle #1: Love Guides the Way

In Proverbs, physical redirection, "the rod," is used the context of love and concern for the well-being of another person. In Proverbs 23:13–14, parents are encouraged to use the rod to correct their child and save their lives from the grave. And in 13:24, only parents who love their children will correct them, just as the Lord corrects those he loves (3:11–12). In other words, the rod—whether physical, verbal, or any other form discipline might take, must always be controlled by love. "The rod" must not be used when a parent is frustrated, angry, embarrassed, or doesn't know what else to do. The sages even warn us that whenever discipline or correction is not controlled and motivated by love, at best it will not work. And more often than not, because it is an unjust behavior, it will create even more problems: "the rod of anger will fail" (22:8b).

Davis offers further support for love-controlled correction by observing that no proverb about the discipline of children is ever more than a few verses away from another proverb cautioning against excessive anger.[14] For example, Proverbs 19:18:

> *Discipline your children while there is hope;*
> *do not set your heart on their destruction.*

This is followed immediately by

> *A violent tempered person will pay the penalty;*
> *if you effect a rescue, you will only have to do it again.* (19:19; see also 29:11, 15, 17)

13. Bland, *Proverbs and the Formation of Character*, 25.
14. Davis, *Proverbs*, 126.

Bland reminds us that within the larger context of the book of Proverbs, the virtue of self-restraint informs all other actions (see 16:32; 25:28), as does patience (12:16; 14:29; 15:18). And sometimes a soft answer is the strongest possible form of redirection (15:1).[15] Consequently, when we lash out at children in any way that is not dominated by love and controlled by self-restraint, we are being abusive. We are not practicing wise discipline as taught by the sages. "Occasionally, love demands tough action," Bland writes, "however, it *never* involves abuse."[16]

Principle #2: First and Last

We know today that, as Davis writes, "The internalization of discipline belongs to an early stage of child development, certainly within the first ten years."[17] In harmony with this contemporary insight, the sages stress early redirection for character development, as opposed to the parental indulgence of allowing children to go their own way, believing that they may intervene when they are older. Parents are responsible for redirecting their "children while there is still hope" (19:18), to act before it will be too late. Do not neglect a child, the sages warn, because skipping action now will cause a child to disgrace the family (29:15). Davis even asserts that failure to help a child acquire self-discipline is "the most grievous form of child abuse."[18] The emphasis on this point in Proverbs may be motivated by a tendency toward laziness or selfishness, perhaps because character formation is difficult. It is difficult to correct in love, difficult to be fair, difficult to be consistent, and difficult not to go too far. In other words, indulgence is the path of least resistance. And wise instruction (in all forms) is not only difficult, it can be exhausting and cause us great pain. Sometimes, wise correction is enormously difficult to practice because as a child, the parent never saw or experienced loving discipline. Their childhood was spent with a foolish parent or maybe parents doing the best they could, but who didn't know how either, which is a growing problem that calls for the community of faith to respond in wise ways.

It is noteworthy that outside the family, the sages in Proverbs only speak of using the rod on fools and those who lack sense:

15. Bland, *Proverbs and the Formation of Character*, 26.

16. Bland, *Proverbs and the Formation of Character*, 25 (emphasis original).

17. Davis, *Proverbs*, 89.

18. Davis, *Proverbs*, 126.

A whip for the horse, a bridle for the donkey,
and a rod for the back of fools. (26:3)

On the lips of one who has understanding wisdom is found,
but a rod is for the back of one who lacks sense. (10:13; see also 14:3a)

In other words, Proverbs indicates that in these cases, the rod is not the first but last recourse in an effort to redirect a person who has moved far down the path of becoming a fool (see ch. 4). The sages do not bring out the rod for a person's first mistake, or the fifth. They only resort to the rod when it is absolutely necessary. When fools are closing in on the point of no return, the rod is their last hope. The implication of this observation for the discipline of children cannot be over emphasized. For ancient Israel's sages, harsh physical redirection did not belong at the beginning of character formation but the end. It was an ultimate act that attempted to reform the youth's character. So while the sages in Proverbs regard character formation as a parent's first task, at the same time they suggest that the rod is the measure of last resort.

Principle #3: From Discipline to Self-Discipline

Davis points out that obedience is not best motivated from the outside, "to make us do things we don't want to do."[19] Rather to have any lasting effect, a child must love and internalize discipline so that it becomes "self-discipline." Ideally, children will learn to listen to those with wisdom, searching for wisdom and committing themselves to living a life that is good (see 4:13; 8:10; 23:23; 24:32). The parents' task is to help children learn to love, search for, and internalize wisdom, not merely force them to do one thing after another against their will. In fact, not every deliberate act of disobedience deserves harsh repercussions, much less forgetful infringement. Can we even begin to imagine what life would be like if God treated us this way? Nor does every act of disobedience merit harsh consequences. Such an approach to parenting fails to capture the bigger picture or our ultimate goal: character development that leads a child to live a life that is good—not the production of perfectly obedient children who demonstrate a parent's skill. In fact, an overbearing approach to parenting is addressed by the apostle Paul, who writes, "Fathers, do not provoke your children, or they may lose heart" (Col. 3:21).

19. Davis, *Proverbs*, 26.

Two Conclusions and a Conclusion

Conclusion One

Many of the individual threads from previous chapters may further help us understand character formation in children and our responsibility: what we have learned about God and the attitudes we are called to have toward those who are vulnerable, usually defined in Scripture as the widow, the poor, and the orphan, to which we may add all children because of their vulnerability. Certainly, we will agree that child abuse is never appropriate. That said, the sages help us identify different ways that adults may abuse children. First, parents may abuse children through neglect, including a failure to provide the structure and instruction they need to develop self-discipline and wisdom. Second, an adult may abuse a child when they act in an uncontrolled manner, whether out of anger, frustration, or any other unrestrained emotion. Third, our objective must stand tall: to help children attain wisdom and a life that is good, not "break their will" or "break their spirit." Such an attitude equates godly parenting with harsh punishment for every minor infraction, a foolish policy that supports a parent's ego rather than the needs of a child.

Conclusion Two

The family values we have discerned here should be placed in their contexts of ancient Israel and the Old Testament as a whole. But even then our task is not complete; in many ways our work has only begun. The sages suggest, and the book of Job demands, that present conclusions always remain open to new insights. So we must learn from contemporary studies of child development and best practices for redirecting children. If we miss this practice of wisdom, I fear we may have seen many trees in the preceding pages but entirely missed the forest.

And a Conclusion

One of the most important themes in the book of Proverbs can be summarized as follows: those who pursue "the good life," who chase wealth, low-commitment sex, security, power, positions of influence in society, and happiness, will ultimately fail. Our pursuit will even chase away the very things we want and lead us to foolish attitudes and detrimental behaviors.

However, those who are wise do not make wealth, security, power, positions of influence, or happiness the aim of their lives. Instead, they pursue wisdom gained through fear of the Lord that enables a *life that is good.* Their expectations follow their goals: developing their relationship with God, knowing what to say and when to say it, making merciful and just decisions, developing qualities suited for leadership, and being satisfied with their wealth and status. If we follow this path of wisdom, we will grow in loyalty and the other character traits that make us a good friend: a pure heart, humility, and love. In short, we will pursue a life that is good instead of the things that attempt to create "the good life." Chasing the good life will ultimately chase life away, but a relentless pursuit of a life that is good will lead to genuine life and its joys.

DISCUSSION QUESTIONS

1. What do the sages promote as wise family values regarding marriage? What most threatened these values in ancient Israel? What most threatens these values today? Why is it difficult to achieve the type of marriage envisioned by the sages?
2. What is your philosophy on the discipline or correction of children? How does your philosophy compare to what you have read in Proverbs? How is it informed by contemporary wisdom? Please explain.
3. Why do you think some parents tend to neglect all forms of correcting their children? What factors contribute to this problem? What does the faith community need to do about it?
4. Review the proverbs that speak negatively about women or wives (e.g., 11:22; 19:13; 21:9, 19; 25:24; 27:15–16). Women: How do these proverbs make you feel? Why? Are you aware of other common or popular proverbs about women or wives? Share these and your feelings about them. Now, rewrite the biblical proverbs as statements about men or husbands. Share and discuss your proverbs with the group. Why do you think such proverbs are absent from the book of Proverbs?
5. I point out three family values in Proverbs. Reconsider these claims. Do you agree or disagree? Why? What additional family values do you see in the text? Explain.

FINAL QUESTIONS AND PROJECT CHALLENGE

How does contemporary wisdom, experience, and insight relate to the book of Proverbs? Does the wisdom in Proverbs always trump contemporary wisdom? Does contemporary wisdom trump Proverbs? How do we negotiate this terrain in specific reference to family issues such as child abuse, spousal abuse, elder care, and other contemporary matters?

How might biblical counseling be understood or redefined in view of your prior answers? Should biblical counseling be open to observations and insights from social scientists, for example, psychology or sociology? What if the new insight contradicts a specific instruction in Proverbs? What if it contradicts specific instruction elsewhere in the Bible?

Bibliography

Bland, Dave. *Proverbs and the Formation of Character.* Eugene, OR: Cascade Books, 2015.

Bland, Dave, and David Fleer, eds. *Preaching Character: Reclaiming Wisdom's Paradigmatic Imagination for Transformation.* Abilene, TX: Abilene Christian University Press, 2010.

Brueggemann, Walter. *Reality, Grief, Hope: Three Urgent Prophetic Tasks.* Grand Rapids: Eerdmans, 2014.

Buckingham, Markus, and Curt Coffman. *First Break All the Rules: What the World's Greatest Managers Do Differently.* New York: Simon & Schuster, 1999.

Coogan, Michael, ed. *A Reader of Ancient Near Eastern Texts.* New York: Oxford University Press, 2013.

Covey, Stephen. *The Seven Habits of Highly Effective People: Powerful Lessons in Personal Change.* New York: Free Press, 1989.

Davis, Ellen. *Proverbs, Ecclesiastes, and the Song of Songs.* Westminster Bible Companion. Louisville: Westminster John Knox, 2000.

Fox, Michael. *Proverbs 1–9.* Anchor Bible 18A. New York: Doubleday, 2000.

———. *Proverbs 10–31.* Anchor Bible 18B. New Haven: Yale University Press, 2009.

Halpern, Bruce. *David's Secret Demons: Messiah, Murderer, Traitor, King.* Grand Rapids: Eerdmans, 2001.

Hausmann, Jutta. *Studien zum Menschenbild der älteren Weisheit.* FAT 7. Tübingen: Mohr Siebeck, 1995.

Hubbard, D. A. *Proverbs.* Communicator's Commentary 15a. Dallas: Word, 1989.

Koch, Klaus. "Is There a Doctrine of Retribution in the Old Testament?" In *Theodicy in the Old Testament*, edited by James Crenshaw, 57–87. Philadelphia: Fortress, 1983.

Kohlberg, Lawrence. *The Psychology of Moral Development: The Nature and Validity of Moral Stages. Essays on Moral Development* 2. San Francisco: Harper & Row, 1984.

Lindenberger, James M., trans. "Ahikar." In *A Reader of Ancient Near Eastern Texts*, edited by Michael Coogan, 207–9. New York: Oxford University Press, 2013.

Longman, Tremper, III. *How to Read Proverbs*. Downers Grove, IL: InterVarsity, 2002.

Lucas, Ernest. *Proverbs*. Two Horizons. Grand Rapids: Eerdmans, 2015.

Malchow, Bruce. "A Manual for Future Monarchs." *Catholic Biblical Quarterly* 47 (1985): 238–45.

McKane, William. *Proverbs: A New Approach*. Old Testament Library. London: SCM, 1970.

Meyers, Carol. *Discovering Eve: Ancient Israelite Women in Context*. New York: Oxford University Press, 1988.

Miller, Henry. *The Books in My Life*. New York: New Directions, 1952.

Murphy, Roland. *Proverbs*. Word Bible Commentary 22. Nashville: Thomas Nelson, 1998.

Pemberton, Glenn. "The Rhetoric of the Father: A Rhetorical Analysis of the Father/Son Lectures in Proverbs 1–9." PhD diss., Iliff School of Theology and University of Denver, 1999.

Purdue, Leo. *Wisdom and Creation: The Theology of Wisdom Literature*. Nashville: Abingdon, 1994.

———. *Wisdom Literature: A Theological History*. Louisville: Westminster John Knox, 2007.

Schwáb, Zoltán S. *Toward an Interpretation of the Book of Proverbs: Spirituality and Secularity Reconsidered*. Journal of Theological Interpretation Supplement 7. Winona Lake, IN: Eisenbrauns, 2013.

Simpson, William Kelly, trans. "Instruction of Amenemope." In *A Reader of Ancient Near Eastern Texts*, edited by Michael Coogan, 191–93. New York: Oxford University Press, 2013.

Tetlow, Elisabeth Meier. *The Ancient Near East*. Vol. 1 of *Women, Crime, and Punishment in Ancient Law and Society*. New York: Continuum, 2004.

Waltke, Bruce. *The Book of Proverbs 1–15*. New International Commentary on the Old Testament. Grand Rapids: Eerdmans, 2004.

Wyse, R. R. "The Proverbial Fool: The Book of Proverbs and 'Biblical' Counseling." *Skrif en kerk* 17 (1996): 237–55.

Yamauchi, Edwin. "Marriage." In *Dictionary of Daily Life in Biblical and Post-Biblical Antiquity*, vol. 3, edited by Edwin Yamauchi and Marvin Wilson, 221–49. Peabody, MA: Hendrickson, 2016.

Zimmerli, Walther. "The Place and Limit of the Wisdom in the Framework of the Old Testament Theology." *Scottish Journal of Theology* 17 (1964): 146–58.

Index of Subjects

Index of Hebrew Words

Index of Scripture